Raise Your Kids
— *without* —
Raising Your Voice

SARAH CHANA RADCLIFFE

Collins

Raise Your Kids Without Raising Your Voice
© 2006, 2009 by Sarah Chana Radcliffe. All rights reserved.

Published by Collins, an imprint of HarperCollins Publishers Ltd

First published in Canada by Collins in an original trade paperback edition: 2006
This trade paperback edition: 2009

HarperCollins books may be purchased for educational,
business, or sales promotional use through our
Special Markets Department.

HarperCollins Publishers Ltd
2 Bloor Street East, 20th Floor
Toronto, Ontario, Canada
M4W 1A8

www.harpercollins.ca

Library and Archives Canada Cataloguing in Publication data
is available upon request

ISBN: 978-1-55468-250-8

Printed and bound in Canada
Set in Adobe Garamond

To my parents

Contents

CHAPTER I

The Parent's Journey

You're on the Journey

Welcome to the parenting journey—the trip of a lifetime! Your ability to raise your children without raising your voice will make this trip a pleasant one for you and your family. More importantly, it will give your children a lifelong advantage. The more respectful your communication, the healthier and happier your children will be. In the short run, while your kids are young, they will suffer from fewer nervous habits, fewer behaviour problems, fewer relationship problems, fewer academic difficulties and even fewer physical health issues. In the long run, when they've grown up, they will have better mental health, better marriages, better parent-child relationships, more success at work and more physical well-being. Even your grandchildren will benefit, since your own kids will be relationship-savvy enough to know how to parent lovingly with patience and self-control. Finally, the more respectful your communication and the less you raise your voice during the two or more decades you spend raising your kids, the more likely it is that you will be able to have wonderful lifelong relationships with your children and grandchildren. You and your family can enjoy all of these benefits when you learn to raise your kids without raising your voice.

Rising to the Challenge

Parenting is meant to bring out the best in you and the best in your children. It does this through a series of challenges, each one inviting you to overcome personal limitations and develop increasing levels of competence, wisdom and emotional power. At the end of the journey, you are light-years away from your starting point, richer in every way. The process, never carefree or easy, stretches your heart and your strength to full capacity; you are the escort for the first phase of your children's journey. You will prepare them for life.

There are so many questions you will encounter—both profound and mundane—and so many emotions you will experience along the way:

- What are the important lessons you should convey?
- What is the best way for you to convey them?
- How do you get your children to listen?
- How do you keep your cool when they don't listen?
- How do you help them overcome their fears and insecurities?
- How do you overcome your own?
- How do you help your children get along with their siblings?
- How do you stop your children from arguing with you?
- How do you get them to do homework, brush their teeth and go to bed?
- How do you get them to clean their room, clear the table and take out the garbage?
- What do you do when you don't like them?
- What do you do when they don't like you?
- How do you teach them responsibility?
- How do you get them to respect you?
- What if your child gets in trouble at school or with the law?
- How do you handle your feelings of frustration and despair?
- What if your child has no friends?
- What if you don't like the friends he or she has?

- What if your spouse disagrees with your parenting approach?
- How do you parent when you are dealing with overwhelming personal stress?

The list goes on and on, challenging your intelligence and skills to the hilt. Parenting actually requires more than instinct—it requires knowledge. There are answers to these parenting dilemmas and the other questions that arise in the course of a parenting day. There are also specific strategies for riding each parenting wave with calm and balance, with know-how and with confidence—a method for staying on top of the crest. Parenting, after all, is no tranquil pond. It is a powerful ocean with constantly changing conditions: over the course of two decades there will be crashing waves, serene stillness, intense storms, bright sparkling sunshine, rushing currents and also the occasional tsunami.

Raise Your Kids Without Raising Your Voice will present you with up-to-date parenting technology and psychology to ease your way. It begins with a map, an overview of the parenting process that will help define the task and point you in the right direction. Next comes an in-depth look at parenting strategies that can help facilitate the healthy development of your children. Finally, there is an examination of the real emotional world of the parent, the inner workings that make it difficult or impossible to carry out the parenting strategies you just learned!

As we all know, there is a huge difference between reading a parenting book and living it, a world between knowing what to do and doing it! You will be lifted off the pages of this parenting manual and settled into your own home at 8 a.m. Telling it like it is, *Raise Your Kids Without Raising Your Voice* will give you the support you need in order to translate theory into action, to make real changes that can make a real difference in the way you parent. You will be provided with vital information to help you settle your emotions and eradicate anger from your parenting toolbox, enabling you to raise your kids without raising your voice. Consequently, the love you have so carefully planted and nurtured will be protected and your family relationships can thrive. Your home can be what you've always hoped for: a haven, a safe harbor, an oasis in a stressful world.

You'll be able to draw on all of this information—philosophy of parenting, parenting techniques, emotional guidance—to tailor your parenting approach to your personal style and your children's individual needs. You'll be equipped to figure out what to do in each parenting situation and—most importantly—to help yourself actually do it.

Your Inner Compassionate Parent

As you work through the material in this text, you will see many references to the "inner compassionate parent." This is your personal companion on the parenting journey. Parenting is hard work, often frustrating and thankless. Parents can become discouraged and even despairing at times. During such moments, you will be advised to call upon this inner parent for support. This practice will enable you to restore your energy when it is depleted and help you to gently acquire new strategies when you need them. This book will give you explicit instructions as to how to access this helpful part of yourself. Regularly employing this strategy will make parenting more relaxing and gratifying than you can imagine.

CHAPTER 2

A Parenting Philosophy

The parenting strategies in *Raise Your Kids Without Raising Your Voice* are presented to you as a series of "less-stress" options. If what you are currently doing is working, leave it alone. If it's not working or if it's exhausting, draining or frustrating, try the less-stress approach. All attitudes and techniques of this approach are designed to save you wear and tear while providing sound education for your children.

Basic Assumptions of the Approach

- Because of the unique, inborn differences in children, no single approach is sufficient. Therefore, the more options we have, the better. Find what works for *this* child.
- Because of the unique differences in adults, no single approach can be used. Mothers and fathers can use different approaches, selecting what fits their style and temperament, providing that each approach is based on sound parenting principles. A united front means supporting each other, not necessarily doing the exact same thing. (The only time *not* to be supportive of a spouse is when the spouse is being truly abusive to a child. In that case, the child must be protected.)
- Parental power comes from a healthy parent-child relationship. A child who likes you also wants to please you, and wants to be something like you, with many of your values, beliefs and ways of being. A child who hates you, on the other hand, wants to distance him or herself from you and your ways. He doesn't care to impress you

and certainly does not choose to emulate you. You won't be able to pass on anything of importance to him or her. Consequently, the most important focus in parenting is on strengthening the warm feelings between parent and child. This goal needs to be taken into account during every parenting moment, and particularly when a child requires correction.

- No matter what you do in parenting, and no matter how well you do it, you cannot actually control the final product of your effort: the child's personality *is not* up to you. What *is* up to you is *how you behave each moment in parenting.*

What You Can Do in Parenting

There are limitations to what you can actually do in parenting. Here are some things you might be able to accomplish:

- You can treat your children with respect—even when you're stressed.
- You can react gently and patiently to their mistakes.
- You can show them affection with hugs, gifts, care and loving words.
- You can attend compassionately to their feelings, giving them emotional support.
- You can set appropriate expectations and goals and help your children work toward them.
- You can expose them to your values and beliefs.
- You can teach them about their history and identity.
- You can teach them a spiritual discipline.
- You can behave consistently and dependably with them.
- You can teach them certain skills.
- You can model behaviors.
- You can implement various types of discipline.
- You can increase your parenting options by continually studying

and learning parenting approaches.
- You can provide for all your children's physical needs.
- You can provide them with every educational, leisure and medical benefit that you can afford or arrange.
- You can provide them with opportunities to develop their interests, skills and talents.
- You can take care of yourself and reduce your stress, enabling you to be a more relaxed, healthy parent.
- You can protect your mental and physical health so that you can operate at your full potential.
- You can work on your marriage.
- You can consult professionals and/or clergy for family guidance.
- You can continue to grow and improve as a human being, giving your children a model for growth and improvement.
- You can pray for your children's well-being and success.

What You *Can't* Do in Parenting

As you see, there are many things you can hope to accomplish as a parent. However, you can't do everything you want to do. For example:

- You can't ensure that your children will be happy.
- You can't ensure that your children will be mentally well.
- You can't ensure that your children will be physically well.
- You can't ensure that your children will succeed in school.
- You can't ensure that your children will have a large circle of friends.
- You can't ensure that your children will have a "desirable" career.
- You can't ensure that your children will get married or stay married.
- You can't ensure that your children will get along with their siblings.
- You can't ensure that your children will hold all of your beliefs and values.
- You can't ensure that your children will choose a life just like yours.

- You can't ensure that your child will enjoy the things you enjoy.
- You can't ensure that your spouse will be an excellent parent.
- You can't ensure that your children will grow up in peace and prosperity.
- You can't ensure that your children will have high self-esteem or confidence.
- You can't ensure that your children will always be safe.
- You can't ensure that your children's teachers will be good.
- You can't ensure that your children's relatives will be supportive and loving.
- You can't ensure that others will always treat your child well.
- You can't save your children from pain.

Often parents believe that, if only they do all the right things, they can raise children who will be happy, confident and successful human beings. When these parents encounter the limits of their control—what a crisis! Not only are the children having a hard time, but the parents feel like failures.

Parents are only failing when they fail to do *what's in their control.*

The Easier Way to Succeed at Parenting

Review the two preceding lists—what you can and can't do as a parent. Notice that in the "can do" list, the parent is in control of everything. The parent is the one who is doing the behavior. Notice that in the "can't do" list, someone other than the parent is in control—the child, the spouse, the teachers, the relatives and the rest of the world. Parents can measure their success as parents only by their own behaviors, not by what happens to their children. In other words, doing a good job as a parent means that you have done all that you can do. It does not mean that you have raised an outstanding human being.

Why Raising an Outstanding Human Being Is Not the Domain of Parents

The child's ultimate outcome is due to many factors, such as:

- Genetic make-up, including all physical, mental and emotional potentials. This includes the child's physical characteristics (physical appearance, physical health and stamina, etc.), intelligence (IQ), learning style and mental health profile (including tendencies to depression, anxiety, personality disorders, psychosis, addictions and so on).
- In-born temperament and character (may be 50% or more of total personality). This includes the "easy-going" child, the "sunny-side up" child, the "perpetually miserable" child, the "spirited" child, the "difficult" child, and all other variations of mood and behavioral tendencies.
- Environmental factors such as birth order, family make-up (number of children, extended relatives, divorce, remarriage, etc.), family conditions (conflicted marriage, handicapped sibling, etc.), living environment (town, city, crowded conditions, etc.), social environment (peer group, culture, media), educational environment (school opportunities, teachers, libraries, media), etc.
- The child's own free will (decisions the child makes based on his own experiences and in-born tendencies).
- *The parents' input.*

As you can see, your input is only one of many determining factors in your child's outcome as a human being.

Whether your input amounts to 50% or more doesn't really matter. Your job, as good parents, is to do the best you can with your part. Parenting is the job that you do—the final outcome is not in your control.

Your New Job Description

Instead of thinking your job is to raise outstanding human beings (something that is clearly out of your control), it may be more helpful to think of your job as "supporting human growth."

This job description can keep you on track, helping you to set an attainable goal. Supporting human growth means that you try to do those things that can help your children reach their unique potentials (see the "can-do" list on pages 5–6). It also means that you refrain from doing those things that would likely stunt their growth or interfere with their achieving what they might otherwise achieve. Knowing how to raise your children without raising your voice is essential if you want to avoid limiting their development.

As a human growth supporter, you clear a path for your children to walk in. It is up to them to walk that path the best they can.

CHAPTER 3

Love: It's All in the Ratio

Remember Your Goals

Parenting is easier if you've selected an easy-going child to raise. Did you do that? No? That was mistake number one.

The easy-going child makes you look like a parenting genius. You ask her to brush her teeth and off she goes to fulfill your request! What a delight!

The difficult child, on the other hand, makes you feel completely inept. It doesn't matter that you're president of a large corporation, that hundreds of people cater to your daily whims in the world outside your home. Junior won't do it. At least, not without a major battle that leaves you both badly wounded. Alas.

Before entering any battle, however, it is essential to remember your parenting goals. Your compassionate inner parent can remind you: you are raising a human being. It is not all about brushing teeth. Relationship is everything.

Getting Through the Day

Some parents operate as if the job of parenting is to get the child dressed, fed, out the door on time, fed some more, "homeworked," cleaned, into pajamas and into bed (and safely restrained, if it's a teenager). Although these tasks exist in parenting, they are primarily a venue, a means to an end: they are not the end in and of themselves. Parenting is about raising a human being. Certainly every parent will get his/her child dressed, fed, out the door, and so forth. The real question is, "how?" It is in the *how* of parenting that we find ourselves either building or destroying a child.

Some parents will scream their way through all of the daily tasks, wreaking havoc with their child's emotional development. Yes, the child is dressed, but also is diminished, demoralized, defeated and destroyed. Other parents get the child dressed in a loving, respectful manner so that the child is dressed and also is encouraged, nourished, cherished and enhanced.

Parenting tasks are only a means to an end. It's as if we are saying, "As I help you get ready for school in the morning, I will demonstrate for you and directly teach you all that I can about how to be a human being. As I help you get ready, I will show you everything I know about love, respect, kindness and patience. I will teach you about responsibility, self-care, care for others and self-respect. I'll teach you about mood management, stress management and self-control. I'll teach you how to be giving, how to receive gracefully, how to show appreciation. I'll do all this as I get you ready for school."

Of course, the same sort of thought process occurs as the parent is helping with homework, serving dinner, encouraging bath-time and bedtime. It occurs as the parent makes requests, teaches household skills and money management, accompanies a child on a shopping excursion, offers driving lessons. It occurs, too, when the parent is occupied with his or her own tasks in the vicinity of watching eyes and listening ears; the parent is constantly aware of lessons being absorbed both directly and indirectly. The focus is always on the larger goal of raising a human being and the larger strategy of maintaining a positive relationship.

Getting kids to listen, then, is really about teaching them self-control, responsibility, respect and empathy.

Therefore, these are the very traits the parent must model during the teaching process. Fortunately, these are also less-stress tactics, techniques that are easy on parents and effective for children.

Less-Stress Strategies for Teaching

Whether the child is easy, difficult or in-between, the same general parenting principles will apply; only specific teaching strategies will vary. For example, no matter what kind of child you are raising, it will be true that relationship is a priority, that consistency is important, and that mutual respect is a requirement. However, the "very difficult" child may need many more learning opportunities and more intense rewards and negative consequences than his "very easy" sister. Moreover, parents should note that temperament tends to be consistent over time. No matter how skilled the parent, difficult children tend to remain harder to raise throughout childhood. In other words, difficult children do not generally become easy children.

If you are raising such a child, your inner compassionate parent will be called on frequently for support. Sit quietly for a moment and create an image in your mind of a truly wise, kind and understanding inner parent. What would this parent say to you when you are in the midst of the most difficult and frustrating interactions you have with your child? Listen now as if that parent is speaking directly to you. Perhaps you'll hear something like this:

> *"You're doing a good job with a challenging child. Not everybody would do so well! It can be really hard and upsetting at times like this. You're holding up admirably. You deserve some rest and refreshment after all this—take care of yourself."*

Your inner compassionate parent is the exact opposite of your inner critic, the part that always finds fault with you, complains about your behavior and generally beats you up. Whereas the critic makes you feel inept and exhausted, the inner compassionate parent gives you renewed energy and strength for your task. Always tune in to the right inner voice!

While doing a good job is important, it is equally vital that parents refrain from doing a bad job. Indeed, the skilled parent helps the difficult child enormously by not using destructive approaches such as a raised voice, insulting words or excessive criticism (where do you think the "inner critic" learns its technique?). This parent helps the difficult child grow up to his or her full potential.

The Importance of the Relationship

The most important parenting strategy is that of building a positive relationship. Although a parent cannot make a relationship all alone (it takes two people!), a parent can do those things that typically create the "soil" in which a positive relationship can grow. Keep in mind that love is the only real power a parent has. You can't beat children into accepting your values. You need to inspire them. Ultimately, children will identify with a loved parent and want to emulate the parent's strongest positive traits. Children will work to please a parent they care for. They will also accept guidance and direction from such a parent. (This may take longer to show up in a "difficult" child, but even here, the effects of a positive relationship are dramatic.) Getting a child to listen or a teenager to cooperate is primarily about setting up the conditions under which they *choose* to do so. Besides being illegal to use brute force to accomplish these goals, it is an impractical methodology. Even children have free will.

What can parents do to lay the groundwork for a positive, loving relationship? They can maintain the magic ratio in parenting. This magic ratio is what I call "The 80-20 Rule."

The 80-20 Rule

Simply put, parents' words and behaviors should feel good to the child 80% of the time. That is, eight out of 10 parenting moments should be pleasant ones *from the child's point of view.* Ideally, 100% of parental interactions are meant for the well-being of the child; however, not all interventions feel good to the child. Although dental work is good for our teeth, it doesn't feel good to us and we don't look forward to getting it done. If we had to endure dental work all day, every day, we'd soon be insane. Similarly, criticism might be good for a child on occasion, but endured all day, every day, it would soon cause severe mental illness. You see, it's all in the ratio.

Typical good-feeling interactions include smiling, telling jokes, laughing, pleasant facial expressions, looks of approval, playing or engaging in activities together, gentle touching, cuddles, hugs, compliments, praise, positive feedback, acknowledgment, using affectionate names ("sweetie," etc.), words of love and affection, listening attentively, naming feelings, showing interest, giving sympathy, giving encouragement, showing understanding, agreeing, giving treats and gifts, giving rewards and privileges, sharing thoughts and feelings, helping, offering assistance, greetings, your own good mood, and pleasant conversation between spouses that is overheard by kids.(How much of this are you doing between 7:30 and 8:30 a.m.?) Even if a parent is singing a tune to himself while he is making coffee in the kitchen, it counts as part of the 80% positive if children are around to hear him. The happy singing sets a good-feeling mood in the house. Similarly, parents having a little laugh between themselves counts as part of the child's 80% if the child overhears it.

Typical bad-feeling interactions include criticizing, reprimanding, lecturing, preaching, teaching, complaining, nagging (repeated requests), yelling, shouting, raising your voice, threatening, punishing, name-calling, insulting, cursing, ignoring, interrogating, supervising, saying "no," limiting, restricting, using an irritated voice, looking angry or displeased, displaying frustration, acting aggressive, interrogating, using sarcasm, mockery, or put-downs, using unwanted touching, giving unwanted help or assistance, saying negative or rejecting remarks, disagreeing, being in a bad mood, having unpleasant conversations between spouses that are overheard by kids, commanding, correcting, requesting, or instructing. Note that the last four essentially amount to "asking a child to do something." Simple requests are included in the bad-feeling interactions because people—even children—don't like being told what to do or asked to interrupt their current activity. If a parent is in his or her own bad mood and is muttering curses under his or her breath and slamming cupboard doors as he or she is making coffee, it counts as part of the 20% negative allotment if the children are within hearing distance. Similarly, if the parents are having a stressful, unpleasant or hostile interaction within hearing distance of their child, it counts as part of the child's 20%.

What's in a Number?

What do you think *your* current positive-to-negative ratio is? If you want to find out, ask your kids and spouse what they think, but make sure they include all of your requests and instructions in their calculation. Alternatively—and probably more accurately—turn on a video camera or tape recorder to record your interactions with your children during three separate hours: the hour before school, the dinner hour and the bedtime hour. Record yourself for several consecutive days or longer so that your "natural" behavior will occur with your children rather than your contrived "good parent" behavior that is inevitable on the first couple of recordings. (Ever notice how most parents in the park, library and store are so patient and pleasant with their children? This is largely due to the effect of being "watched." Parents who want to improve their daily performance in the privacy of their homes should imagine that there is a camera recording their behavior in every room of the house. Those with a spiritual bent may have already internalized this concept with their understanding of being constantly watched by an "Eye that sees and an Ear that hears"—and they may recognize that they themselves will be revisiting their "private family moments" in a later life-review process. Such a belief can help raise those ratios!)

After you've recorded your interactions with your children, select several 10-minute sections to play back, stopping the tape every minute and noting whether your behavior in the minute seems to be a "good-feeling" behavior (from the child's point of view) or a "bad-feeling"

behavior. Be sure to include all sarcastic remarks, instructions, direc-
tions, requests, criticism and threats in the "bad-feeling" communications. Remember that there are no "neutral" moments because human
interactions always have a feeling quality to them, even if only a very
slight one. When you are standing beside a man in an elevator, for example, you can get a slightly bad or a slightly good feeling from him even
if he is not directly talking to you; you read subtle signals in his face,
posture and other body language, as well as in his physical appearance.
A "neutral" parental face may actually appear to the child to be either
disapproving, tense and unhappy, or relaxed, calm and pleasant. Calculate
your ratios with all of this information in mind. How did you do?

Do you want to know how the average parent does? Remember, the
average parent "loves" his or her child! Most parents feel that they are
giving lots of positive attention to their kids. However, when they add
up their minute-by-minute interactions, the ratio is not likely to be anywhere close to 80-20! Research shows that the average parent is giving
94% negative to only 6% positive attention! How is that possible? Easy.

Picture a typical parent-child interaction at 5:30 p.m. in a home
where there are two boys aged 8 and 10. Look at Mom's words and
decide whether each statement would likely feel good or bad to the boys:

> "David, please put your jacket in the closet, where it belongs."
> "Josh, stop teasing the cat right now."
> "Boys, let's get started on the homework. Get your books out."
> "David, where is that page you were supposed to do? Why isn't it
> here? I asked you to make sure you brought it home. I'm going
> to have to give Mr. Spencer a call again. This is totally unac-
> ceptable."
> "No, Josh, you can't eat until we've finished this work."
> "I know you don't like fish, but that's what we're having tonight.
> Now get started on these questions. . ."

It's not that Mom doesn't love the boys. She obviously does! She wants
them to do well in school, she's clearly concerned about their habits, and

she's prepared a healthy dinner for them. Yet her sons experience her as a pain in the neck. The ratio in the above communication is 100% negative to 0% positive. It's no fun being around Mom! Would that ratio work in marriage? (I don't suggest you try it to find out.)

Because so much of the parenting day consists of giving kids instructions, making demands, offering corrections and criticisms and making threats, it is actually quite challenging to create that 80-20 ratio. Challenging, but not impossible. Practice makes it second nature (after 20 years or so), but even after only a few weeks, you'll find it easier. And you will find that this ratio makes parenting much less stressful.

Here's a trick to get you started: in the morning, in the hour before the kids leave for school, put 8 pennies and 2 quarters in your right-hand pocket. Each time you give a positive form of attention (a positive stroke), move one penny to your left-hand pocket. Each time you give a negative form of attention, move one quarter over to your left-hand pocket. You only have 2 quarters, so when you've used them up, you must move the remaining pennies before you can give any more negative strokes. When all the pennies and quarters are in your left pocket, move them back to the right—positive strokes move pennies and negative strokes move quarters. You can continue this game when the kids come home from school. Soon you'll be an 80-20 expert!

Now you might be wondering why the ratio has to be 80-20. Wouldn't 50% positive and 50% negative be good enough? No! The reason that a 50-50 ratio just won't do is that negative attention weighs much more than positive attention. One criticism can wipe out 20 pleasant remarks. Just think of a time you spent an evening with someone and the whole night went well except for the one negative comment they made about you. Didn't it ruin the whole evening? Indeed, a single intensely negative remark can sometimes ruin an entire relationship. In parenting, think of each mild bad-feeling action as "undoing" 20 positive ones and each intensely bad-feeling action as wiping out hundreds of good-feeling words and actions that you've invested in your child. It is clear that, as unfair as this seems, we need to give out many more positives than negatives in order to keep the overall atmosphere positive.

The 50-50 Rule

For you 50-50 fans, don't despair. There is a place in parenting for this ratio. The good-feeling attention is divided 50-50 between "free" positive attention and "earned" positive attention. Another name for free positive attention is "unconditional love." Earned positive attention is called "conditional love" or "positive reinforcement."

Both types of love are necessary for a child's growth. Here are some ways of showing *unconditional love:*

- saying things like: "I love you!" "You're the greatest in the whole wide world!" "You're the most brilliant, wonderful, beautiful. . ." "You're delicious!" "You're gorgeous!" and any other exaggerated form of global praise.
- buying a child a gift for no particular reason
- making a favorite meal for no reason
- playing and/or joking together
- talking together "adult-to-adult"
- hugging or affectionately touching a child for no reason
- listening and showing interest, sympathy or support
- sharing a pleasant activity (e.g., watching a movie together, shopping, baking)
- going on an outing just for fun.

All of these kinds of behaviors convey general acceptance, adoration and support. They help give the child a strong inner security. However, children also need to know when they're on the right track. Is it better to eat with your hands or with your fork? Is it better to make your bed or leave it? Does it make a difference whether you write neatly or not? Does it matter whether you shout or whether you speak quietly? Is being clean a real necessity or an optional lifestyle? As soon as a parent indicates pleasure at a preferable behavior, they have given a conditional form of attention. All parents have preferences. Some will be pleased by a young-ster's good grades, some will be delighted with a child's wit and some will be proud of the child's ability to be assertive. What parents are pleased about varies. However, the result of the unavoidable expression of parental pleasure is that the child gets positive attention because he or she is on track. Because it is generally pleasant for the child to receive positive con-ditional attention, this intervention contributes to the strength of the relationship even as it helps the child to achieve age-appropriate goals.

Here are some ways of showing *conditional love:*

- acknowledge the desirable behavior ("I see you're getting dressed by yourself.")
- praise the desirable behavior ("That's very neat handwriting. You've done a great job!")
- label the desirable behavior ("That was really *brave* of you.")
- reward the desirable behavior ("I think that deserves a game of chess.")
- hug, pat or smile at a child *because* he just performed a desirable behavior
- give the child a treat or gift *because* he just performed a desirable behavior
- go on an outing with the child *because* he just performed a desirable behavior.

As you can see, the same parental action can be given either condi-tionally or unconditionally to the child. When it's given conditionally, it tends to increase desirable behaviors. When it's given uncondition-ally, it builds inner security.

Using Positive Attention to Guide and Teach

Some parenting experts frown upon the use of rewards and other con-ditional forms of positive attention, suggesting that these parenting tactics are manipulative and controlling. Purposely using techniques that bring out the best in a child and guide his or her behavior in a socially acceptable and healthy direction is indeed manipulative and controlling on the part of parents. Manipulation and control is only a bad thing when it is done for the sake of harming the child or when it is the *only* form of positive attention being offered. In other words, if a child is only offered affection, treats, smiles and other kinds of pleasant attention when he or she behaves "correctly," the youngster will ultimately feel manipulated and completely unloved. That is why conditional positive attention can never exceed more than 50% of the good-feeling attention offered by a parent.

In its correct proportion, conditional positive attention acts to guide and teach children how to behave appropriately. Desirable behaviors are reinforced by pleasant consequences of many kinds. This motivates children to continue to engage in new behaviors until the behaviors eventually become self-reinforcing. By adolescence, for example, most kids are quite happy to keep themselves clean. For the first 10 years, however, parents sometimes need to use conditional positive attention to encourage kids to wash up. "Manipulating" and "controlling"—when it comes to parenting—are essentially equivalent to "guiding" and "teaching." Parents do indeed hope to *raise* their children—not just by feeding them until they've grown to adult size, but by instilling values, ideals and standards of behavior.

Conditional positive attention is unavoidable in parenting. The trick is to use it consciously and wisely, thereby reducing the need for bad-feeling interventions. Parental displeasure is also unavoidable in parenting, the natural consequence of not approving of what the child is doing. However, it has potentially dangerous consequences as an intervention. It is highly preferable, therefore, to help children stay on track using good-feeling attention.

Optimal development requires an equal dosage of I-love-you-for-no-reason messages and I-notice-you're-on-the-right-track messages. It is easy and natural to give our very young children this ratio. However, as children mature, their cuteness wears off a bit. We stop adoring them all day long and begin to focus in on their performance. As a result, we have a tendency to forget to give the older child his or her needed unconditional positive attention. Instead, the positive attention we give tends to be largely conditional. Unfortunately, when a child receives plenty of conditional positive attention and not enough unconditional positive attention, he may, as discussed earlier, feel deep insecurity. "Do you only love me if I get an A on my report card, mow the lawn, look attractive and succeed socially? Do I always have to earn love? Do I have to be perfect for you to find me acceptable?" This sort of insecurity can, in vulnerable teens especially, lead to perfectionism, anxiety and depression. Always be careful to balance conditional love with unconditional love, no matter what the age of the child. Even adults need a generous dose of both! Ideally, unconditional positive attention should be sprinkled like sugar throughout the parenting day, every day for the first 20 years.

Conditional Love Shapes Behavior

As we've already seen, unconditional love builds inner security, while conditional love shapes behaviors. In the following chapter we will examine how to use positive attention (conditional love) to increase desirable behavior in children. Getting children to listen using good-feeling attention is the least stressful way to parent. More importantly, it is the healthiest approach to use with children, contributing to high self-esteem and emotional well-being.

CHAPTER 4

Positive Tools for Getting Kids to Listen

Positive tools—all of the "good-feeling" techniques—form the basis of our most powerful means of discipline. Discipline is guidance and education; it can feel pleasant or unpleasant to a child, although it is always meant for the child's welfare. In this chapter, we will learn many different positive tools that can be used in "good-feeling" discipline interventions.

Positive Tool #1: Comment

Commenting on a child's appropriate behavior is one way to ensure that it will occur again. Of course, commenting on a child's *inappropriate* behavior is one way to ensure that *it* will occur again as well. That's why we want to avoid giving poor behavior unnecessary attention (more on this later). For now, we will note that comments are powerful reinforcers. We can use our comments wisely to maintain and to shape desirable behaviors.

There are actually three types of comments we will want to use:

1. Acknowledgment: "I *see* you picked up your toys." "I *notice* you cleaned off your desk."
2. Praise: "You did a *great* job picking up your toys!" "You did a *fantastic* job with your desk!"

3. Appreciation: "*Thank you* for cleaning up your toys." "*Thanks* for cleaning up your desk."

Acknowledgment involves making a simple observation. The parent notes that the child did something appropriate.

- A child sits down to do his homework. The parent comments, "I see you're starting your homework."
- A child shares his treat with a sibling. The parent comments, "I see someone's sharing."
- An 11-year-old gets up with his own alarm clock. The parent comments, "I see you got up by yourself this morning."

Positive acknowledgment may seem unnecessary or unnatural to parents. What is natural, however, is offering acknowledgment for a child's inappropriate behavior: "I see you slept in again." Giving attention to undesirable behaviors can lead to their increase. Simply acknowledging appropriate behavior is a powerful step toward maintaining it.

Praise occurs when a parent makes a comment that contains a positive evaluation of the child's performance. It is a verbal form of attention that follows a child's appropriate behavior.

- A child makes his bed. The parent says, "You did a good job!"
- A child does a thorough job of cleaning up the kitchen. The parent says, "You did an amazing job in here! It looks great!"
- A child selects a nice outfit to wear. The parent says, "You put that together really nicely!"

When praising, the parent gives a direct statement of approval—he or she does not use *comparative* praise. That is, a child is told that her handwriting is very good, not that it's better or that it's good *now*. To see why we follow this approach, imagine that you are receiving the following compliments after you show up to work with your new haircut:

- "Your hair looks great!"
- "Your hair looks so much better that way!"
- "Your hair looks good now."
- "What an improvement!"

Indeed, the last three statements are usually called "backhanded compliments" when given to adults. Yet parents and teachers routinely praise children this way. Children have the exact same feelings as we do—they might even be more sensitive. Just tell them what's right about what they're doing and ignore the improvement part of the equation. Review the praise statements above and note that they are purely straightforward words of praise.

Appreciation involves thanking a child for some sort of pleasing behavior. Communicating appreciation provides a good model for the child, showing how a person should convey gratitude whenever possible. Appreciation is also a "good-feeling" interaction that reinforces whatever it follows.

- A child helps with the groceries. The parent comments, "Thank you for helping."
- A child calls home to say he'll be late. The parent comments, "Thank you for remembering to call."
- A child waits patiently to speak. The parent comments, "Thank you for waiting."

When to Comment

The time to comment is when a child is already engaging in a desirable behavior (something he's supposed to be doing). The parent notices and comments on the behavior.

- Alex comes right away when his father calls him. "That's great listening," praises Dad.

Positive attention lets the child know that this sort of behavior is important to the parent. When children know that positive attention is easy to come by, they continuously strive to earn it by doing those things their parents value. However, when positive attention is a rare commodity, children often give up attempting to please their parents. They come to feel that they won't be noticed anyway, so why bother trying.

If the child is not yet doing the desirable behavior, the parent can shape the behavior with a comment. This involves helping the child to succeed, sometimes in small steps leading to the complete goal.

- Four-year-old Jamie is not getting his coat on promptly. Mom hands the toddler his coat and comments, "You're getting your coat on quickly! That's great!"

In this example, Mom starts Jamie off, since he is having trouble getting started. Perhaps the next time, she will simply hold the coat up for him to come and get it. After that, she may not touch the coat at all, but simply give him instructions to get it himself. These increasing demands are each supported with generous praise. When shaping behavior, the parent focuses only on the correct element in the child's current actions. For example, suppose a child has messy handwriting. To shape neat handwriting, the parent finds one letter on his page that is sitting neatly on the line and comments, "Hey, this letter is sitting perfectly on the line. That's really nice!" The next day, the parent finds one letter that is written at the right slant and comments, "Look at this letter! It's slanted exactly the right way! Good for you." The next day, the parent finds a letter that's at the right height and comments on it. The parent continues finding correct aspects of the child's handwriting to praise or acknowledge each day. Most likely, the child will soon have beautiful handwriting! Notice that no mention is made of any weakness in the handwriting during this shaping process. This same approach can be used to build up skills in many different areas. For example, use the comment technique to help a child learn to keep his room clean, to help a child learn to speak more clearly or to help a child get into bed on time.

Another use of the commenting strategy is called "distract and praise." It is particularly effective for very small children. The technique involves quickly shifting a child's attention from an inappropriate behavior to a more appropriate or desirable one.

- Ruthie is a toddler who wants to play with the toilet. As she starts to run toward it, Mom very quietly says, "no," picks the child up and places her in front of some appropriate toys, commenting loudly, "Here we are! This is where we play! Good for you!"

Notice that in this scenario Mom does not say, "good girl!" We should always refrain from using this expression—and its opposite, "bad girl." We're not judging the child's worth as a human being; we are only teaching her how to behave appropriately.

The major principle behind the positive comment is that human beings work "from strength to strength"—or, to put it another way, "success leads to success." Helping children to feel that they're on the right track helps them to get on the right track. Be generous with your positive comments! As you remember to comment, notice that your inner compassionate parent will be praising you for smart parenting.

Positive Tool #2: Label

The positive label is a second essential parenting tool. Positive labels are used for "Positive Programming," a conscious use of parental hypnotic power. The truth is that children are highly suggestible to the words of their parents. Therefore, whether parents want it or not, they have the power of hypnotists. What parents say to their children deeply affects them, at times influencing their behavior lifelong. You probably remember words your own parents said to you in the course of your childhood, words that your parents may have long forgotten.

Labels—adjectives that describe personality—often have the most potent effect on a child's development. Suppose, for instance, a parent calls his child "lazy." The child may absorb that label into his permanent self-concept. Once there, the label will influence the child's behavior in a consistent fashion. The child behaves like a lazy person—can't get up in the morning, can't do his exercise, can't do his homework. What do you want from him? He's lazy! The more the label is used, the lazier he becomes. Moreover, it will take a lifetime of hard work for him to remove that label from his consciousness. The power of words on a child's mind is awesome.

But the child *is* lazy, you might argue: that's why his parent called him that. True. However, the child cannot be helped by being labeled. Indeed, the negative label itself increases the problem behavior. The child needs help of a totally different kind. His self-concept needs to be organized around successful behaviors, not failing ones. Let's look at another way the parent could have corrected this child's "lazy" attitude: "Hey, you've got tons of energy—use your energy to get out of bed right now and get going!" Every time the child demonstrates lazy behavior, the parent reminds him that he's got lots of energy. Eventually, the child will see himself as someone who has lots of energy. The word will gradually do its work on both his conscious and subconscious mind.

Parents will be using labels on their kids for at least the first 20 years of their lives. Imagine a child hearing herself called "selfish" or "stupid" or "careless" or "irresponsible" over the course of a 20-year period—the most vulnerable and suggestible period of her life. While the parent is using such labels in an attempt to correct a child's faults, the parent is only succeeding in assuring that the faults will become ingrained! Negative labels are destructive! Therefore, the rule in parenting is *never use a negative label.*

Positive Labels

Precisely because of the power of labels, parents can use them productively in parenting. The trick is to use only positive labels.

Try this exercise: sit down and write all the labels you would like to be able to use to describe your grown-up child's personality. It will probably sound something like, "I'd like to say my child grew up to be generous, kind, responsible, reliable, prompt, organized, creative, considerate, helpful, productive, talented, smart, independent, innovative, resourceful..." and so on. Whatever words you choose, these should be the words you use daily in the 20-year period of raising your child.

There are two occasions on which parents can use positive labels:

1. directly following praise, and
2. when correcting a child's behavior.

Following Praise

Every time praise is used, its power can be enhanced by adding a positive label. Here are some examples:

- "You're sharing your candies! That's so *generous* of you."
- "Thanks for doing the dishes without my asking! That was very *responsible* of you."
- "That's a beautiful drawing! You're so *talented!*"
- "You figured that out all by yourself? Aren't you *clever!*"
- "I like the way you put that outfit together—you're a smart dresser!"

When labels are used following praise, they are highly believable (and consequently digestible). Since the child is sharing, it is obviously true that he is being generous. Since the child figured out a difficult problem, it is clear that she is clever. The child can assimilate this information into her identity and use it to go forward.

When Correcting a Behavior

Correcting a behavior is considered a negative form of attention and therefore doesn't actually belong here in the section on positive teaching strategies. However, we will take a moment to illustrate the use of positive labels in this context.

Keep in mind that negative labels are toxic and they are always processed by the child, no matter how you try to hide them in your grammar. Consequently, all the following statements are equally detrimental:

- "You are being *disgusting*."
- "Don't be so *disgusting*."
- "What you did was absolutely *disgusting*."
- "That was *disgusting*."

No matter how you say it, the negative label will be heard and digested by the child. That is why it is essential that no negative label should ever be used in any context.

Changing Negative to Positive

Try this exercise: imagine your child is yelling at you and calling you names. Think of a negative label that would describe his behavior. Now, try to correct the child's behavior, using *the exact opposite* of the word you came up with.

Did you think of the word "rude" or "disrespectful"? Your correction might then have sounded like this, "You need to speak more respectfully to me before I can listen."

The rule here is: always use the exact opposite of the label that would best describe your child's incorrect behavior. Here are some examples:

- "Rude" becomes "polite" or "respectful."
- "Messy" becomes "neat" and "clean."
- "Dirty" becomes "clean" and "shiny."
- "Loud" becomes "quiet."
- "Selfish" becomes "generous."
- "Careless" becomes "careful."
- "Late" becomes "on time" or "prompt."
- A statement to a careless child who almost knocked a plate to the

floor might be, "You need to be more careful around the plates."

- A statement to an irresponsible teenager who spends too much money could be, "You need to be more responsible."
- A statement to a mean 4-year-old who enjoys teasing the toddler could be, "You need to be kind to your brother."
- A statement to a rude 7-year-old could be, "Please say that more politely."

Don't worry. Your inner compassionate parent will always use positive labels with you. If you ever hear anything else, rest assured it is not your inner companion. Ask the culprit to leave promptly and call your inner parent for help! Culprit: "How could you be so stupid?" Inner compassionate parent: "You're paying attention now. You're improving, getting better every day. I know you can do it."

Positive Tool #3: Rewards

Rewards are particularly useful for helping children to develop new behaviors. The child who constantly teases the baby might benefit from a reward system, as might the child who has trouble listening. Rewards are suitable to help train children to wait more patiently, to function more independently, to behave more kindly, to eat more neatly and much, much more.

Rewards can be anything a child finds pleasing: extra privileges, food treats, gift items, quality-time with a parent, even hugs and kisses. In order not to create addictions, be sure to rotate your use of rewards (i.e., don't use only one type of reward: sometimes use food, sometimes use privileges, sometimes use quality-time and so on).

The correct use of rewards is employed in two parenting contexts:

1. as part of a method of positive discipline, the CLeaR Method (see next page), and
2. as part of a reward-chart system.

The CLeaR Method of Positive Discipline

The CLeaR Method uses the first three positive tools we have just learned: Comment, Label and Reward. For easy recall, use the word "CLeaR"—"C" for Comment, "L" for Label and "R" for Reward.

When a child is engaging in a recurrent problematic behavior (i.e., always calling people names, routinely "not listening," regularly forgetting his homework, etc.) a parent should make a *parenting plan* to solve the problem once and for all. Simply making corrections "on the spot" is ineffective, unpleasant and destructive, as will be explained in detail in the next section. A parenting plan starts with "good-feeling" methods and moves on to "bad-feeling" methods if, and only if, the positive strategies fail to produce the desired change. One of the most powerful "good-feeling" forms of discipline is the CLeaR Method.

Let's say a child has trouble waiting patiently for Mother in the bank. He tends to run all over the place, creating havoc. The inner compassionate parent has made note of the problem and devised a parenting plan using the CLeaR Method.

The next time Mom goes to the bank, she's all ready. Two minutes after arriving (before trouble has started), Mom catches Junior being so-far-so-good quiet.

> "C": Mom **comments**—"I see you're waiting *quietly*."
> "L": Mom **labels**—"That's very *patient* of you."
> "R": Mom **rewards**—"I think that deserves a candy, which I just happen to have in my purse!"

Junior is delighted, of course! He finds it easier to wait for the next few minutes. Notice the positive discipline sequence:

1. **C: Comment.** Name a specific appropriate behavior. "You listened to Mommy right away!"
2. **L: Label.** Use a positive label that describes the kind of person who performs the behavior that was just displayed. "You're a good listener."
3. **R: Reward.** Give a reward. "I think that deserves a big hug and kiss!" (Rewards don't have to be concrete prizes of food and toys; they can be any pleasant form of attention.)

The three steps should be used repeatedly until the new behavior is established. Once the child is consistently performing the new behavior, the reward is "thinned." This means that Steps 1 and 2 (comment and label) are given each time the behavior is performed, but Step 3 (the reward) happens every second time for a while, then every third time, then every once in a while and, after about a month of winding down, it is not given at all. However, the commenting and labeling should be continued for many months after a new behavior has been established. After a time, a comment alone will maintain the behavior indefinitely.

Rewards vs. Bribes

Let's take a moment here to clarify the difference between rewards and bribes. Rewards are the second step in the CLeaR Method. They always *follow* a comment for appropriate behavior that has already occurred. Bribes, on the other hand, *precede* the desired behavior. Bribes are put forth as pleas to a child: "*If* you cooperate, I'll give you such and such." The reward is offered, though the child has not yet performed. In the CLeaR Method, rewards are not mentioned beforehand at all. Mom "just happens" to have a candy in her purse—she knows what she's planning to do, but Junior doesn't. Mom "catches" Junior behaving appropriately, comments on his behavior and "decides" to reward him. Mom is in charge. However, when Mom begs Junior to cooperate and offers him a prize for doing so, the cards are in Junior's hand. His attitude will be, "Let me think about that . . . hmmm. . . . I think I might consider doing it if your offer were a bit more generous. . . ." This puts the child in the wrong position. When he feels in charge, he also feels abandoned. Psychologically he's wondering, "Where have all the grown-ups gone? Gosh, I'm only three and calling all the shots! This is fun, but also scary! Is anybody home?"

It is true that once a child has received true rewards for a couple of times, he will attempt to initiate a bribe process with the parent. For example, our youngster at the bank will soon figure out that Mom may have a treat for him if he behaves nicely. At the next trip to the bank, he asks her, "Will you give me a treat if I behave?" Mom must not encourage the bribe dynamic. She answers, "It's not right for you to ask me that. You do what you have to do, and I'll do what I have to do." In other words, she refuses to play that game.

Isn't the CLeaR Method a Lot of Work?

Eventually (after 20 years or so!) it becomes second nature. But what are the alternatives? Most parents don't bother with this sort of planning. Instead, they do the "hit and miss" and "nag till they hate you" approach. These more stressful techniques are also a lot of work and a lot less gratifying. Here is a typical Mom in the bank with her impatient preschooler:

> "David, come back here. Just wait beside me. Put the pen-
> cil down. David, come back now. Just sit here. You're mak-
> ing too much noise, David; quiet down. David, I'm warning
> you. David, if you don't behave, there'll be no treat this
> afternoon. David!"

One consequence of this approach is that the child comes to hate his name. This is the natural consequence of hearing it said frequently with tension, irritability and obvious displeasure. Indeed, it is good practice *never to use the child's name when correcting a child's behavior.* Hating one's name is quite problematic, as one's name is so completely tied in with self-concept.

A second negative consequence of this approach is that it reinforces negative behavior. The more Mother attends to David's disruptive behavior, the more disruptive behavior is likely to occur. Attention reinforces anything it follows. It doesn't matter what kind of attention is given (positive or negative). *Behavior + attention = more of that behavior.* In other words, this strategy isn't going to work. Mom will probably be repeating the same scene weekly at the bank for several years.

A third negative consequence of parental nagging is that it corrodes relationship. Nobody likes to be around a critical, complaining person. If David's mother doesn't change her tune, her behavior may eventually destroy the possibility of a warm relationship between herself and her son—both because her son may dislike her and also because she may dislike him for not being cooperative. Indeed, parental helplessness often leads to the parent distancing from the child! This is possibly the most serious consequence because, as we learned previously, a positive relationship is the key to all parental power of influence. *No positive relationship – no positive influence.*

We can see, then, that it is worth becoming comfortable and competent with the CLeaR Method, as this approach to discipline has virtually no negative side-effects. Moreover, it will be your easiest and most successful intervention for daily behavior problems.

Now that we have looked at the use of the first three positive tools in the context of the CLeaR Method, let us revisit Positive Tool #3, rewards, to see how this technique can stand alone for another "good-feeling" form of guidance.

Rewards as Part of Reward Charts

Once or twice a year, you might want to try a reward chart with your child. It is not advisable to use such charts more often, because they may set up an unhealthy expectation on the part of the child that everything he does should be paid for! However, used rarely and carefully, they can be very helpful.

Set your reward chart to last five or six weeks. This is about how long it takes to make a permanent behavioral change. Create a series of tasks that increase in difficulty and that are matched with prizes of increasing value. End the chart with a special "grand prize."

It's important to have a single focus for the chart. For example, work on having the child do his chores independently, or clean his room, or play more nicely with his siblings. Do not have one chart that includes all kinds of different things like brushing teeth, going to bed on time, doing homework and cleaning the room!

Break down the single behavior into five or six steps. For example, room-cleaning could be broken down into picking things off the floor, making the bed, hanging up clothes or putting them in the laundry, cleaning the surfaces of chairs and clearing the desk. If the behavior you are targeting is a single behavior (getting the child to stop hitting his siblings, for instance), create a series of time periods of increasing duration. For example, the first one might be a five-minute period in which no hitting occurs. The second one might be a 10-minute period in which no hitting occurs. This could continue to increase, so that there are periods of a quarter-hour, a half-hour, an hour, two hours, a morning, an afternoon, an evening and a full day. Always start with the period in which the child could *easily* succeed. Reward charts should be easy. The child moves from strength to strength. If you think the child can only succeed for 30 seconds, then start your chart there!

Make the first task very easy. Give a sticker for each day or each period the task is accomplished. Arrange the chart so that young children will earn their first prize after three days and children over 5 years old will earn their first prize after about a week. Allow in your calculations for the child to miss earning a point occasionally.

Let's see how it would go with the clean room as our target. Suppose we are working with a 9-year-old. We make her first task very easy— she just has to make sure there's nothing on the floor when she leaves for school in the morning. Succeeding at this each day earns one point. We want her to get her first prize by the end of the week; therefore, we ask her to earn five points for the prize. This gives her two days that she could "forget" to clean her floor and she'd still succeed at receiving her first prize by the end of the week, when she doesn't succeed in her task, no comment is made and no sticker is earned. (If you find that the child cannot easily succeed in her task, you have set the task too high for a reward chart program. Make it easier.) Do not remind the child to do her task. The reward chart *replaces* nagging—it doesn't supplement it!

After the child earns her five points and receives her first prize, she starts the second task. The task is slightly harder and the prize is slightly larger. In our example, the first task was clearing the floor. The second task may be both clearing the floor and putting the clothes away.

The third task is still more difficult (clear floor, put away clothes, clear chairs). Tasks continue to increase in difficulty and the size of the prize increases correspondingly until the entire behavior is accomplished (in our case: clearing the floor, putting away clothes, clearing chairs, clearing furniture and making the bed). At this point, a grand prize is offered, something special that the child will really value.

The behavior is then reinforced with praise and positive programming. If the targeted behavior slackens off, negative-feeling discipline will be used.

Use your imagination in creating reward charts. Just remember to break down a behavioral goal into a series of smaller tasks. Have the child start with the easiest task and the smallest reward. Increase the size of the next task and the size of the accompanying reward. Continue in this way until the total behavior is accomplished. Young children should be able to earn each reward within three to five days and older kids must earn them within a week. The chart should continue for four to six weeks, and it always ends with a grand prize. Have fun!

CHAPTER 5

Emotional Coaching

This technique is so simple, yet it is unbelievably powerful. Because of its power, we will examine it in depth. Emotional coaching is one of the best tools for strengthening the parent-child relationship. It affects both security and behavior.

Emotional coaching is the skill of accompanying our children on their journey, much as our inner compassionate parent accompanies us. The concept was coined by Dr. John Gottman in his wonderful parenting book, *Raising an Emotionally Intelligent Child*. Dr. Gottman found that emotionally coached children became emotionally intelligent: they were smart about the world of feelings. They were aware of both their own feelings and the feelings of others. They could relate empathetically to people and therefore had better social skills. He also found that they were better able to regulate their own emotions. They demonstrated better academic performance and experienced better physical health. Like emotionally intelligent adults, these children did better in every area of life. And they engaged in much less misbehavior than other children.

What's the secret to raising emotionally intelligent children? Emotions. Parents need to acknowledge, accept and "be with" their child's emotions. That's all there is to it.

How Is This Done Exactly?

1. **Acknowledge.** When a child shows any kind of emotion (happy, sad, scared, disappointed, angry, frustrated, excited, confused, annoyed, etc.),

acknowledge it. Do this by *naming the feeling*. For instance, say, "I see that you're upset," or "You look worried," or "You're mad at me." Do this before saying or doing anything else.

As you do this, be sure that your own facial expression, tone of voice and general manner are reflecting the feeling—in other words, *say it with feeling*. For instance, in a low, slow tone, say, "You seem sad about it." Or in a strong, energetic tone say, "I can see that you *really* don't want to go swimming!" Neither children nor adults will accept the naming of a feeling from someone who shows no emotion or the wrong emotion. In fact, the cold or incorrect naming of a feeling actually causes rage in the listener. Imagine how *you* would feel if your heart was breaking and someone said to you in a dry, emotionless voice, "I see that you're very broken up over this," or if you were utterly furious at your spouse and he or she said in a calm, cool voice, "I understand that you're mad." Chilly communications like these will make a child feel *less* understood, not more. Feelings are hot, vibrant, passionate and intense. They must not be named in the same factual voice that one uses to note that two plus two makes four.

2. **Accept.** Rather than argue with, correct or otherwise attempt to change the child's feeling, simply accept it. "You don't want pizza tonight. I understand." This is different than saying, "Why don't you want pizza tonight? You love pizza!" This latter statement is an attempt to get the child to change his feeling. Saying "I understand" or "I see" lets the child know you accept his feeling.

3. **Be With.** When feelings are strong, the parent should just "be with" them or "sit with" them. Sometimes this means literally sitting beside the child quietly, after acknowledging and accepting a feeling. For example, suppose a child told Mom in a dejected manner that he failed the science test he studied so hard for. Mom can acknowledge the feeling by saying, "I can see you're very sad about it." She can accept the feeling by saying, "Your being down makes sense. You studied so hard for it and you didn't get the results you wanted to." She can then be with

or sit with the feelings by literally sitting down beside the child and putting her arm around his shoulders without saying anything further.

These three steps (acknowledge, accept, be with) allow the child to process his feelings. They help the child release his negative emotion rather than suppress it. Released emotions lead to healthy functioning, whereas suppressed emotions may be channeled into physical pain and/or emotional difficulties. Released emotions are the key to emotional intelligence and all of its positive consequences.

Remember to Welcome Negative Feelings

Although Steps 1, 2 and 3 (acknowledge, accept, be with) are all easy and straightforward, emotional coaching is emotionally challenging for parents. Parents often have a hard time acknowledging, accepting and being with *their own* negative feelings, let alone their child's! Indeed, when a parent is confronted by a child's bad feelings, the parent herself can feel overwhelmed, disturbed, saddened, frightened, angry and otherwise upset (these and other parental emotions will be explored in detail in chapters 12, 13 and 14). In some cases, it will be appropriate for the parent to actually share her reaction. Most often, however, the parent must set aside her own feelings temporarily while she attends to the child's emotional needs. When the child is settled, the parent may take some time to help herself process her own feelings privately. (Techniques for doing so are provided in the chapters on parental emotions.)

Parents want their child to be happy. It's hard to allow a child to have scared, sad or troubled feelings. There is a great tendency for a parent to try to make bad feelings go away by trying to cheer up the child, distract him, downplay his feelings or correct his perceptions. Note the following example:

Eli comes in after school looking sad and dejected.
Mom: *What's wrong, sweetheart?*
Eli: *Nobody likes me.*

Mom: *What do you mean? Everybody likes you! Danny likes
          you, Leah likes you, Sarah likes you, Nathan likes you,
          and Daddy and I like you most of all!*

Poor Mom! She just can't tolerate Eli's negative feelings. Without even
recognizing her own fear and panic, she tries urgently to talk him out of
his feelings. This is not emotional coaching! Emotional coaching involves
listening and accepting. What Mom should have said when Eli said
"nobody likes me" is "Really? That's so sad. I can see you're feeling really
badly." With this sort of acknowledgment and acceptance, Eli probably
would have gone on to explain that he had a fight at school earlier that
day and he feels so rejected. Most likely he would also be able to do some
problem-solving with Mom after his emotions are released.

While acknowledging and accepting Eli's feelings helps to release
them, offering reassurance actually increases insecurity. Mom's attempt
to reassure Eli by naming all the people who like him, distracts him
momentarily from his inner reality. It does not, however, remove the bad
feeling. Bad feelings must be *released*, not covered over. When covered
over with reassurance, the bad feeling is suppressed, stuffed deeper down
into the personality. The clue to this syndrome is hearing yourself say,
"No matter how often I reassure her, she keeps coming back with the
same concerns." Indeed, reassurance itself reinforces insecurity. Let's look
at how another mom uses emotional coaching to help her daughter
process a negative feeling:

Rachel: *I feel fat.*
Mom: *Really? That must be hard for you.*
Rachel: *Well, I'm not that fat . . . it's just my stomach. I hate my
           stomach.*
Mom: *Oh, you hate your stomach.*
Rachel: *It's puffy.*
Mom: *Mmm…*
Rachel: *And there's nothing I can do about it. I do sit-ups all
           day and it doesn't help!*

Mom: *Mmm. That's too bad.*
Rachel: *It's not fair!*
Mom: *No, it certainly isn't!*
Rachel: *I've got to go now. Patty's waiting.*
Mom: *Okay. See you later.*

What's happened in this conversation? First of all, Mom has accepted Rachel's feelings. She hasn't argued with her or tried to "enlighten" her. As a result, Rachel is able to continue expressing her feelings till she feels relieved—she's cleared her own upset. This is a powerful skill. Rachel's also learned that feelings aren't scary. Mom is modeling that she can handle all of Rachel's feelings without needing to change them or run away from them. This enables Rachel to process every difficult emotion successfully. Moreover, Rachel has experienced the kind of support that will allow her to have a healthy inner parent one day, a small, supportive voice that accompanies her everywhere. She'll never be alone.

If Rachel needed advice, she could have asked for it and received it. However, problem-solving always comes *after* emotional coaching. Feelings are addressed first and solutions are worked on second.

What if Mom wanted to teach Rachel some important things about body image? Would it be all right for her to give a short speech after the emotional coaching? The optimal word here is "short." If Mom can get her point across in 10 or 15 words or less, it might be all right. Kids don't benefit much from speeches and lectures. Neither do adults, come to think of it. Perhaps, for example, if Mom felt a very strong urge to share her wisdom, she might say, "Anyway, women are meant to have soft tummies—it's very feminine." Such a comment, however, must come at the very end of an emotional coaching session. If offered at the beginning, it could actually lead to a fight!

More Examples

Emotional coaching can be used both with a child's small worries and with his largest concerns. When a child says he can't stand life and wants to die, it's time for emotional coaching—for naming, accepting and being with feelings. A child who is able to share this kind of pain with you needs your response. Even though you may later arrange an appointment with a mental health professional, he's talking to you now. Just name the feelings: "You sound as if you're feeling completely hopeless." Let's look at this example of extreme negative emotion more closely:

Child: *I can't stand life. I want to end it all.*

Parent: *You sound incredibly discouraged. What's going on?*

Child: *Nothing. That's the problem. Nothing's happening in my life. There's no point in living.*

Parent: *"There's no point in living." That sounds so empty. It's like you're in a dark tunnel or something.*

Child: *Black. Everything's black.*

Parent: *Black. Mmm.*

Child: *It's no use. I'll never get what I want anyway. What's the point of trying?*

Parent: *I see. It feels like nothing will work, so why try, why not just give up?*

Child: *Well, I can't see any other way.*

Parent: *Yes, I see how hopeless you're feeling right now.*

Child: *So what should I do?*

Parent: *Do you want to see a counselor—someone who could help you sort it all out?*

Child: *Maybe.*

Parent: *I'll look into it for you and let you know what I find out.*

This would have to be one of the most challenging conversations a parent could have with a child. The parent will instinctively want to try to talk the child out of his feelings—"Don't talk like that!" "Never say that!" "Don't ever think of doing that!" The untrained parent will rush in with advice, warnings and dire threats. Unfortunately, this will only cause the child to clam up completely, keeping his thoughts to himself, turning inward to his pain. The child may feel criticized and abandoned, rather than supported and assisted.

In the above dialogue, we see that a parent can support a child even through deep, painful emotions. The parent simply names the child's feelings in each of his statements, right down to the deepest feeling near the end of the dialogue—"hopeless." When the child has gone down to this depth of feeling, his feelings do what most people's do—they start upward again. After Mom says "I see how hopeless you're feeling," the child actually starts the process of problem-solving ("So what should I do?"). It's only because Mom had the courage to go all the way down with him that he's able to start the ascent. Mom also did one other thing: she added the words "right now" in her sentence ("I see how hopeless you're feeling right now"). By doing this, she helped bring her child's experience into the present moment, implying that his feeling of hopelessness won't last forever. This is a helpful approach when dealing with overwhelming emotions. Draw the child's attention to *this moment, this specific difficulty.* It is a calming technique. (In another example of this technique, a father helps his child who "hates math" by acknowledging that "problem #9 on the homework sheet is really tricky and not fun to do," which brings the big problem right down to the specific issue and moment in time. See Martin Seligman's *The Optimistic Child* for an in-depth look at this listening strategy.)

Emotional Coaching Doesn't Change the Facts

In its more common, everyday usage, emotional coaching addresses many passing moods and small issues. A child is frequently frustrated, displeased, disturbed, upset, anxious and bothered. All of these feelings can be named. However, just because a parent has named his child's feelings doesn't mean that the parent will then give the child whatever he wants. The parent can acknowledge that Junior hates swimming lessons and then still send him for swimming lessons. It helps to put the acknowledgment of feelings in a separate sentence, apart from the statement of facts. "I see you don't want to do your homework. Unfortunately, it's time to get started on it." It's very important *not* to join the feelings with the facts using the word "but." For instance, "I see you don't want to do your homework, but it's time to get started on it" sounds completely different from the first example. The word "but" acts as an eraser, rubbing out the previously offered emotional support. The word "but" ends up sounding like, "I know you have such and such negative feeling, but I don't care." It's helpful at times for the parent to sympathize with the child's feelings or show that he has had similar feelings himself. This helps the child feel that the parent truly understands. Note the differences in the following two comments:

- "I understand that you don't like your teacher, but you still have to go to school today."
- "I understand that you don't like your teacher. No wonder you don't want to go to school. I remember having teachers I didn't like and that was no fun at all, believe me! Unfortunately, you still have to go to school today."

Or these:

- "I can see you're disappointed, but we'll try to go to the park another day, when the weather is better."
- "I can see you're disappointed. You were really looking forward to going to the park and now our plans are ruined. I was looking forward to going also, and I'm really disappointed too. All we can do is try to go another day, when the weather is better."

In emotional coaching there is a "period" after the acknowledgment of feelings—a full, complete stop. This stop is long enough that the "period" can be heard clearly. The period gives the emotional acknowledgment weight and substance; it gives it importance of its own. If the period is replaced by the word "but," the acknowledgment of feelings becomes insignificant, whereas the "facts" become the focal point. Even when an unpleasant situation cannot be changed, the child benefits from being heard and emotionally supported. This is accomplished by creating a true pause after the naming of feelings.

One of the lessons of emotional coaching is that feelings are only feelings. They are not dangerous to own or to acknowledge. Even when they are painful or unpleasant, they needn't interfere with appropriate functioning. A child is allowed to feel unhappy. It doesn't mean, however, that he is excused from his responsibilities or the realities of life.

Emotional Coaching Increases Cooperation

Sometimes a parent needs to teach a child something. Teaching can only occur in a "teaching moment," a moment in which both parent and child are calm. Emotional coaching helps calm a child and ready her for listening. But it does more than that. It actually creates a learning condition. Look at the difference between these two dialogues:

> Child: *I'm not going to any more swimming lessons. I don't like it anymore. Anyway, I know how to swim already.*
> Parent: *You need to get stronger in the deep end. I still want you to continue lessons.*

Or this:

> Child: *I hate going!*
> Parent: *Well, you have to go until I feel you're safe.*
> Child: *I hate it! I'm not going!*

> Child: *I'm not going to any more swimming lessons. I don't like it anymore. Anyway, I know how to swim already.*
> Parent: *Sounds like you're tired of your lessons. They aren't fun anymore?*
> Child: *No. I don't like the new teacher either.*
> Parent: *Oh, that's frustrating. It's not much fun to go when you don't like the teacher. The problem is, I want you to get a little stronger in the deep end. I want you to be perfectly*

safe in the water and I'm not comfortable that you're quite there. Probably one or two more sessions will be enough, but I don't want you to stop until I know you're really safe.

Child: *All right. But just one or two more sessions—not more!*

Parent: *Okay. We'll keep it to that, as long as you pass the deep end test. Okay?*

Child: *Okay.*

Keeping in mind that dialogues in books are only dialogues in books (they don't necessarily unfold exactly that way in real life), these two conversations do illustrate an important aspect of parent-child communication. When we try to teach a child something *before* we've done emotional coaching, we're wasting our breath. The conversation will feel like a struggle or outright fight. The child feels unheard and not understood. Until the child feels heard, she will not be ready to listen, learn or cooperate. *Therefore, always use emotional coaching before teaching or instructing an upset child.*

To further understand why this is so essential, consider this analogy: Parent and child form a train. The parent is the engine, and a little way behind him is the caboose—an upset child. The two parts are arranged like so:

Suppose the parent tries to teach a lesson or give information or instruction, without first providing emotional coaching—in other words, "lecture, lecture, lecture." What happens is that the engine moves down the track alone, like this:

If the engine wants to bring the caboose with her, she must first *back up* to where the caboose is, *hook on*, and then proceed down the track together, like so:

This action could be described as "teach-learn-teach-learn." Backing up to where the child is and hooking on (bonding) is the act of emotional coaching. When the child is securely attached, the parent can teach, inform or instruct and hope to be heard. Without that attachment, the parent is talking to himself. The child remains isolated, feeling misunderstood and abandoned. He neither processes the parent's words of wisdom, nor inclines himself to cooperate. Rather, he remains stuck on the track.

Emotional Coaching Soothes Upset Feelings

In addition to helping children learn and cooperate, emotional coaching can help them resolve feelings of frustration or unhappiness, enabling them to accept compromises and consolation. Examine the following two dialogues. In the first conversation, the parent answers by stating the facts and omitting any acknowledgment of the child's feelings. In the second conversation, the parent reflects the child's feelings using emotional coaching, and then engages in problem-solving. Note the differing results:

Child: *Why does Becky get to go out with you and I never get to go! It's not fair!*

Parent: *I'm just taking Becky to get some shoes. We'll be back very soon.*

Child: *But I want shoes! You never get me any shoes!*

Parent: *That's not true. I get you shoes when you need shoes. Right now Becky needs shoes.*

Child runs away and slams door.

Child: *Why does Becky get to go out with you and I never get to go! It's not fair!*

Parent: *You don't like that Becky's coming with me and you have to stay home right now. That doesn't seem fair; you want to come too. You're upset with Mommy.*

Child: *Yes. Why can't I come? I want to come!*

Parent: *Yes, you really want to come, I can see that. And I'd like your company too. It's just that Becky needs to get some shoes and it's hard for me to get her shoes and look after you at the same time. I know it's disappointing for you not to be able to come. What if I bring you back some bubble gum from the candy store—would that help at all?*

Child: *No! I want to come! You never get me any shoes!*

Parent: *Oh, you just want to come. Bubble gum won't help. And Mommy never gets you shoes; she only looks after Becky. That's sad.*

Child: *Yes.*

Parent: *Yes.*

Child: *What kind of gum?*

Parent: *I was thinking of your favorite—red bubble gum.*

Child: *Can I have two pieces?*

Parent: *Yes, I'll bring you two pieces. We'll be back very soon. Bye-bye, sweetie.*

When feelings are accepted ("that's sad"), they clear, leave the system and vanish. The way to change a feeling is to accept it. There is no other way. Once the painful feeling leaves, solutions can be found. In the example you just read, Mom offers Becky some comfort food to ease the pain of disappointment. She could have offered other treats instead, such as a few minutes of special quality time, bubbles in a bath, a privilege such as a video and so on. In fact, it is important to vary the types of comforts that are offered so that addictions are not formed. However, comforting pain in some way is an important step for parents to take with their children. It helps kids learn to comfort themselves in healthy ways throughout life. Soothing pain by talking about it, feeling it and comforting it replaces the need to drown it out or numb it with unhealthy addictions such as drugs, alcohol, gambling, eating and so on. The "talking about it" and "feeling it" steps are absolutely crucial: had Mom simply tried to hush Becky up by bribing her with bubble gum, Mom would have been contributing to a numbing/addictive cycle rather than a healthy cycle of emotional release and soothing.

Feelings and Behaviors Are Different

An important rule to remember is that all feelings are acceptable; not all behaviors are acceptable.

Suppose Junior is very upset because his favorite cereal box is empty. There's nothing wrong with him being disappointed or even angry. Those are just his feelings. However, if he starts to throw things all over the kitchen and scream at the top of his lungs, he's going to need some lessons on emotional expression. Children need to learn how to express anger, sadness and even fear, in ways that are socially acceptable. While it is perfectly normal and acceptable for a child to be afraid of thunder, for example, it is not acceptable for her to scream and cry at the top of her lungs throughout a storm. A child must often be taught how to use her words to express feelings and how to calm herself enough to restrain her behavior when upset. In a later section, we'll discuss in detail how to teach a child to express his negative feelings in a healthy manner.

Similarly, it would be fine for a child to be furious at his brother for breaking his toy. It would not be fine for him to punch the brother for doing so. It would be totally okay for a teenager to hate eating dinner with the family. However, it may not be okay for her to be absent from the table.

There are some feelings a child has that his parent wishes he didn't have. These feelings, too, need to be accepted rather than corrected. Only by accepting feelings can parents hope to change them. Acceptance of feelings releases them and allows them to clear out of a person's system. Acknowledging and welcoming an emotion actually opens a door, permitting the feeling to move out of the room that it is stuck in. On the other hand, telling a child to change his feelings is futile. Feelings cannot change on command. They can be silenced in that way, but they cannot be healed. Indeed, ignoring a feeling (slamming a door on it) keeps it permanently locked inside, where it remains an active part of the child's inner world. Note the following two dialogues:

- "I understand you hate your brother, but that isn't right. You should love your brother because that's who you're going to have to count on your whole life long."
- "I understand you hate your brother. Sometimes he makes you really mad and he hurts your feelings."

A parent may be afraid to acknowledge a child's "hatred" of his sibling. However, if the feeling is acknowledged, the child will be quicker to heal and self-correct. On the other hand, if the parent attempts to talk a child out of his feelings ("you should love your brother") this can send the feeling underground, where it may fester for a lifetime.

Don't Punish Feelings

It may be necessary to use discipline for the inappropriate *expression* of feelings, that is, the inappropriate behaviors. However, we do not punish the child for having his feelings. We would not, for example, tell a child to go to his room because he's so miserable. Similarly, we would not make fun of a child for having fears. "Afraid of the elevator? What are you—a sissy?" We would not humiliate a child for his sensitivity. "Crying again because she called you names? What are you—a baby?" Remember, all feelings are acceptable. Moreover, the only way to change a feeling is to accept it. That is the basis of much psychotherapy. Once the fear, sadness, anger (or whatever) is acknowledged and even welcomed, it diminishes automatically.

Nonetheless, a parent must be careful not to accidentally reinforce the child's tendency to have problems. If Patty comes home from school on Monday complaining bitterly about the mean math teacher, her parent should offer emotional coaching along with a bit of sympathy (emotional coaching is the naming of the *child's* feelings; sympathy is the expression of the *parent's* feelings). If she comes home on Tuesday with the same story, emotional coaching should be offered, followed by an invitation to begin problem-solving (figuring out how to cope with this teacher for the whole year). If she comes home on Wednesday with the same miserable tale, however, the emotional coaching should be limited to one or two sentences ("Oh, that's so frustrating") and the emphasis should be put on finding solutions or quietly adapting to a difficult situation. If the parent were to sit down for 20 minutes of quality-time listening every day, the child would inadvertently learn that having problems earns excellent attention. In order to avoid such a lesson, a parent should only give top-notch coaching on the first and second run of a problem; after that, attention needs to be pared back. In addition, parents should be careful to give quality, intense attention when the child is *not* unhappy. Otherwise, the youngster learns that being in pain is the only way to get that kind of care.

Chronic Negative Feelings

At times, a child's distress does not subside no matter how much emotional support and problem-solving has been offered. Hours of unhappiness turns into days, and days turn into weeks; in some cases, weeks turn into months. When negative feelings become chronic, it is time for a trip to a mental health professional. Competent professionals have many more tricks up their sleeves besides naming feelings and finding solutions (acquaint yourself with the training and approach of the prospective therapist to make sure he or she will be able to do more than you have done!). Just like most folks can brush and floss their own teeth but choose to go to the dentist when they have a cavity that needs filling, average parents can handle the normal issues of child-drearing but choose to consult a professional when situations are more complicated. Even though a child may be engaged in therapy, the parent will still want to welcome all feelings in the home. Good mental health for all the members of the family is assisted by the regular expression and acceptance of feelings.

The Importance of Emotional Coaching

Emotional coaching may seem like a parenting "frill" to you. Believe me, it is not. It is virtually the core of parenting. Helping a child to acquire emotional intelligence is one of the greatest gifts a parent can give. Moreover, when a parent can support his or her child through trying times and difficult moments, the parent has an opportunity to build tremendous trust, intimacy, understanding and love with that child. These are valuable "relationship-builders" and—as you know—relationship is everything.

CHAPTER 6

Staying Calm
Under Pressure

Your Feelings

Children aren't the only ones with feelings. We parents have them too. And ours aren't all "happy" either! Parents feel sad, helpless, insulted, upset, scared, worried, stressed, pressured, overwhelmed—sometimes all before breakfast! In other words, we're human. In later chapters we will examine some of these emotions in depth and study their effects on our parenting style. We'll even learn some powerful techniques for healing our distress. For now, however, we will look at only one emotion and its impact on childrearing: parental anger.

Feelings are just feelings and are all acceptable—including anger. However, not all behaviors are acceptable. (Does this sound familiar?) Thus parents need to know that being human is fine; being irresponsible is not. Recognizing that our emotions affect our children both directly (through affecting our parenting style) and indirectly (through exposing our children to our moods and personalities) allows us to engage in more conscious parenting. We can actually choose not to hurt our children no matter how upset we *feel*. We can choose to raise our children without raising our voices once we realize the destructive impact of the raised voice. Of course this choice involves a commitment to learn how to harness our angry feelings. In this chapter we will look at some behavioral strategies for doing this. In later chapters, we will examine ways of actually removing anger at its source, thereby obliterating the need to "manage" it.

As we successfully control our mouths and actions, we gain a twofold benefit: 1) we make our family emotionally safe, and 2) we show our children by example how to manage stress, cope with disappointment and handle frustration.

Why Do We Raise Our Voices?

Why do we yell at our "loved" ones? The subject of why we yell at our spouses deserves a book of its own, so we will limit the question for now to why we yell at our children. Why do we do it? Here are the popular reasons for this pervasive habit:

- Kids don't listen.
- Yelling seems to get results.
- We were programmed by our parents to do it.
- We're stressed.
- Our buttons get pushed.
- We're overwhelmed.
- We're tired and hungry.
- We have "yelling" genes.
- We don't know what else to do.

The problem, of course, is that a raised voice interrupts the flow of love. It's like a knife that cuts right through the warm flow of affection. Anyone who wants to enjoy the benefits of loving relationships—happiness, joy, wholeness, contentment, security, physical health, mental health and more—must find a way to parent without yelling. No matter how well a raised voice seems to work in getting kids to cooperate, it is simply not worth the price that must be paid: yelling hurts parents, children and their relationship. The negative consequences may last a lifetime.

Curing Raised-Voice Addiction

Many modern parents are fully aware of both the dangers of an angry parenting style and the need to teach their children how to be respectful and loving. They just can't do it. Every day they wake up intending to do it, but they just can't. Their neural pathways propel them along directly from an upset feeling to a raised voice. It's like there is a little switch in the brain. To turn it on, a parent need only feel some sort of upset. This could be a frustration of some sort, a hurt feeling, or perhaps a fear. It could be the result of an interaction with a child or it could be the result of thinking about something disturbing. Once the switch has been flipped, however, an energy pulse moves along the pathway directly to the muscles of the mouth. The mouth opens and out comes the raised voice!

The neural pathway may have been inherited from Mom or Dad, or it may have been learned from them and practiced in childhood, or it may have been developed in the process of parenting and practiced until it is like a piano tune that flows on automatic pilot from the fingertips. It doesn't really matter how it got there. What does matter is knowing how to get rid of it!

Brain surgery is never easy. The old pathway must be deactivated and a new one, the peaceful one, must be installed. Many different interventions can help with this process, involving thought, action and emotion. In this chapter, we will examine our beliefs and our behavioral options—the first two steps in getting a grip!

"You're Making Me Mad"

Have you ever said that to your kids? Let's just put it this way: while we shouldn't actually say this to children, the truth is that they *do* make us mad. However, as we shall presently see, that's not actually their fault.

Here's why:

1. It's not their fault. They're children. Young children run around with lots of energy, getting into everything, experimenting and exploring. That's healthy for them and annoying for us. Only a very ill child does not engage in this kind of activity. Older children are experimenting, trying on different activities, relationships and roles. This is their job. Failure to branch out, individuate and take risks in adolescence may cause problems later on in life, when the urge to grow suddenly manifests at middle age, wreaking havoc.

2. It's not their fault. Their misbehavior is necessary in order to test the environment, discover rules and boundaries and learn right from wrong. They are programmed genetically to unfold in this manner. Our job is to give them feedback. Gently. Just like your inner compassionate parent does it.

3. It's not their fault. We may be short on patience because we've had too little sleep and too much stress. We may be running on adrenaline, caffeine or pep pills. Our resistance may be low.

4. It's not their fault. We may be frustrated with our own lack of effectiveness, our helplessness in getting them to do what we want. It's our job to know how to do this, not theirs. We may be short on strategies and options and in need of study or professional guidance.

5. It's not their fault. Telling them it's their fault gives them a "blaming" model of the world. It teaches them not to take responsibility. Try asking your 7-year-old why he hit his brother. You might hear something like this: "It's his fault; he took my book." To which a wise parent answers, "You have choices as to how to handle that. He didn't make you hit him." This lesson becomes

hard to teach when we insist on blaming our children for our own actions and feelings. Yes, we are responsible not only for our behaviors, but also for our feelings. If we find that we are often getting angry, we need to discover the root cause and remedy the tendency to experience this emotion so frequently. We may need to check our physical health (being tired, sick or run-down leads to irritability). Or we may need to check our mental health (temperament issues, mood issues, chemical imbalances and unresolved emotions can lead to excessive anger). *It's up to us* to find our path to emotional serenity and balance. Our emotional health is not dependent on our children's behavior.

In any case, it's our problem, not theirs.

For all these reasons, we never say to a child, "You're making me mad."

So What Do We Do?

Review the possible reasons for yelling listed on page 51, and ask yourself and your spouse which one likely applies to you. Then start a program of rehabilitation that addresses the real source of your behavior. (Hint: it frequently helps to seriously consider your spouse's explanation of your outbursts, even—or especially—if it differs from your own. Your spouse is an expert on you.) You can also use the following guidelines to help determine your "anger style."

If you were never really an angry person till you had children, the most likely cause of anger lies in the state of your health, unresolved stress or inadequate parenting skills. Hold this book close to your heart for a few minutes and meditate. Meditation reduces stress and restores physical and mental health. Then read the book from cover to cover! Focus your attention on those strategies that help to prevent behavior problems and those strategies that address it once it's occurred. Study the "2x Rule" especially carefully—it is a true antidote to anger. (The 2x Rule is explained in detail in Chapter 7.)

If you've always had a temper, the cause probably lies somewhere in your family background and/or inborn characteristics. If you want, you can just say, "This is the way I am," and proceed to ruin your children's lives. Or you can seek the help of a psychologist, anger management specialist, psychiatrist, naturopath, homeopath, flower essence practitioner or other health professional who deals with long-lasting anger difficulties. Let your inner compassionate parent guide you appropriately.

Once you've determined the likely underlying causes of your temper, you can begin an appropriate program of rehabilitation. While occasional experiences of frustration and irritation are part of the normal human experience—and particularly, part of the normal parenting experience—regular and frequent occurrences of upset, anger, rage, annoyance, resentment and so forth indicate an imbalance that requires treatment. If you feel this kind of emotion on a regular basis and have not been able to determine any particular cause, seek professional guidance. Psychologists and other mental health practitioners can often help reduce both the angry feelings and the angry behaviors that accompany them. Since there are many professional approaches to accomplishing this, look around until you find a practitioner with an approach that appeals to you.

Meanwhile. . . How to Manage Anger

Till you're completely cured, here are some tips on how to manage anger that you are in the midst of feeling:

1. **Name your feeling.** If possible, name your feeling out loud as soon as you are aware that you are feeling tense. If it's long past that, do it anyway. Your sentence should sound something like this: "I'm starting to get frustrated." (Notice the difference between this sentence and "You're making me frustrated." Always use "I am" instead of "You are.") If you're already further down the line with your feeling, that is to say, you missed your first anger signals, you should still name your feeling. Try, "I'm feeling very frustrated." It is better to use words like "frustrated," "upset,"

"irritated" and so on, than to use the words "angry" or "mad." These latter two words have an implied "at you" attached to them, as in "I'm angry *at you*," or "I'm mad *at you*." They imply that the child is at fault. Words like "irritated," on the other hand, can be understood as internal states and are less inherently blaming.

2. **Announce the steps you are going to take to calm down.** Say out loud, "I'm going to sit down, breathe slowly and think about how to solve this problem." This provides a terrific model for your children to learn to calm themselves down. *Anger is a signal, not a tool.* It signals that something is wrong and needs your attention. Once you have heard the signal, *turn it off by sitting down to breathe or leaving the room to start your calming process.*

These calming steps contain powerful anti-adrenaline properties. Here's what happens in our bodies when we get angry. When we feel threatened (like when we can't get our kids to take a bath or when our adolescent starts bellowing at the top of his lungs), adrenaline is released in the body. This puts the body into emergency-mode, draining blood and oxygen from the brain's cortex (the problem-solving part) into the larger muscles of the body that are designed for fight-or-flight activity. The angry parent, aided by adrenaline, now suffers a deficiency of oxygen in his brain—which is why parents say the dumbest things in anger! Moreover, the brain, now operating on "automatic pilot," starts spewing out programmed messages from the parent's own childhood. This is why we find ourselves suddenly sounding awfully like our own parents of yesteryear, saying things we promised ourselves we'd never say. Help—we need oxygen badly!

Fortunately, the sitting down and breathing technique provides that oxygen and turns off the fight-or-flight emergency response, thus restoring physiological and emotional calm. Anti-anger breathing involves breathing in, to a slow count of 4, and breathing out, to a *slow* count of 8. Do this for one full minute. (This magic 1:2 breathing ratio turns off the adrenaline response in both anger and panic attacks.) With oxygen restored, we can begin to think about what to do next.

3. **Do it: sit down and breathe slowly in to a count of 4, and out to a count of 8.** Listen to your inner compassionate parent telling you that you're doing the right thing. Feel it stroke your back gently, as it praises your efforts and commends your actions. Listen to its statements of confidence in your parenting skill and its reassurances that the children will be grown up before you know it, and that this moment will certainly pass and there's something pleasant for you to look forward to this evening. (It's a good stress-reduction practice *always* to arrange something pleasant for yourself to look forward to each day.)

When you're quite calm, create a parenting plan to handle the type of situation that prompted your angry response. Suppose the kids were calling each other names. Decide what intervention you'd like to use on a long-term basis to solve this recurring issue. Decide if it is appropriate to do anything right now or if it would be better to discuss the plan with the children later on. Remember, very few things must be taken care of in the moment. In fact, they can be taken care of hours or even days later. Timing is important: wait for a "teaching moment,"—a time when both parent and child are calm. With the exception of danger to limb or life, you can sit and think calmly while the misbehavior actually continues. In those times when the situation is dangerous, remove the danger and then follow Steps 1 to 3.

Raise Your Children Without Raising Your Voice

If you really want to raise your children without raising your voice, there is a sure-fire method of doing it. This method can be used even if you don't know any other parenting techniques. After using it, you may not be a perfect parent, but at least you won't be a yelling one! Here's how it works:

After every episode of expressed anger (a raised voice, unkind words, aggressive body language, etc.), sit down and write out lines. Your lines should be expressed in a positive form, such as "I speak quietly to all people at all times" or "I speak quietly no matter what." For the first three days of the program, write one full page (one side of three-ringed lined paper) of these lines after every angry episode. Lines should be written as soon as possible after an "incident" but definitely completed by the end of each day. For the next five to seven days, write two sides after every episode. If your angry outbursts have been reduced to close to zero during this period, continue to write two sides for another couple of weeks; if they have not improved significantly, increase your pages to three or four and note the results. Keep raising the number of pages in your assignment until you find the number that actually lowers the incidence of your poor behavior. If this technique doesn't appeal to you or lacks effectiveness, feel free to modify the negative consequence to something more personally frustrating than writing out lines. The key is to choose something that you are willing to actually do. Some people find it effective to charge themselves a generous sum (to be donated to charity) for each angry outburst. Again, the sum can be increased over the course of a couple of weeks until it becomes too expensive to yell! Other folks fine themselves with added work: every inappropriate communication requires them to clean out a drawer or work on their taxes or do some other normally dreaded task. Some people lose weight and get fit by assigning themselves 10 push-ups per yell, moving up to 15, 20, 50 or whatever is necessary. Select your medicine and get started! Providing that you actually carry out your negative consequence each time (don't let yourself off the hook by deciding that your behavior wasn't really so bad), you ought to be cured of yelling within a month.

A bonus to using this method is that the children are quite likely to express curiosity about your line-writing or other negative consequence—in fact, don't try to hide it. Explain openly to them that you are working on yourself. Let them know that you are training yourself to speak respectfully at all times and that when you are finished, you will begin training them as well. Children will be quite impressed with your willingness to improve yourself and with your obvious concern for them. They will see that people can change and grow through conscious effort and will learn that growth is a lifelong process that leads to greater love and happiness.

Why Manage Anger?

Why do all this? Why not just let those kids know loud and clear when you're not happy with their behavior? Won't that help them know right from wrong? Especially if you've really had it, if they've really gone much too far, if they really deserve what for—shouldn't you give it to them?

No.

While it's true that we have to let our children know right from wrong, it is not true that we have to do this loudly, forcibly or otherwise disrespectfully. When we use anger to teach a lesson (in other words, use anger as a teaching tool), we are always teaching the basics of disrespect. We're effectively telling our children, "When a person has something really important to say, then it's okay for him to lose his own dignity and to ignore the dignity of others. Emotional or verbal abuse is acceptable, as long as your message is important." Is that what you want to teach your children? Such a lesson will guarantee them a life of troubled relationships. Raging at people is always costly, no matter how "justified" it is. Sometimes the damage is beyond repair. Think carefully before you fall back into the "let 'em have it" routine. Besides harming them, you can very well harm yourself: many parents have lost their children this way.

Another reason for doing all we can to prevent our anger—and this may be the most important reason—is to maintain our power of influence. Keep in mind that if we use anger frequently with our children, we will destroy the relationship, the seat of our influence.

How frequently would be too often? Can you blow up at your child once a year with no harm done? How about once a month? Would once a week be okay? Once a day? Several times a day?

To answer this question, decide how long you'd like to be married to someone who yelled at you several times a day. What would the quality of that relationship be? What would it do to the relationship if your spouse blew up at you only once a month? How often do you think you deserve to be screamed at by your partner? Children have the same sort of feelings and reactions as we do. They don't like people who mistreat them any more than we do. Please remember that if your children can't stand you, they will not identify with you, your values, your principles, your beliefs or anything you hold dear.

In the first 10 years of life, children appear to put up with an angry parent. They don't have much choice because they're very much in need of the parent. It is not until they are big enough and old enough (typically in the second decade of life), that their reaction becomes clear. At this point, they withdraw from the angry parent or more openly defy him or her. It is fairly common for the later adolescent to cut off relations with his angry parent altogether, stopping communication completely. The relationship may not ever be repaired.

Your anger may not be so intense as to drive your child away. Does that mean it's okay to leave it where it is? This question is like the dentist asking if it would be okay to leave a little bit of an abscess in your gums. Now why would you want that? Sure, a little bit of dysfunction is better than lots of dysfunction. But anger is a poison to your own body and to everyone around you. Whenever you're angry, you are bathing your children's minds and bodies in your toxicity, bequeathing to them a lifelong struggle. Perhaps you yourself have inherited your parents' yelling tendency. Notice how difficult it is for you to shake it. Notice how it harms your health and your relationships. Is this the gift you want to pass on?

On the other hand, imagine what it would be like if you could teach your children how to handle disappointment, frustration and helplessness. By practicing anger-management strategies, you can actually give your kids skills that will allow them to deal successfully with stresses at home, at work, wherever they find themselves. By eliminating your own tendency to rage, you can give your children skills that will help them enjoy life and maintain excellent physical and emotional well-being.

Not only is anger management good for the children—it's also good for you. You might have noticed the references I've made to the health benefits of not being angry. Some people are under the impression that "letting off steam" is good for the heart and prevents ulcers and other diseases. However, research in the last decades of the last millennium showed that the tendency to rage is just as bad for health as the tendency to hold feelings in. Indeed, the only strategy that has health benefits (such as reducing the risk of heart disease, cancer and other autoimmune deficiencies) is that of processing emotions and respectfully communicating feelings. Therefore, even for your own benefit — never mind your child's—find a way to eradicate chronic anger! You'll live a longer, happier life.

Now back to the kids.

CHAPTER 7

Rules to Relax By

Rules Reduce Stress

Rules can reduce parenting stress and help the whole family relax. For example, the "no-cookies-before-dinner" rule prevents daily discussion and/or argument about snacking before supper. The "no-computer-after-10-p.m." rule stops a nightly dispute about shutting down the system. Instead of upset, battle and anger there is order, calm and peace. Once the rule has been established, there simply is no discussion. (There may be consequences for breaking the rule—see further in this and the following chapters—but there is no talking, debating or arguing.) The issue becomes a non-issue, replaced by a pleasant, quiet void.

While a carefully selected bunch of rules can make family life smoother and easier, overuse of rules can have the exact opposite effect, creating a rigid and tense milieu. Excessive parent-driven rules may create an authoritarian atmosphere that inhibits individuality, creativity, flexibility and other mental and emotional factors essential to the development of healthy youngsters. (Of course, there may be times when this seems like a small price to pay for some peace and quiet!) However, numerous psychological studies have verified that authoritative parenting—characterized by a combination of clear rules, clear expectations and emotional warmth—produces the healthiest development in children.

Although it is important, then, to avoid burdensome rule-making, parents can certainly take advantage of the fact that a simple, well-placed rule can help prevent the eruption of anger.

It used to be so unpleasant every evening. The kids would ask if they could watch T.V. or a movie and if I said "no" they would start begging and whining and complaining. Eventually I would get fed up and yell at them, or if I was too tired to fight, I'd cave in. Whenever I felt they'd "won," I'd be resentful and disgusted the rest of the night. We solved the whole problem recently by making a rule for school nights: after homework and bath, Monday night and Thursday night are "media" nights; Sunday, Tuesday and Wednesday are media-free. That put an end to all the fighting.

Parents and children can make rules collaboratively or parents can make them alone (most appropriate when dealing with very small children). When a parent has noticed a chronic difficulty that could be resolved by the formation of a rule, he or she can ask the children for suggestions. The parent can then take those suggestions into consideration when forming the rule. ("I seem to be making four different dinners every evening and I'm no longer prepared to do that. I'm open to suggestions from you kids regarding a reasonable dinner rule. The one I'm thinking about right now is 'everyone eats the one meal that is prepared.' If you have any better ideas, I'll be happy to consider them.") Often kids have excellent ideas—especially if they have experienced reasonable rules when they were younger.

Coming to the table for supper used to be such an ordeal: Myra and Robyn would practically attack each other trying to get the chair next to me. I couldn't keep track of who sat where, when, and I didn't want to. Finally, I asked the girls to make some sort of rule that could solve this once and for all—and they did just that. They worked it out that Myra got to sit beside me Monday, Wednesday and Friday; Robyn got to sit beside me Sunday, Tuesday and Thursday, and Saturday was divided into two six-month periods—one for each of them. I thought it was a bit odd, but they were happy!

Although children's suggestions are always a welcome part of rule-making, it is important that adults maintain the leadership position.

This, after all, is their job. Parents raise and guide their youngsters, protect and nurture them—until they are ready to leave the nest to lead independent lives. Parents are not necessarily smarter than their kids, but they have more life experience and information, and they have the child's best interests at heart. Most important, however, is the fact that parents have the ultimate responsibility for any decisions that are made on behalf of a child. It is ultimately the parent who must decide on matters relating to health, behavioral standards and values. Therefore, giving undue weight to a 5-year-old's suggestion that bedtime should be when the adults go to sleep, or sweet snacks should be available two times a day, can actually be viewed as an abdication of parental responsibility. Even accepting a 16-year-old's suggestion that curfews are no longer necessary is more often the result of a feeling of parental helplessness than it is the product of reasoned consideration. Excess neglect in the area of limit-setting is viewed legally by family service agencies as a form of negligence and emotional abuse!

The purpose for including children's opinions at all in the process of rule-making is for their benefit: to help them learn how to create self-imposed limits that will serve their overall well-being. Grownups who can't say "no" to themselves may end up with health problems, substance addictions, obesity, financial difficulties and other challenges brought on by excess. Sometimes these problems develop because parents have made unreasonable rules, saying "no" too often to their youngsters (e.g., a rule barring all sweets often creates a sugar-holic child). However, parents who fail to develop rules at all, or who do not give their children experience in contributing to the construction of rules, are also creating fertile conditions for the development of problems in the area of self-control.

Rules regarding permitted and prohibited speech patterns can illustrate this point. Children who learn the rule that everything must be said in a respectful way (i.e., no shouting, swearing, name-calling, etc.) generally grow up to be adults who speak respectfully to their spouses, children, colleagues, bosses, employees, service providers, store staff, neighbors—everyone that they come into contact with. On the other hand, children raised without such rules often struggle throughout adulthood, sometimes paying a heavy price for their inability to use verbal self-control during critical moments in professional and personal life.

Making Helpful Rules

Rules are meant to help reduce conflict and increase peace. They should be employed when they will achieve that purpose. But how do parents know when a rule is needed? For instance, must a 10-year-old child have a bedtime rule or is it okay for the child to simply go to sleep when he is tired? Does it make a difference if the child is 6 years old or 13? Is it negligent not to make a formal bedtime rule? Should children have rules about eating? Is it right for parents to insist that a child eat a portion of protein or at least one vegetable? What about computer rules, T.V. rules, homework rules and so on?

Actually, there are no hard-and-fast rules about rules. Since every child is different and every parent is unique, each home will have its own individual set of rules to relax by. Parents must look at themselves and their children to come up with rules that are appropriate for *their* household. Rules might even vary for each child in a family. For example, 10-year-old Alexa manages to get up for school every morning bright-eyed and cheery, and continues to maintain her energy throughout the day. She puts herself to bed at night when she feels sleepy. Some nights this may be 9 p.m. while others it may be 8 or 10 p.m. Alexa does not have a formal bedtime rule, nor does she seem to need one; she is functioning well without it. However, her brother Howie has a lot of trouble getting up in the morning. He sleeps through all the alarm clocks and then ignores his parents' calls. He drags himself through the school day, under-performing along the way. In the evening he is irritable and short-tempered. Like Alexa, he does not have a bedtime rule. Unlike her, he needs one.

Flexible parents assess the situation to determine whether or not a rule will be helpful. When a child does not need a rule, it is not always necessary to impose one just because others in the family will do better with it. For instance, a parent can tell one child that she must be in bed by 9 p.m. while another child—one year older or younger—doesn't have a formal bedtime. Children are quite capable of learning the definition of "fair" as "each child gets what's right for him or her." Of course, it will sometimes be necessary to make a household rule, even though it will have a different impact on each member of the family. For instance, the "everyone-eats-the-one-dinner-I-make" rule will impact the most on the fussiest eater in the family.

Rules will reflect the values and priorities of the parents. Some parents are very health conscious whereas others take a more relaxed attitude. Obviously, parents who aren't worried about the harmful effects of sweets aren't going to set up rigid limitations about how many sweets a child may eat. However, those same parents may feel that academic performance is very important and they may set up limitations concerning an amount of permissible socializing on school nights. The following scenarios illustrate several different ways of handling the food-rule question.

> *Ben seems to live on cheese and bread. Somehow he is growing—he's taller than both of us. I've never seen him eat a vegetable other than a potato. Dr. Silver says he's healthy. I never made the kids eat vegetables if they didn't like them because I remember how much I hated vegetables when I was young; now I can't get enough of them. I'm figuring the same thing will happen to all of them eventually, including Ben.*

> *We have a rule in our house: "No dessert until the main meal is eaten." The kids grumble sometimes but we're firm. We both feel it's important that the kids get all of their nutrients.*

> *We let the kids eat whatever they want and however much they want of it. None of them are fat or sick, so I guess it works for us.*

> *Jennifer doesn't like to eat in the morning. If I left it to her, she would go to school on an empty stomach and not have anything till lunch.*

I believe that kids should eat a good breakfast, a balanced meal includ-
ing protein, carbs and fat. But I also believe that you shouldn't force
anyone to eat. So I've compromised and made a rule that Jennifer
must have at least a small glass of milk before leaving the house. She
cooperates because she knows I'm meeting her halfway.

Flexibility means being willing to change our minds when the situation calls for it. As long as the kids in the examples on the previous
page are thriving, each mealtime rule is acceptable. However, if children are suffering from lack of energy, obesity, excessive cavities or any
other food-related problem, their parents might consider changing
their rules.

When Caitlin was a baby, I took her with me everywhere—to the
bank, to the mall, to the supermarket, to business meetings. She
would fall asleep when she was tired, whether that was in the car
seat, in the stroller, in my arms or in the shopping cart! I didn't
believe in rigid rules and schedules for babies, and I could see that
my philosophy of parenting was really working. But then Mendy
was born and my plan completely fell apart. He simply could not
settle down unless he was in his own crib! At first I just dragged him
with me, as I did Caitlin, but after a while I could see that he was
getting exhausted and frantic because he couldn't sleep on the run. I
actually had to be home with him at 10 a.m. and 2 p.m. for nap-
times for 18 months! He turned me into a rigid rule-keeper.

Actually, the parent in the above example was totally flexible, adapting her parenting style to the individual needs of her kids.

Rules in the Context of the 80-20 Rule

Like all parenting interventions, rules must be assigned as either "bad-
feeling" or "good-feeling" to children. Their assignment allows their

use within the 80% (for rules that feel good to children) or the 20% allotments (for rules that feel bad).

Rules, while protective for all concerned, have a slightly "bad-feeling" quality to them when they involve limits (and also, as we shall see in the next chapter, when they involve negative consequences). The slight bad-feeling of rules is highly preferable, however, to the intense bad-feeling of parental anger. It is also preferable to the risky whining, demanding and escalating behaviors of children who aren't happy with a parent's response to their request. Although restrictive rules must be placed within the 20% allotment for bad-feeling interventions, their use only slightly negates the amount of good that a parent otherwise achieves. Rules are only mildly bad-feeling. On the other hand, intensely negative parental actions—yelling, insulting, door-slamming and other abusive communications—negate hundreds or thousands of positive-feeling actions that a parent performs for a child. Where rules are lacking, parents can, out of frustration over endless demands, find themselves behaving in destructive ways.

Limits are restrictions on activities that kids or teenagers enjoy— like eating junk food, playing on the computer, staying up late, driving the car, using the phone, spending money and so forth. Having to curtail an enjoyable activity is unpleasant; hence the bad-feeling quality assigned to restrictive rules.

Good-feeling Rules

Rules are not, by definition, bad-feeling. For example, a family can have a rule that whoever is in bed on time gets a story. This is a rule that may provide a good-feeling motivation to cooperate (conditional positive attention). It can fall within the 50% of positive-feeling interventions that are allowed to be "earned," along with praise, rewards and other kinds of attention that are used to reinforce desirable behaviors. As mentioned earlier, it is important to carefully balance earned positive attention with "free" positive attention—the former guides behavior while the latter conveys love and acceptance. Good-feeling rules may be part of a parent's tool chest for raising healthy, functional children. Here are a few more examples of these kinds of "educational" rules:

- Whoever has dressed, made her bed and eaten breakfast may watch television until it's time to leave for school.
- Whoever finishes his homework can help himself to a snack.
- Playtime happens from the time you get home till the time we have dinner. (After dinner, it's homework time.)

These kinds of rules are made *once* and intended to hold in place for some months (or even years!). They are meant to reduce the need for daily struggles and arguments. Like all rules, they help the parent avoid the yelling trap. A variation of the good-feeling rule structure, intended for use on an "as-needed" basis ("Grandma's Rule"), will be explored in the next chapter.

Good-feeling rules can also be sources of unconditional positive attention. Used this way, they can just be silly or fun—excuses to convey love and affection. For example, a family may have a rule that whoever hiccups gets a kiss!

Establishing the "I-Don't-Argue-With-You" Rule

One helpful rule to live by is the "I-don't-argue-with-you" rule. Because of its powerful anti-yelling contribution, we will look at this rule in detail. The principles involved in setting and maintaining this rule will be useful for any other rule a parent wishes to establish. Moreover, knowing how to apply this one rule is essential to the ability to carry through with all other rules. It enables parents to state a rule firmly, without unwanted debate (discussion about a rule can be made *before* a rule is formed, not in the middle of applying it!).

However, in order to successfully establish the "I-don't-argue-with-you" rule—or any other household rule—parents need to prove that they are reasonable and caring people. Dogmatic, authoritarian, unthinking and unkind parental behavior hurts children, causing a breakdown of the parent-child relationship. Children may become uncooperative or outright rebellious under such conditions. They will argue, possibly loudly and disrespectfully. Indeed, "no" parents—parents who offer hasty, automatic "no" answers—invite arguments from their children; the youngsters will argue relentlessly to move such parents into a more reasonable position.

Round 1

To avoid these problems, parents should always take a moment to seriously consider a child's request. It is good policy to refrain from answering immediately. Rather, a parent can pause and say something like, "Let me think about that." If a parent misses saying this phrase the first time he responds to a child's query—what I call "Round 1" of the conversation—he should definitely add it on the second response to the same query—"Round 2." ("Round 3" is called "arguing.") Although the terms "Round 1," "Round 2" and "Round 3" are hauntingly reminiscent of a sports competition, they are not used here to denote an aggressive game between parent and child. Rather, they reflect the repetitive nature of a child's request: a child asks a question and gets an answer she doesn't like; the child asks again (and again, hoping to get the "right" answer). From the parent's point of view, this can feel like Round 2 (and 3 and 4 and...)—hence the terms I use. However, no matter what the parent feels about being asked again, Round 2 is his or her last chance to think about it, so this thinking should be done carefully. After due consideration, the parent can inform the child of the decision, and if the answer is in fact "no," the parent should offer one brief explanation for that conclusion.

Reconsider on Round 2

Some children are natural arguers, born to lead the school debating team. However, all children—even the meek and mild—can discover that arguing "works." They can accidentally learn that carrying on long enough with rational arguments or irrational strategies such as crying, tantrum throwing, whining, begging, relentless nagging or other painful techniques may lead to a parental change of heart. Even if they find that these kinds of behaviors only effect a change once in awhile, children will be inclined to use them indefinitely. This means that there may be years of arguing occurring in the family. Sometimes the parent will remain firm and "win." However, sometimes parents will not be able to remain firm in the face of a child's endless objections; they will eventually throw their arms up in defeat, snarling in disgust, "All right then. . . just for tonight . . .but never again!" When parents give up, the child wins the battle but loses the war; he gets what he wants but loses the feeling of parental love. The look of frustrated, helpless loathing on the worn-out parent's face sends a strong message of rejection. It is all too clear to the child that he or she is "bad." Parents protect the child's long-term emotional well-being by following the "I-don't-argue-with-you" rule.

Does this mean that parents can never change their minds for fear of creating incessant arguers? No. Parents can harmlessly change their minds when responding to a child's request—but only on Round 2 of the request. Parental flexibility occurs on Round 2. At this point, a parent can pause, think a little longer about what the child is asking and, if it seems warranted, change the initial response. The parent can also change the response at this juncture simply because he or she is too fatigued to cope with the child's disappointment or anger at receiving the "wrong" answer. Perhaps the parent is under the weather, stressed or otherwise not up to dealing with a very unhappy youngster. Perhaps the issue is just not that important. Or, even though the issue is important, maybe the parent has already been too negative with the child throughout the day, achieving a ratio of 20-80 rather than 80-20; in this case, the parent can have a change of heart just to raise the positive-to-negative attention ratio. Sometimes the parent just wants to show love for no reason at all (unconditional positive attention), simply wanting to make the child happy. Or, maybe the parent is uncertain about the correctness of the initial response. Indeed, the parent might be ambivalent for other reasons as well; perhaps carrying out the limitation will be too difficult. Maybe the parent has no backbone, is co-dependent or even mentally ill—it really doesn't matter why the parent wants to change his or her mind on Round 2. Any reason—or no reason—is fine! There is only one non-negotiable condition for having a change of heart, however, and it is this: the change must occur on Round 2 and not later. Later—Round 3 and beyond—is the realm of argument.

What If the Child Makes a Good Point on Round 3?

Of course, parents who are only willing to ponder a child's request twice may miss something important. If further discussion were permitted, the child might actually raise a valid objection that the parent hadn't properly considered. Indeed, on Round 4 or 5 or 10, the child may come up with a brilliant reason why permission should be granted or the answer should change. This possibility, however, does not warrant the encouragement of arguing. Parents who let their children continue to point out reasons for a mind change are actually letting them be unpleasant to be around. They are aiding and abetting the development of poor social skills. People don't like to be brow-beaten or bullied, and the arguing child is doing just that. Such children can grow up with an inability to let an issue drop. They may become inflexible adults, unable to go with the flow and adjust to new realities. Worse yet, they may become abusive spouses who can't back down, but instead must exercise their will till the bitter end. Although children can develop these kinds of painful and rigid traits all by themselves, parents do not need to partner that development by reinforcing the arguing tendency.

Most importantly in the short run, parents themselves tend to respond poorly to being harassed and harangued. In other words, parents who allow their children to argue are setting up the conditions for their own eventual frustration and subsequent bad parenting behavior (i.e., a show of temper or a capitulation of responsibility). It is protective of everyone to end discussions on the early side, even if it means missing an occasional good point. It is more important for parents to teach the "I-don't-argue-with-you" rule than to make a child happy on any one specific occasion.

The Strong-Willed Child

The parent's brief explanation of the original "no" response is offered only to show the child that some thought has gone into the decision. It is not necessary for the parent to consider the matter from every angle and knock down every objection one by one. Home is not a court of law. When parents usually say "yes" and show themselves to be generally reasonable and loving, the child usually learns to trust the occasional "no." Ideally, the child comes to see the parents as beneficent caregivers rather than as careless inflictors of senseless pain. Certainly, strict adherence to the 80-20 Rule for young children (and the 90-10 Rule for teenagers, which we'll get to in Chapter 11) should accomplish this goal.

However, there are some children whose nature dictates that everything should be just as they want it. "No" is not an answer they can live with. Most such children will respond well to the interventions described in this chapter. Some who are particularly challenged by their need to have things go their way may additionally benefit from naturopathic interventions such as Bach Flower Therapy. Sometimes—when the child's inflexibility makes family life truly challenging—such children may benefit from a psychological assessment and treatment plan.

All three groups of youngsters, however, share some commonalities. Like adult "control freaks," these children often use methods of intimidation to ensure that no one even considers trying a "no" on them. They may yell, curse and become violent and/or hysterical in the face of the "wrong" answer. No matter how kind, sensitive and caring the parent, these children freely hurl accusations of abuse, mistreatment, injustice and cruelty when faced with a "no."

It is essential that parents stay grounded during such episodes. They need to affirm their own fair and benevolent tendencies. Then they need to clearly recognize the child's verbal abuse, manipulative strategy and lack of emotional regulation—so that they can help the youngster. These children need guidance. If parents change their minds because of aggressive and offensive behaviors on their child's part, they are actually rewarding the child's dysfunctional behavior. They are teaching the child to be a tyrant and thereby guaranteeing the child a life of adult misery through failed relationships. These children need to learn that drama does not lead to a parental change of heart. In fact, when drama occurs after the first "no"—on Round 1—the parent no longer has the option of flexibility on Round 2. The change of mind on Round 2, in this case, might be interpreted by the child as a pay-off for his tantrum. Therefore, the parent must stick to her first answer whenever the child throws a fit after Round 1.

Moreover, the child must eventually be taught how to express disappointment appropriately. This skill will not only lead to successful interpersonal relationships throughout life, but will also enhance the child's enduring mental and physical health. (The tendency to be explosive has been found to be physically and emotionally detrimental in adults.) Techniques for teaching children how to express their negative emotions are described in Chapter 9. These techniques, as well as the general skill of emotional coaching, can be combined with anti-arguing strategies. In such cases, emotional acknowledgment will precede the parent's answer in Round 2.

Round 1
Child: *Can I please stay outside a little longer?*
Parent: *Hmm, let me think about that…No, sorry, Ben—it's*

time for bed; we've had too many late nights this week already.

Round 2

Child: *N0-0-0-0! Everyone is still outside!*

Parent: *Oh, that's frustrating! Everyone is still outside and you have to come in. That's hard...Unfortunately, honey, it's bedtime—let's go.*

Round 3

Child: *Please! I promise I'll go right to bed when I come in— I won't have any stories or juice—please please please!*

Parent: *The conversation is over.*

Round 4

Child: *You're the meanest parent on the block! Everyone else's parents let them stay up! Why do you have to be so mean? I wish I didn't live here!*

Parent makes no comment; holds the door open for the child to come in.

In the above scenario, the parent uses an anti-arguing strategy: refusing to discuss the issue after Round 2, despite the good suggestion offered by the child in Round 3. The parent also uses emotional coaching in Round 2, just before repeating the answer.

This same scenario is presented in Chapter 9, where there are strategies for teaching the child how to express his disappointment in a more appropriate manner. As will be seen in Chapter 9, there are four possible parental responses, depending on which step the parent is currently teaching. In the above example, the parent has chosen to temporarily ignore the abusive speech patterns of the child (such as shouting and name-calling). The parent has chosen to reserve use of negative-feeling techniques, such as correction or negative consequences, for other, more priority misbehaviors at this particular time. The need to maintain the

80-20 Rule is an overriding priority. Not all misbehaviors can be corrected in any one day. Therefore, in our example, the parent ignores the disrespectful speech for the moment and chooses a future time to teach the child how to reply respectfully when feeling upset.

In responding to the child's request to stay out later, it would also have been possible for the parent to omit everything except the anti-arguing strategy itself. In other words, emotional coaching in Round 2 is optional. The parent could simply have said at that point, "Unfortunately, it's bedtime—let's go." Nonetheless, parents should keep in mind that emotional coaching—naming feelings—often helps a child to accept a negative answer more gracefully. Even when it doesn't seem to ease the pain, it is valuable as a tool for strengthening the parent-child relationship and raising the child's emotional intelligence.

It is important to note that the child in the bedtime scenario is *arguing* about the need to come in the house, but actually comes in the house when the parent holds the door open. Anti-arguing strategies are meant to handle conversations, not behaviors. If this child did not *listen* to the parent (i.e., actually refused to come into the house for bedtime), the parent would have to use a discipline strategy in addition to the anti-arguing strategy. Discipline strategies for such circumstances are described in Chapter 8.

End the Discussion

In Round 3 of the bedtime scenario, the parent announces that the conversation is over. This anti-arguing strategy is called "ending the discussion." A parent can end a discussion by announcing that the subject is closed and, if necessary, by becoming actively involved in some other activity (like making a phone call or picking up the newspaper or getting on the computer). This announcement should preferably occur at the end of Round 2 but, if forgotten, can be the response to the child's attempt at Round 3. It is "ending the discussion" that is the critical skill in the anti-arguing program. Ideally, when the second answer is given, the parent adds a phrase that indicates the discussion is over. For example, a parent might say, "No, I don't want you to have a sleepover here tonight and I don't want to talk about this anymore," or "No, I don't want you to have a sleepover here tonight and that's the end of the discussion," or "No, I don't want you to have a sleepover here tonight and that's my final word on the matter." It is *essential* that no further words come out of the parent's mouth after the announcement. The parent is finished. If the child continues (as he or she is likely to), the parent gets deeply involved in some other activity. It is important to avoid the following kinds of communications:

Round 3
Child: *Could I please, just this once, I'll never ask you again, please have the sleepover here tonight?*
Mother: *I told you that I'm not discussing it anymore.*

Round 4
Child: *I'll clean everything up myself—we won't leave any mess; you won't even know we were here!*
Mother: *I am not talking about it.*

Round 5
Child: *Why not? Just tell me what you're concerned about and we'll take care of it. Just tell me.*
Mother: *I SAID, I DON'T WANT TO TALK ABOUT IT ANYMORE!*

Mother's error was in continuing to respond to the child at rounds 3, 4 and 5. Saying "I don't want to talk about it anymore" is a form of engagement. Disengagement involves saying *nothing*.

Ending the dialogue is an important tool for the prevention of verbal abuse both on the part of the parent and the part of the child. While the child's verbal abuse is never the parent's "fault" and it will always have to be addressed (see Chapter 9 for methods of addressing it), it is still preferable not to set up conditions for its almost inevitable appearance. Consider the following two dialogues. A child is asking permission to stay at his friend's summer cottage for the weekend, despite the fact that there will be no adults present. The dialogue, without the "end-the-discussion" strategy, could sound like this:

Round 1

Child: *Dad, can I please stay at Colin's cottage for the weekend? His parents say it's okay, even though they won't be there this time.*

Father: *I don't like the sound of that. Hmmm…no, I prefer not.*

Round 2

Child: *I promise we'll be responsible—you have nothing to worry about. He has neighbors just across the lake if we need any help.*

Father: *Let me think again…no, I'd rather not—I like the parents to be home.*

Round 3

Child: *Why not? What are you worried about?*

Father: *I just don't feel comfortable with it. I don't know who else is up there or what you guys could get into. I don't like the idea.*

Round 4

Child: *Oh, so you're saying you don't trust me—is that it? Why? Did I ever break the law or something? I can't believe this!*

Father: *I'm not saying I don't trust you. I'm more worried about the other kids. Who knows what could happen up there— maybe everybody will get drunk and someone will jump into the lake. I don't know—I just don't like it.*

Round 5

Child: *Well, you've got to let go sometime, Dad! You can't keep me tied to the bedpost forever. If someone drowns, they drown. You must think I'm really stupid—like I can't take care of myself. What am I supposed to tell Colin? That my dad thinks I'm stupid?*

Father: *Look, I've answered you already. I don't want to discuss this anymore.*

Round 6

Child: *Yeah, well, I don't want to talk to you anymore either. This is garbage.*

Why did Dad let the conversation go on so long? Because he's such a nice guy. However, in the end, his son is disgusted with him and doesn't see him as a nice guy at all. If Dad had ended the conversation at Round 2, things might not have degenerated so badly. Undoubtedly the child would not have liked the "no" answer, and might even have viewed Dad as unreasonable. However, short conversations breed less hostility than longer ones.

In this scenario, Dad doesn't really have much of a leg to stand on, and his son knows it. Dad offers flimsy excuses for his refusal to give permission, excuses that just don't cut it for the child. When the parent's logic is flawed, children attack the weakness with a vengeance. The result is an unsatisfactory conversation for both parties.

During the years of childrearing, there are countless confusing dilemmas. Things are not always black and white; the answer is not always obvious. Many times a parent must rely on his or her "gut" feeling in decision-making. In fact, experts are beginning to tell us that the "gut" is an important and reliable source of information, a source not to be discounted or ignored. Can a parent always offer a completely logical explanation for a particular decision? No. Sometimes the parent just has a "feeling." Now if the parent is a "no" person, as mentioned earlier, always limiting and restricting a child, there will be inevitable conflicts as well as undesirable consequences for the parent-child relationship. However, when the parent is

generally a "yes" person and has a track record of considerate and reasonable decision-making practices, he or she can offer the "gut" as a
reason for "no" once in a while. This kind of parent does not have to
sound intelligent to the child on every single occasion. The child
must learn to trust the parent's benevolent intentions.

The worst-case scenario would be one in which the parent, under
the child's pressure to be "rational," sidestepped the gut feeling and
allowed the child to do something that resulted in actual harm. At that
point the absolute responsibility of the parent becomes totally clear:
the parent should have erred on the side of safety. Parents must have
the courage to disappoint their children when necessary. The following corrected scenario illustrates this point:

Round 1

Child: *Dad, can I please stay at Colin's cottage for the week-*
        end? His parents say it's okay even though they won't be
        there this time.

Father: *I don't like the sound of that. Hmm…no, I prefer not.*

Round 2

Child: *I promise we'll be responsible—you have nothing to worry*
        about. He has neighbors just across the lake if we need
        any help.

Father: *Let me think again…no, I'm afraid not—I like the par-*
        ents to be home. It's just the way I feel about it. So you
        can't go this weekend—you can go when his parents are
        there. (Father turns his back and walks away.)

Round 3

Child: *Why not? What are you worried about?*

Father gives no response; ignores the child and gets on with
his affairs. Child walks away feeling frustrated.

In the corrected scenario in which the father uses the "end-the-discussion" technique after Round 2, the child is left feeling unhappy with the answer. However, the parent's goal here was not to make the child happy; the goal was to keep the child safe. The father relied on his own sense of what was necessary to achieve that goal, refusing to be swayed by the child's displeasure.

Note that the father gives a perfectly clear answer on Round 2, just before ending the conversation. There is nothing wishy-washy. There is no "I'd rather not." Instead, there is a succinct "No." This is very important. Ambivalence invites argument. Moreover, the father openly admits that his reason is based on emotion rather than logic. This admission short-circuits the child's strategy of pointing out holes in a weak case.

When parents *routinely* end the discussion after a clear answer on Round 2, children learn that arguing is a waste of time. They simply stop doing it. They will not always be happy with the answers they get. However, chances are that they will have a much better relationship with their parents than do children who are allowed to argue. Argument and conflict destroy relationships. Of course, unreasonable, restrictive and over-controlling parents will always have troubled relationships with their children, even without the presence of arguments. On the other hand, reasonableness combined with anti-arguing strategies helps protect the parent-child relationship.

The Practical Side of Rules

We don't make a big thing about rules. There are a few routines we hold by and I don't even think we call them "rules" but I guess it amounts to the same thing: the kids each have a bedtime, dinner is served around 6 p.m. every night, candy isn't available on weekdays, we don't have the T.V. on in the morning. I don't even remember how we established the routines in the first place—I must have said something like: "I don't want the T.V. on in the morning" or "Candy is for the weekends." I guess that was enough. I know that when the kids fight, I always say things like, "no name-calling, no hitting"—maybe those are rules too.

Of course, the kids are always asking for something or other—to go here or there, do this or that, or have something they don't have. I try to say "yes" to my children's requests whenever possible. They know that about me. But sometimes they ask for things that just aren't realistic, like permission to stay up an hour later on a school night or permission to have some cereal 15 minutes before dinner is being served. I think they, themselves, realize that these are inappropriate questions, so when I say "no" they aren't particularly surprised and they don't even think I'm being unfair. I guess they just figured it was worth a try. I also think that if I were to answer "yes" to some of that stuff, they would feel like I couldn't be bothered to parent them, like I just didn't care enough. I don't think that would be very good.

Rules are not always highly structured affairs. They can, as in the above example, simply be the stated and unstated expectations in a home. Whether rules are explicit or implicit, however, doesn't matter at all; what is important is the sense of order and calm that is created by clear standards. Structure is the opposite of chaos. It helps both adults and children utilize their energy for the important things in life rather than squandering it on excessive and exhausting daily negotiations. It helps maintain a peaceful, functional atmosphere in the home.

Rules for Older Children and Young Adults

When my kids were little, I thought I had a handle on things. In fact, I'd say that Donald and I ran a tight ship. The kids knew they had to do their homework right after school and there was no going out on school nights. Each one had household responsibilities and there were consequences for failing to carry those out. We always had strict bedtimes. But everything seems to have fallen apart now that they're older. In fact, as soon as they entered junior high school, it seemed the game was over. Now they tell us they have to stay out late for the drama rehearsal, the sports team or the party. They say they can't do their homework after school because the store closes at 6 and they have to get new running shoes for the game. Every day it's a different story. We don't even eat dinner as a family anymore. We're all over the place.

Today's parents are often intimidated by their older children. Although some parents abandon ship when their kids are teenagers, many begin the process of total abdication when their twenty-somethings are living at home. "How can I lay down the law for my 22- and 25-year-old kids? You can't tell adults what to do!" As a matter of fact, you can. It's your house and therefore *you* make the rules. Children are free to make their own rules as soon as they live on their own. For example, if they decide that they don't ever want to take the garbage out once they are living in their own apartment, then they certainly don't have to react to the "garbage truck comes on Tuesdays" rule. It's their choice. However, if they're still living in your home and your household follows the "garbage truck comes on Tuesdays" rule, then you can insist that they cooperate.

Moreover, your lifestyle may involve all kinds of implicit and explicit rules. In fact, you may still be trying to pass certain value-based rules on to younger siblings in the house. You have a right to ask your older children to comply with the rules as far as appearances go both for your own sake and for the sake of the younger children. For example, suppose you are trying to teach the little ones to follow certain religious practices but the 14-year-old is no longer interested. If the younger ones see that the older one doesn't have to play by the rules, they may find it harder to follow along as well. You have a right to insist that the older one follow your rules as long as he or she lives in your house. Kids don't have to believe what you believe or feel what you feel—parents cannot intrude into the minds, hearts or souls of their offspring. However, they can certainly *do* what you do. Even if there are no younger children to influence, you and your spouse have the right to live in a house that runs by *your* rules. Indeed, in previous generations, older kids often did whatever they wanted to do, just as today's children do. The difference, however, was that young people respected their parents enough not to contradict their rules right to their faces. *Out of respect*, they would follow their parents' rules whenever they were in their presence. Rather than considering such behavior to be hypocritical, both parents and children viewed it as a form of consideration and sensitivity. This same philosophy is mirrored in the popular adage, "When in Rome, do as the Romans do." This is how goodwill and good relationships are fostered.

Suppose that a certain couple has a rule that there is no swearing allowed in the house. It doesn't matter whether the rule was formed out of personal preference, religious doctrine, or even anxiety disorder—this is their rule. Their 16- and 18-year-olds swear along with their buddies all day at school. It would be "hypocritical" of them not to continue swearing at home, since they obviously feel that swearing is a valid form of personal expression. Can the parents insist that the kids follow the no-swearing rule at home? Yes! Just because smokers smoke all they want in their own homes does not mean that they can smoke in the no-smoking sections of airplanes, restaurants and public buildings. They must follow the rules. Will insisting that the kids respect this rule absolutely destroy the parent-child relationship, stifle the children's development or otherwise cause harm? No. It is always more dangerous for the parent to be disgusted with the child for not choosing to cooperate than it is for the child to follow a reasonable rule. ("Reasonable" here means that the rule exists in the proper proportion of negative-feeling interventions, designed in the context of a fair-minded and loving relationship.)

Rules do not damage the parent-child relationship; unhealthy and unbalanced parenting does. Imbalance can come just as much from failing to establish rules and boundaries as it can come from employing excessive restriction, showing hostility, being unpredictable or dramatic and relating in any number of other dysfunctional ways.

What kinds of rules, then, can be used in a household of older children to help the family live more peaceably, safely and efficiently? Here is a selection of rules that families with children of this age group have found helpful:

- A child must either be in school, apprenticing or working in order to live in the family home.
- All people must contribute to the tasks involved in running a home (select from: cleaning, cooking, shopping, laundry, lawn care, etc.).
- All people must clean their own dishes.
- No substance use in the home.
- Respectful speech must be used at all times.
- Curfews for school nights and weekends.
- You must say where you are going when you leave the house.
- You must call home when changing plans or expected time of arrival.
- Observe a respectful dress code (e.g., don't come to dinner in your underwear).

Note that all such rules help to establish lifelong habits of consideration and responsibility.

Can parents of older children insist on everyone meeting for dinner every night? Maybe not. Some rules may have to change in order to adapt to new, practical realities as the family grows. However, if dinnertime is an important value, a family meeting can help produce a solution to scattered schedules and new demands. Perhaps everyone will agree to be together for one or two or three regular meals (e.g., every Friday and/or Sunday night). Perhaps "together time" can occur at breakfast or Sunday brunch instead. Perhaps it won't involve a meal at all. Each family will have its own creative solutions. However, it will be parents that establish the priorities, structures and values in the home the entire time the children are there. Parents lead the way, and whatever choices they make—including abdication—will play a major role in the child's development.

I make lots of rules for my kids—the problem is that they never stick.
The kids follow along for a day or two and then it's all forgotten.

The question, of course, is *who* has forgotten? Undoubtedly children would like to forget restrictive rules such as always wear your seatbelt in the car, put away your toys after playing, no sleepovers on school nights, no snacks before dinner, no liquor taken without permission, no telephone calls after 10 p.m. and so on and so on. However, the question of forgetting really concerns only the parent. When the parent forgets, there is effectively no rule.

For example, imagine that the government made rules that drivers must follow the posted speed limit, stop at stop signs and obey all other road signs. After making the rules, nothing more is said or done by government agencies: there are no tickets, fines or other consequences for failing to follow the rules. Indeed, the government puts a few commercials on the air, reminding people to follow the rules, but then never mentions the rules again. How long would it be before people just parked wherever they wanted, for however long they wanted to park there? Despite the intelligence of adults, how long would it take before they "forgot" about stopping at stop signs, driving within speed limits and refraining from turning onto selected streets during rush hour?

Making a rule is obviously only part of the task. The second part—the part that completes the task—is carry-through. In the next chapter, we will look at effective techniques for carrying through with both rules and ordinary requests.

CHAPTER 8

Anger-Free Discipline

Preventing Anger

It's important to know how to manage anger, but it's even better to know how to *prevent* feelings of anger from occurring in the first place. As we've seen, parents get angry for a variety of reasons. All parents would benefit from practicing a variety of stress-management strategies, since these calm the system and prevent anger. Here is a partial list of some such strategies:

- Eating healthy meals and taking vitamins.
- Getting adequate sleep.
- Practicing some form of daily relaxation, breathwork, yoga or meditation.
- Engaging in exercise each day.
- Taking calming therapies as needed throughout the day: anti-stress herbal teas (consult a herbalist), mood-lifting and stress-reducing essential oils (aromatherapy), self-help reflexology (hand and/or foot massage), stretching, and whatever else you can incorporate into your self-care routine.
- Having a fun period each day (doing something you enjoy, even if only briefly).
- Listening to soothing music.
- Building and maintaining a circle of friends, including one or two close friends.
- Refraining from over-commitment, overspending and over-stimulation.

There are many more activities that reduce stress. It's a good idea to make your own collection of stress-reducers and use them faithfully.

Interestingly, refraining from yelling, shouting, arguing and other kinds of fighting also lowers stress. Thus, the fewer angry-sounding techniques that you actually use, the less angry you will tend to feel.

Obviously, having effective parenting tools also lowers stress. That's what this book is all about.

"Bad-Feeling" Interactions

No matter how calm, mature and wise we are, we will not be able to parent using good-feeling techniques alone (100% positive). This is not a failing on our part; it is the nature of the job. Children—like adults—need clear boundaries at times; like it or not, these must be established using bad-feeling techniques (for example, telling a child to stop engaging in an activity or using the word "no"). Moreover, there are things that children must do that they don't consider "good-feeling" and parents are often the initiators of such activities. The result is that, even when limited to their appropriate 20% allotment, the following negative comments inevitably appear in daily parenting:

- requests ("Please turn the computer off now.")
- instructions ("Put your schoolbag in the closet where it belongs.")
- corrections ("Please ask me again in a more pleasant tone of voice.")
- criticisms ("Your socks aren't very fresh.")
- limits and other versions of "no" ("I can't drive you there right now.")
- reprimands ("I'm very disappointed with your performance.")
- complaints ("You left your computer on again!")

This is not an exhaustive list. Our body language, tone of voice and behavior can also be included in bad-feeling interactions. Now re-read the examples given for each type of communication. Note that all the words are positive, nothing is abusive or even negative. But just imagine that these seven sentences constituted the entire communication a parent had with a child within an evening. Pretend that you are the child listening to this. How does it feel?

It's essential to constantly keep the power of negative communications in mind. The power we're talking about here, of course, is the power to completely destroy parenting power. Use negativity with great caution!

Threats of discipline, and discipline itself, must be *added* to the list of seven communications on the previous page. You can see, therefore, that there isn't much room for bad-feeling discipline techniques in parenting.

Unconditional Negative Attention: Free Bad Feelings

You might be wondering why anyone would give their child unconditional negative attention. It's not really that we want to do this—it's more like an accident. Unconditional negative attention is bad-feeling attention given to the child for no reason. Recall that unconditional positive attention is good-feeling attention given for no reason, apart from the fact that the child is loved. Unconditional positive attention leaves the child feeling loved and secure; unconditional negative attention leaves her feeling unloved and insecure.

It can happen so easily. For example, imagine that you wake up one morning after a very bad sleep. You're grumpy, in a bad mood, snappy and irritable. It's the child's "bad luck" that she happens to be around you when you're a walking disaster. Now you're yelling at her for petty reasons or you've just got a sour expression on your face.

Even when we're not attending specifically to our children, they "receive" our energy—our good vibes or our bad ones. A parent who is in the kitchen making her own breakfast while the kids sit nearby may not be interacting directly with the children at all. If, as she pours her coffee, she's humming a pleasant little tune and is obviously cheerful, the children will feel relaxed and safe in her presence. They are receiving a long-distance, unconditional positive stroke. But if Mom is slamming the cupboard doors and cursing under her breath, snarling and mumbling in an agitated way, the innocent children sitting nearby will be picking up her negative energy. They'll be receiving a long-distance, unconditional negative stroke. Imagine the effect if they had to endure that every morning.

It's not just fatigue that can make parents treat a child harshly or unpleasantly for no reason. Unprocessed emotions can do this as well. As we saw in the section on anger, a build-up of stress or unresolved childhood issues can result in miserable adult behavior. Current overwhelming stresses (marital difficulties, divorce, financial problems, health problems and so on) can temporarily unbalance a parent. Chemical imbalances and temperamental challenges can cause chronic dysfunction. These factors can contribute not only to excessive anger, but also to chronic, low-level grouchiness, chronic mild sadness or to full-blown states of depression. The result is that some children find themselves sitting in the presence of an unhappy adult. The attention may not be hostile, but it may be withdrawn, mildly displeased, deeply distracted or otherwise negative. Children take the feelings of their parents personally. If a parent can't be happy with them, they feel it's their fault; they must be defective. They cannot consider the possibility that the parent has his or her own issues. The parent is not intending to cause harm, but is "accidentally" doing so by virtue of his or her own personal issues.

The only solution is for the parent to be healthy and happy. Sorry. I know it's a drag. Refer to the anger section in Chapter 6 and to upcoming sections on emotions in parenting for a set of interventions that restore personal well-being.

By the way, tune into your inner compassionate parent if you see yourself in any of the above conditions. Listen to the words of support and encouragement. Perhaps you'll hear some of the following whispers: "You're doing the best you can and getting better every day. You're a great parent, really pushing your limits for the sake of your children. Your heart is in the right place and it will lead you to success—every step on the way counts. It doesn't matter if the journey is slow; what's important is that you're on the path. Just keep moving forward. Take my hand. I have faith in you. Even though you've been struggling a long time, healing can come at any point. It's never too late."

Discipline: Where to Start

The CLeaR Method—a good-feeling intervention of Comment, Label and Reward, which we discussed in Chapter 4—is actually our most powerful discipline tool. If you're trying to get your kids to behave, try this strategy first. Although it doesn't bring immediate results that very moment, it brings sure and permanent results over the course of a few days or weeks. Remember that attaining immediate results is not our goal. If that's all we wanted to do in parenting, we could just yell at our children. Yelling seems to yield immediate results, although it doesn't tend to lead to long-term changes in behavior and it has a few nasty side-effects like destroying love, our educational power and our child's mental health. What we're actually looking for in behavioral change is a fairly permanent result delivered via a relationship-strengthening strategy.

"I" Messages

Here is an introductory method of mildly bad-feeling discipline. This technique has a low success rate with children under the age of 10, but it is so respectful that it is worth using now and then even with that age group (just to show them that you think they deserve a chance of being treated like a grown-up). In fact, this is a technique that we do use with grown-ups. If everything goes well, you may be able to use it frequently with your preteens and adolescents.

Basically, it involves expressing your feeling. Using the word "I," you state what you feel or what you need, as in the following examples:

- "I need it to be quiet now."
- "I don't like being disturbed when I'm sleeping."

- "I need some help in the kitchen."
- "I'm unable to concentrate on my work."
- "I can't listen to two people at once."

Older children and adults tend to understand the implied requests in these sorts of statements. For them, "I need it to be quiet now" is equivalent to "Please be quiet now." If you have a respectful relationship with your older child, your "I" message will usually be enough for him or her to perform the implied behavioral change. However, young children don't always get it, so you may need to actually proceed to a direct request after stating your "I" message. For example:

- "I need it to be quiet now. Please lower your voices."
- "I need some help in the kitchen. Jan, please load the dishwasher."

The important part of the "I" message is that it is all about the parent. It is not about the child at all. "I need it to be quiet now" is very different in meaning from "You're being too noisy." The first statement is about the parent's needs, whereas the second suggests there's something wrong about the child. Refer back to the section on positive programming for a review of this important principle.

Grandma's Rule

Grandma's Rule stands somewhere between a bad-feeling technique and a good-feeling technique. This is because it contains both an unpleasant instruction and a pleasant reward. Here's how it sounds:

- "As soon as you've cleaned up the toys, you can go out to play."
- "When you've finished your homework, you can go on the computer."
- "When you've written an apology, I'll consider your request."

As you see, the phrase starts with an instruction to do a comparatively unpleasant chore or task and ends with the opportunity to have some sort of treat or benefit.

Grandma's Rule actually *prevents* problems. Rather than permit little Junior to go play and then struggle to get him to clean up his toys when he returns, Dad cleverly uses the playtime as a motivator for the chore. Similarly, any pleasant opportunity can be used as a motivator for any less pleasant activity.

The trick with Grandma's Rule lies in its structure: "As soon as/when (unpleasant task is completed)…then (pleasant time can be had)."

The structure differs from a bribe. Bribes start with "if." The "if" puts the ball in the child's court. As explained earlier (see the section on rewards in Chapter 4), this is the wrong place for the ball to be. Grandma's Rule leaves the parent in charge, which is as it should be. The parent is not dispensing any pleasant activity or benefits until the unpleasant task is completed. The assumption is that the unpleasant task will indeed be completed. Of course, it is possible for a child to decide that the benefit is not worth the effort of the unpleasant precursor. Even if the child turns down the offer, however, the parent has still maintained a position of authority. There will be no computer, since the homework was not done. Parents do not actually force their children to do anything; rather, they set up conditions to inspire and motivate. Children have free will.

The 2X Rule

The 2x Rule is a form of discipline that, when used according to the following instructions, prevents parental anger. This in itself is a great accomplishment. Equally important, it leads to lasting behavioral change in your child.

The 2x Rule is essentially about making requests and rules. It involves asking a child something no more than two times. Most of us have enough patience for asking twice, whereas we don't have patience for asking three, four, five or 10 times. Indeed, it is following the 10x Rule that makes raging lunatics out of all of us. The 10x Rule works like this: say it once in a normal tone of voice. Say it a second time a little more firmly. Say it louder on the third time. Say it more impatiently on the fourth time. Continue for six more times, until you are red in the face, smoke is coming out of your ears and you are screaming at the top of your lungs. Now your child will respond. He has learned that he doesn't actually have to respond until you're hysterical. He trains you to be hysterical (by responding only when you are), and you train him to be deaf to a normal, pleasant tone of voice. That's the 10x Rule.

It's Very Simple

So the 2x Rule is really very simple: never ask more than twice. What follows is commentary.

There are actually three steps to the 2x Rule:

Step 1: Give **information** or make a **request**.
The **information** approach is used to correct a chronic misbehavior. Suppose, for instance, that a child leaves his clothes on the bedroom floor almost every day. An example of an information statement would be, "We don't leave clothes on the floor because they might get trampled on and ruined. Clothes belong in the cupboard or in the hamper." As you can see, the structure of the information statement is, "We don't do X because of Y. We do Z instead." The child is told what is incorrect about his behavior and why it is incorrect. He is then directed to a correct behavioral choice. Another example is that of the child who chronically calls his brother names. The parent might make an information statement such as, "We don't call people names because it hurts their feelings. If we're unhappy with their behavior we can just say so." Similarly, if a child hits his sibling when frustrated, the parent might offer the following information statement: "We don't hurt people when we're upset because everybody deserves to live in safety in this house. Use your words instead." For the child who regularly neglects to call home to say he'll be late, the parent might form this informa-

tion statement: "It's important not to stay out past your curfew without calling home because it causes us to worry. You need to figure out a reliable way to remember to call when you're going to be late."

The **request** form of Step 1 is used when a parent makes a specific request. The request is not concerning a chronic problematic behavior and may not be concerning any misbehavior at all. It can be a simple case of wanting the child to do something like take his cup off the table or start his homework or lower his voice. An example of a request would be, "Please put your shirt in the cupboard" or "Please eat with your mouth closed."

Step 2: Repeat your information or request and add a **warning of a future consequence.**

An example of Step 2 following an information statement (for a chronic misbehavior) is as follows: "I asked you yesterday (two days ago, last week or whenever) not to leave your clothes on the floor because they may get ruined. I want you to put them in the cupboard or in the laundry basket if they need to be washed. *From now on*, when I find your clothes on the floor, ABC will happen. (ABC is a specific negative consequence. We'll discuss what that could be in an upcoming section.)

Notice that Step 2 for an **information** statement is a rule (*from now on*). This means that on the third occasion that Junior has left his clothes on the floor, and forever into the future, he will experience a negative consequence for that behavior. Here are some other examples: "From now on, when you forget to call home, ABC will happen." "From now on, when you leave your books on the sofa, ABC will happen." When making a rule, try to make it as broad as possible. If, for example, your child has been biting the baby, don't use the word "bite" when making your rule. Rather, keep it as vague and open as you can. In this case, the word "hurt" would be good, as in "from now on, if you hurt the baby in any way at all, ABC will happen." If you don't do this, the child will say, "You said I shouldn't *bite* him—you never said anything about pinching him!"

An example of Step 2 following a **request (for a specific action)** is as follows: "I asked you a moment ago (a few minutes ago, half an hour ago or some other very recent time) to put your shirt in the cupboard. If it's not done in the next two minutes, I'll put it away myself and ABC will happen to you."

Step 2 for a request is a warning that in the very near future—"by the time I count to five" or "within the next five minutes" or "by six o'clock tonight"—a negative consequence will occur if the request is not fulfilled.

It is worth mentioning here that if you should select a counting option ("If you don't do it by the time I count to..."), then the preferred number to count to is five. Counting to three does not give a child enough time to do a turnaround. Especially for those children who feel a strong need to save face, or those who suffer from inflexibility, a few extra moments can help them succeed. When counting, just count. Don't talk in between numbers ("That's 1—I mean it. ABC will happen if you don't do it. That's 2—do you want ABC to happen? That's 3 and —. That's 4 and —, etc.). Definitely not. The correct way to count is as follows:

- That's 1.
- That's 2.
- That's 3.
- That's 4.
- That's 5.

That's it. And count nice and *s l o w l y*. You want the child to succeed. However, if you actually pronounce the number 5, it's too late: the negative consequence must occur. Make sure you explain that to the child before you start counting.

Step 3: Fulfill your promise.
You promised a negative consequence. If you didn't get what you asked for at Step 2, you must fulfill your promise.

Failure to fulfill your promise has dire consequences in parenting. It causes your entire program of discipline (read "education, socialization and guidance") to falter. You lose credibility and therefore your children will feel that it's never really necessary to do what you ask. They know they can always wrangle their way out of a nasty consequence. They'll continually do what you've asked them not to do (they have no fear of punishment) and you'll eventually resent them for doing so. Your helplessness puts them at great risk. When you feel overwhelmed and resentful, you stop enjoying and liking your children, and they'll feel this. Your rejection of yourself and them harms the relationship—your true source of power to educate. Moreover, the experience of parental rejection can be developmentally disastrous for children, sometimes having lifelong negative effects. Your job is to protect that relationship for the sake of the child's mental health.

Your ability to discipline a child is actually a form of protection, helping the child to remain loveable. The most a child should ever lose is a privilege or a possession—and only for a very short time. A child should never lose parental love. As long as you like the child, it doesn't really matter if he or she is unhappy about receiving a negative consequence. When you follow the correct procedure for selecting appropriate consequences (described on next page), you will never cause emotional scars. "Punishment" and "negative consequence" are synonymous for our purposes and distinct from "abuse." Abuse—physical or verbal assault—is never an acceptable part of any relationship and certainly not the parent-child relationship. Abuse of a child can cause enduring emotional consequences. However, rejection of a child is also a form of abuse, since it involves neglecting the child's most basic need for love. Rejection is almost guaranteed when a parent lacks the courage to discipline a child. The damage will come from the obvious disgust that parents will eventually show the undisciplined youngster.

In summary, it's never healthy for parents to be unable to discipline children. The inner parent sends warning signals galore—that out-of-control feeling is all wrong! You're supposed to be the grownup, the teacher, the wise guide and the loving parent. The bells start ringing when you lose your place.

Why Punish?

Some people feel that punishment or negative consequences shouldn't be necessary in raising children. They ask, "Do we want children who only do what they're told because they're afraid of negative consequences? That's such a low level of functioning! Children shouldn't do the right thing out of fear—they should do it because they're good, they're intelligent and they're reasonable. They should be inspired to choose the correct action on their own. Why should we need to threaten punishments? Rational explanation should be sufficient." Most people who hold this position actually use negative consequences with children but have failed to identify them as such, tending to confuse punishment with abuse. They feel that logical and respectful consequences, since they aren't abusive, are not negative consequences. For our purposes, however, any bad-feeling intervention that occurs as a result of a child's undesirable behavior is a negative consequence. Thus when Mom tells her toddler that he will have to stop screaming in her ear or get off her lap, she is (according to our definition) offering a negative consequence. Similarly, when a parent tells a teenager that she is disconnecting his cellphone until he has paid the excess portion of the bill he ran up, she is giving him a negative consequence. In democratic societies, adults are subject to the same sorts of negative consequences—note what happens to your phone service if you don't pay the bill for a few months!

Moreover, the idea that children will naturally do the right thing once they "see the light" on their own is also open to question. Do adults always do the right thing because they're reasonable, intelligent and capable of problem-solving? Not always. Let's look at the case of speeding while driving, for example. We imagine that reasonable adults ought to understand that speeding on the road could lead to accidents, including not only damage to expensive vehicles but also loss of life and limb. But there are many grownups who only slow down after they receive hefty financial fines (punishment). These folks have already learned about the reality of death due to accidents. They aren't short on information. Yet, when they're in a rush, all their knowledge flies out the window. And it is not only in the area of driving that grownups fail to follow the rational approach. How rational is it to smoke cigarettes in light of the known medical consequences? How rational is it to eat generous amounts of sugar and white flour? Despite a plethora of information, adults routinely engage in unhealthy habits. The "natural consequence" for some people is deadly disease. Is it really fair to assume that children should be able to function at a higher level than adults, doing the right thing only because they understand that it is right?

Yes, there are some kids who will behave appropriately once things have been explained to them, and they may never need negative consequences to get the point across. However, very few children are capable of operating on that level. In the same way, some adults will never overstay their welcome at a parking meter, for example, but most will need to experience the negative consequences of getting a few parking tickets.

Certainly, we should appeal to a child's rationality first, before moving to a consequence approach. However, when it is necessary to apply consequences, we can feel confident that we are employing a form of education that is effective, fair and respectful. After all, in the 2x Rule, a child must actually choose his consequence himself, since he is always offered the choice of either complying with the parental request or accepting the consequence. No child is ever punished without first being offered this choice. No child is ever punished for a "first-time" offence, no matter what it is; for regular misbehaviors, the soonest he can be punished is the third time he's done the same incorrect behavior. The child is given every opportunity to choose compliance, along with the freedom to choose punishment.

And yet, some parents cannot actually bear to carry out Step 3. *This is the sad step, the part where the child receives a negative consequence and becomes unhappy.* Now, if you've learned how to tolerate, welcome and work with your child's negative emotions (see Chapter 5 on emotional coaching), this shouldn't be such a problem. But if you need to see your child happy all the time, you're going to have a big parenting problem. Not only will you have difficulty carrying out discipline, but you will probably also struggle with setting healthy boundaries, saying "no" appropriately and so on. If this is you, turn to your inner compassionate parent. It will hold you up through these difficult parenting moments, reminding you that you are doing the right thing for your child, the best thing, in fact, in that you are providing your child with a strong parent and a strong support in life. You are providing a good model of healthy boundaries, courage and selflessness to do what's right and best, even when it's personally inconvenient or unpleasant. The inner parent will reassure you that your child's love and respect for you will grow, not diminish. The inner parent will praise you as you keep your word, reminding you that you are just where you should be in the parent-child relationship.

There is one more problem, however. Step 3 is more than sad for some children; it can be intensely infuriating, causing some children to become hysterically dramatic and even outrageously violent. In other words, it can scare the wits out of parents. Many children accidentally discover their ability to gain the upper hand by emotionally and physically intimidating the big folks. This discovery often takes place while the youngster is still a toddler. Have you ever seen a situation in which a 2-year-old has managed to get all the grownups—including the nanny, the mother and the father—to do it "her way"? In the olden days, before the age of enlightened parenting, this would never have happened because the adults would have been only too ready to literally slap some sense into the small child and take back their control. However, we know better than to use thoughtless violence in modern parenting. But do we know our other options? Is capitulating to the child the only other choice? No.

The fact that a child is making a lot of noise and an enormous fuss is no reason for parents to avoid Step 3. Even if that child is 17 years old, 6 feet tall and 225 pounds, parents need not worry about doing Step 3. Remember: Step 3 *is the sad step, the part where the child receives a negative consequence and becomes unhappy.* For this group of kids, we can rewrite our description of Step 3 as follows: *This is the hard step, the part where the child receives a negative consequence and becomes intensely dramatic.* So what if the child decides to engage in high-intensity negative affect (screaming)? If the child is making a lot of noisy threats, they can just be ignored. In the case of destruction of property or violence perpetrated on people, the small but feisty child can be constrained or moved to a safer location, or the other people can move away from the child. If the child is larger, the parents can call in resources, other adults to surround and contain the child's aggression. This can be neighbors, relatives or law enforcement agents—whatever works. Giving in to violence (terrorism on a small scale) only ensures that there will be lots more of it. Parents need to show children that they are not afraid. Indeed, all throughout the drama, parents need to demonstrate reasonableness, maturity and calm. It is important—in fact, crucial—that the parent not join the child in immature, unhealthy and destructive ways of behaving. Someone has to be adult. Someone has to provide a model. Someone has to take charge of the situation. Someone needs to be normal. Guess who that someone should be!

If you are dealing with a child who pulls out all the stops when you dare to give him a negative consequence, do practice sessions in your imagination. A few times a day, create a story in your mind in which you deliver a consequence, witness the tantrum of a lifetime and calmly hold your ground throughout. Your daydreaming will help plant the neural pathways you will need when you actually carry out discipline with this youngster.

The Policeman in You

Now let's get back to business. How does one deliver a negative consequence? What are the exact steps involved?

In using a system of negative consequences, it is useful to look at our adult justice system. Correction of crime begins with a police officer. In the home, this is the parent. However, in order to understand the role of the officer, let's examine the process that occurs when he or she stops a speeding driver on the road.

Let's use a male police officer for this illustration and imagine that you are the speeder. The policeman flags you down, directing you to stop your car on the side of the road. He approaches you and asks you to roll down your window. Does he turn all red in the face and scream at you? Not usually. That would be a very exhausting thing to do all day long on the job. It's more likely that he'll politely ask to see your license. He very quietly writes some things down, and gently hands you a little yellow slip of paper. He tells you to have a nice day, and drives away.

- He doesn't get mad; he certainly doesn't yell and scream at you.
- He doesn't lecture you (about the terribly irresponsible and dangerous behavior you were engaging in).
- He doesn't reject you emotionally (he doesn't stop liking you or treating you respectfully).
- He effectively disciplines you (helps you to drive more carefully in the future).

How does he help you to drive more carefully in the future? He gives you a ticket.

What Is a Ticket?

A ticket is a negative consequence. In order to be effective, it must be a "right-priced" ticket. A ticket that is too cheap does not teach its lesson. For example, the tickets they give out in my town for staying too long at parking meters are relatively inexpensive. It may even be cheaper to pay the ticket than to pay the local parking lot. As a result, many people aren't very careful about coming back before the meter expires. Some don't even pay the meter to begin with! Now just imagine that coming back after the meter expired was going to cost $500. Folks would make more of an effort to be there on time, don't you think?

They'd actually change their behavior.

Of course $500 would probably be overdoing it. The trick is to find the lowest price at which the average person would change his or her behavior. Let's just say that we think most people would change if they had to pay fines of $100 for their misbehaviors. We'll call this the "right-priced" ticket for now.

Or suppose a policeman gives a speeder a $100 ticket. This is actually an "illogical consequence" for speeding. A more logical consequence for not following the laws of the road would be to take away the offender's car, or at least his license. And, if the speeding is truly chronic, this could eventually happen. However, for the "regular" occasional offender, a monetary fine is all that is given.

The effectiveness of a ticket does not depend on its being logical. *The effectiveness of a ticket depends on its being the right price.* Therefore, illogical tickets—punishments that are completely unrelated to their crimes—are fine to use. In parenting, we can try to find a "right-priced logical consequence" first, but if that isn't readily available, the "right-priced illogical consequence" is just fine.

What If the Speeder Doesn't Pay His Ticket?

That's a good question! Before I answer that, let me give you another scenario to contemplate. Suppose the speeder is really annoyed at the police officer for stopping him in the first place. Suppose he takes that ticket, rips it to shreds and spits in the policeman's face. What would happen then?

A person could go to jail for defying the authority system. A person who punches the policeman in the nose, swears at him or spits in his face is going to get a lot more than just another ticket. In our civilized society, we must show respect for authority. Failure to do so earns a very big punishment (jail).

And here's something else to think about. Suppose the driver of the speeding car is actually driving a stolen vehicle with a murdered kidnap victim tied up in the trunk. Does he get a ticket? No, he goes to jail. *A person goes to jail for committing serious crimes.*

Finally, let's get back to your question (my question really, but we won't quibble). What happens if, after the policeman has left the scene, the driver crumples up the little yellow ticket and throws it out the window? At first, he'll receive a notice of summons to pay the ticket. Then he'll receive a higher-priced ticket. And if he continues to ignore these escalating punishments, then ultimately, he too can go to jail. *A person goes to jail for not paying tickets.*

Now, Think Like a Policeman

- If your child kicks you in the shins, swears at you or trashes the house when you give him a ticket, he's defying the authority system in your home (you); *he's in line for jail.*
- If he is punching his sibling in the eye, writing with magic marker all over your furniture or sitting in the middle of the road to see what will happen, he is engaging in "a serious crime." For children, a serious crime is any truly dangerous or destructive behavior; *he's in line for jail.*
- If you have given your child a punishment (read "ticket"), and the child does not comply with it (read "pay it"), then *he's in line for jail.*

Negative Consequences That Really Work

Junior is leaving his clothes on the floor. This has been going on for weeks. Mom decides to use the 2x Rule. On Monday, she does Step 1. Although she's mentioned the problem to him numerous times already (nagging), when she does Step 1, she acts like she's never spoken of it before. On Tuesday, Mom sees that Junior has picked up his clothes. Very good. However, on Wednesday, clothes are on the floor again. Mom does Step 2. She says, "Junior, on Monday I asked you to not leave your clothes on the floor because clothes that lie on the floor tend to get ruined. I said they should be put in the cupboard or in the laundry basket. From now on, when I find clothes on the floor, I'll put them away and you'll owe me one page of lines stating 'Clothes belong in the cupboard or in the laundry basket.' The lines will be due by 6 p.m." (See section on consequences, starting on the next page, for more information on choosing tickets.)

On Thursday, Junior somehow forgot to put his clothes away again. Mom noticed this after Junior had left for school already. She put them away. When Junior arrived home at 4:30, she greeted him, offered him a snack and mentioned that he owed her one page of lines by 6 p.m. She said this quietly, and only once. *The ticket does all the teaching. It replaces all speeches, lectures, reprimands, reproofs, complaints and raised voices.*

Mom figured these lines would take Junior about 10 to 12 minutes to complete. However, by 5:45 Junior has not started them. Mom now notifies Junior, for the first time, that *failure to pay the ticket leads to jail.* She says to him, "Junior, your lines are due in 15 minutes. I just want to let you know that if I don't get them by then, you can forget the lines and instead you'll lose computer time for the week."

For Junior, who is a computer addict, losing computer time would definitely be a jail-level punishment. If he believes Mom will do as she says, he'll probably start writing his lines. However, if he doesn't believe she could ever be that "mean," then he'll ignore her and figure he'll be able to sweet-talk her into giving back his computer privileges later on. In order to establish credibility, Mom will have to keep her promise!

Please note that if a jail-level punishment must be administered, the ticket and the entire issue surrounding it is temporarily dropped. The parent is taking a time-out to teach the very important lesson that tickets must be paid.

Ticket-Level Consequences

Remember that tickets are meant to be just annoying enough to change behavior; they should be comparable to a $100 speeding ticket. Jail-level consequences, on the other hand, are meant to be drastic enough to put an *immediate* end to jail-level behaviors. They are like a measles injection: one properly delivered application should last a decade.

Since tickets are no more than annoying, they should not elicit an intense emotional reaction in a child. A child who is crying for more than 10 minutes because of a ticket he has received is likely trying to prove a point: "I'll punish you if you try to punish me!" Therefore, if a child regularly has a hysterical or dramatic response to tickets, the parent may eventually consider such behavior a "defiance of authority" and treat it accordingly. (For example, the parent may warn the child that excessive displays of grief over a ticket will result in a jail-level consequence in the future.) On the other hand, a child can be expected to cry a long time for a jail-level punishment. Jail-level consequences may be painful for both parent and child, whereas ticket-level consequences should really only bother the child.

Here is a list of possible "tickets" to choose from. They are in random order. Choose one if you think it has a $100 value for the child who needs it. *When applying Step 2 of the 2x Rule, name the specific ticket you are choosing as a consequence.* For example, you could say, "From now on, when you throw the ball inside the house, you will lose the ball for the remainder of the day." You would not say, "From now on, when you throw the ball inside the house, there will be a punishment."

- Removal of possessions. A parent can take away any possession belonging to the child, for as little as one minute and for up to a maximum of 24 hours. The shortest time period that is worth $100 should be chosen. (Small children should be taught that everything they have, no matter how they came into possession of it, belongs to the parents until they are paying room and board.) Thus, the parent can remove a child's sticker collection, baseball bat, cellphone (or even car keys, if a teenager has keys to a parent's car).

- Removal of privileges. The child is not allowed to do something he enjoys, for as little as one minute and up to a maximum of

24 hours. Examples are: not being allowed to see a video, not being allowed to have a friend over (providing the arrangement was not already made—we don't punish other people's children), not being allowed to ride a bike, use a baseball mitt or bat, not being allowed in the same room as a sibling, not being allowed to stay up till normal bedtime, not being allowed to go out with the parent, not being allowed to have story-time, not being allowed to borrow the car, not being allowed to use the computer, not being allowed to take phone calls and so forth.

- Removal of non-nutritious food items. Removal of one junk-food item per ticket (one dessert, one good lunch snack or one after-school treat). This is generally applicable to pre-adolescents.

- Time-out. There are two types of time-out. One is not a punishment at all. It is called "renewal time" and is useful for children who need to collect themselves during or after a tantrum or who are entangled in a fight with someone. It sounds like this: "Go to your room until you are calm and then you can come out." Renewal time is not a negative consequence; it is a cooling-down period. Time-out that is a true negative consequence is a restrained time-out, meaning that the child is not free to roam around. For children aged 4 and under, a "thinking chair" is good for this purpose. The child must sit in the chair (which should be in the same room as the parent) for about the minutes of his age, plus or minus two. Thus a 4-year-old could be sent to a thinking chair for two to six minutes. Children aged 4 to 9 can be sent to a corner where they must stand, facing the wall, without talking or playing. They stay there for the number of minutes of their age, plus or minus two. In the privacy of home, the corner is not a humiliating experience; it's just a boring one. It's the boredom that gives it its $100 ticket value. This ticket is applicable to children under 10 years of age.

- Addition of work. There are three types of addition of work. Type

A is called, literally, "more work" and involves giving the child more work to do as a consequence for not doing the work he was asked to do originally. For instance, young Junior who couldn't be bothered to pick his clothes off the floor would pay the ticket of having 15 minutes of extra chores after school. This might be called a "logical consequence," with the logic being, "Since you won't spend three minutes cleaning up when I ask you to, you'll spend 15 minutes cleaning up later!"

Type B addition of work is called "over-learning." Here the child practices the skill she seems to be missing. The practice need only take a few minutes. For instance, Junior's mom could have made the rule as follows, "From now on, when I see you've left clothes on the floor, I'll call you to put them in the laundry basket, take them out again, put them in again, take them out again, 10 times, just to practice that motion." Similarly, a child who slams the door might be asked to practice shutting it quietly 10 times; a child who stomps down the stairs might be asked to walk down quietly five times; a child who calls his sibling names might be asked to say five nice things about her, and so on. Over-learning is generally applicable to children under 10 years of age.

Type C addition of work is called "writing things." It includes writing out lines, passages from a book on a relevant topic, passages on an irrelevant topic, a creative essay on the topic, an action plan for the topic—whatever. The ticket value of this consequence is the boredom aspect: the child is stuck writing out things when he could be playing or out with his friends. The writing exercise replaces the corner for children over the age of 9, but can also be used for younger children. This ticket can be used throughout the teenage years.

When selecting a ticket, the parent chooses one that she thinks is worth $100 to this child. She uses it on *three* separate occasions. If the child's behavior does not show improvement, it means that this ticket was not worth $100 to him or her. Maybe it was worth $20 or $50, but it wasn't worth $100. The test of the ticket's value is the child's behavior. If it improves, the ticket must have been worth $100; if behavior fails to improve, the ticket was obviously not worth $100 to that child. What the child says about a ticket is irrelevant. Therefore, if a child says "I don't care" when you deliver a ticket, you can just ignore that. The measure of caring is determined solely by whether or not the problematic behavior improves after three experiences of the ticket.

By the way, never negotiate tickets with children. They are trying to bargain you down from a $100 ticket to something cheaper. Remember, cheaper tickets don't change behavior! After three uses of a non-productive ticket (or two uses of a non-productive "jail" sentence), the parent tells the child that she sees the punishment doesn't bother him all that much and therefore a different consequence will be used. The parent then selects *another ticket*—not jail. There are only three occasions that justify the use of a jail-level consequence. (See page 100, "What If the Speeder Doesn't Pay His Ticket?" for a review of the indications for jailing.)

In general, all discipline should be carried out within the privacy of the family. Humiliation is a costly bad-feeling intervention; it can harm a child severely and also have severe negative consequences for the parent-child relationship. Therefore, when children are out in public with you or visiting others, or when others are visiting your home, Steps 1 and 2 of the 2x Rule should be done inconspicuously (by discreetly calling the child aside and whispering in his or her ear), if they must be done at all. It is preferable to note problems and mention them to the child *afterwards*, when alone again. However, some things must be taken care of at the time, such as aggressive or destructive behaviors. Even then, Step 3—punishment—must never occur in the presence of other people. It can wait until the family is alone again. If the matter is urgent, it may be necessary to remove the child from the public arena.

For example, a child may sometimes behave loudly and inappropriately in a supermarket. A parent can whisper a request to the child to quiet down (Step 1). A few moments later, the parent can make the request again, with the warning that they will have to leave the supermarket right away and there will be a subsequent loss of privileges at home (Step 2). If the child still does not quiet down, the parent may have to leave the shopping cart and take the child home. The subsequent punishment is for causing the parent such inconvenience.

Jail-Level Misbehavior

The 2x Rule is modified for jail-level misbehavior. Steps 1 and 2 are combined into one step: the child is told what not to do and what jail-level (awful) consequence will happen if he or she tries it in the future. This is a place in parenting where a stern facial expression and stern tone of voice are recommended. Here are some examples of the modified 2x Rule being used on a 9-year-old computer addict:

- "We do not slam a door in a parent's face! If you ever do anything so disrespectful again, you will lose computer privileges for a month!" (defying authority)
- "Never, ever play on the roof again! If you ever play anywhere other than inside this house or in the backyard without my express permission, you will lose computer privileges for a month!" (very dangerous or destructive behavior—a "serious crime")
- "Your punishment was to lose dessert and I see you just helped yourself to it when my back was turned. Well, let me tell you something: if you ever again disregard a punishment your mother or I have given you, you will lose your computer privileges for a month!" (not paying the ticket)

Notice how these jail-level behaviors have been treated. In each case the child has done something very unacceptable that must never happen again. Yet the child is not punished on this occasion. The reason for this is that the parent is not trying to hurt the child: he is trying to educate her. If the child believes the parent will carry out the negative consequence, she will refrain from the unacceptable behavior from then on. It may be necessary to actually carry out jail one time in order for all the children in the family to come to believe that it could actually happen to them. When children see that their sibling has indeed received a terrible "jail-level" consequence, they may decide not to put themselves through it themselves. They are learning vicariously. The jail-level consequence may be averted completely if a parent has established a sufficiently trustworthy track record with ticket-level consequences.

Jail-Level Consequences

The principles for selecting a jail-level consequence are similar to those for choosing tickets, the main difference being the intensity (cost) of the consequence. Recall that a ticket should be annoying, whereas jail should be much more upsetting. Jail-level consequences are meant to permanently curtail dangerous and out-of-bounds behaviors.

To create a jail-level consequence, a parent considers his child's greatest vulnerabilities. What is the *most* important thing/activity for this child? Is it sugary treats? Is it time with friends? Is it a particular T.V. show, computer time or other media activity? Is it the keys to the car, or access to the phone? Is it freedom to leave the house? Something that is a ticket for one youngster may be jail for another. For instance, there are some children who are extremely attached to their things. Threatening to take away a toy for this kind of child might be a jail-level punishment, whereas the same punishment might only be a ticket for a second youngster. It might not be possible to use it at all for a third child who does not get attached to her things.

Tickets can also be turned into jail-level consequences by expanding the parameters of a ticket. For instance, 24-hour time limits are removed so that the same punishment is extended over days or weeks. A child might lose T.V. privileges for a night as a ticket and for a week as a jail. For older children, particularly over the age of 12, a jail might go as long as a month. Try to keep it to a week or two for children under 12. Over-punishment is always dangerous to the relationship.

A parent must make the jail-level punishment truly painful—softening it means having to give several jail sentences or, worse yet, jailing indefinitely. This must be avoided. Jail-level punishments are very negative. If overused, they can harm the parent-child bond. Therefore, they should ideally be employed only once in 10 years. Twice maybe. The punishment must be made strong enough to do the job. Here is another example of a jail-level consequence being used to train a child to pay his ticket, a crucial lesson for the child to learn because it is what will make the rest of his education effective. The child who will not pay his ticket-level consequences is too far out of control to be guided. Consider the following scenario:

> There is a new rule in the house that hitting results in being sent to the corner. Junior, 5 years old, thinks the new rule is a bit of a joke. He punches his little brother for "stealing" his soldier. Mother sends Junior to the corner, as promised. Unfortunately, Junior runs the other way. Mother stays put and calmly states: "That's okay. I'll count to five and if you're not in the corner by five, you can forget the corner. Instead, you'll lose the special chocolate-sprinkled donuts we're having for dessert tonight." (Mother actually bought these in order to train Junior to go to the corner. She knew he'd never do it the first time he was sent.) As it turns out, she is right. Junior just runs away. Mom says no more about it until two hours later, when dessert is being served. She hands out donuts to everyone in the family except Junior, the sugar addict. Salivating, Junior asks if he could have a donut, pretty please. Mother says only once: "I'm sorry. You didn't go to the corner when you were told to. You've lost your donut." Junior proceeds to try every trick in his book: pleading, offering to make up his time in the corner now, bargaining, grabbing, crying, and finally, throwing a major tantrum. It's truly a painful scene. The family is instructed to keep eating their donuts and just ignore Junior, who is now crying hys-

terically, foaming at the mouth and pounding his head against the floor. It's not easy to ignore, but having to do it gives the other children a vicarious experience of jail that may inoculate them for the next 10 years as well. The next day, when Junior is sent to the corner for hitting his brother, he decides to go. In fact, he goes whenever he is sent for the next several years.

The ideal time to expose children to "jail" is when they are very young; the lesson stays with them throughout childhood. It helps them to always pay their tickets, which means that they will always accept the discipline (instruction, guidance) of their parents. These children don't have to fight their parents to the bitter end, but simply accept fair consequences. They are "civilized." They're careful not to cross lines of safety and morality. They're "normal." Just as you don't have a show-down with the police officer who gives you a ticket, they don't have a show-down with you every time you set limits. Your children are balanced and healthy when they work within the 2x Rule.

How to Use the 2X Rule: A Summary

For simple requests, use the 2x Rule as follows:

1. Make a request. ("Please put your schoolbag away.")
2. Think about where you are in your 80-20 ratio right now. Can you afford to have a negative communication? Are you feeling up to it? Do you have time now? If you didn't answer "yes" to all questions, drop the request. (Either you put the schoolbag away yourself without saying any more about it or let it sit there till it rots. Either way, you don't ask the child again.) If you answered "yes" to all questions, then you can go on to the next step.
3. Make the request again, but add a warning of a negative consequence (ticket) for failure to comply. ("I asked you to put your schoolbag away. If you haven't done it by the time I count to 5,

I'll do it and you'll lose dessert tonight: 1, 2, 3, . . .")

4. If necessary, apply the consequence with minimal attention (very briefly and quietly). ("I'm sorry. You've lost dessert tonight.")
5. If the child does not accept the consequence, offer jail as a substitute for the ticket and apply if necessary.

For correcting a misbehavior that has been occurring over a period of time, do not use the 2x Rule until you have tried the good-feeling strategies. Only if these have not been successful should you consider the 2x Rule. In this case, proceed as follows:

1. Give an information statement such as "We don't eat with our hands, because it's not polite and it gets messy. We use our cutlery."
2. The next time the problematic behavior occurs, go to Step 2 and create a rule with a consistent negative consequence (e.g., "From now on, when you eat with your hands, you'll be excused from the table").
3. Apply the consequence as necessary.
4. If the consequence is not accepted, offer jail as a substitute and apply if necessary.

In Conclusion

The 2x Rule is a powerful antidote to parental anger. Because you don't ask more than twice, you don't lose patience. Ask once in a normal, pleasant tone of voice. Think before asking again. Ask again with a warning, if so desired. Apply a consequence if necessary. There you have it: you're a competent, calm, take-charge parent. Using the 2x Rule, you are now able to model for your children how you can, even under pressure and upset, maintain your self-control and self-respect without losing your sensitivity and respect for others. In the next chapter we will see how you can actively teach these principles to children, in addition to modeling them. Teaching and modeling is the winning combination.

CHAPTER 9

The Relationship Rule

Helping Your Child Acquire Relationship Skills

As you may recall from Chapter 2, there are limits to parental control. One of the things that parents cannot completely control is the quality of the parent-child relationship. This is unfortunate because, as you know all too well by now, relationship is everything.

The reason that relationship is not entirely in your control is because there is another player—a person with his or her own free will, experiences, genetic make-up and so on. You can only do your part.

Your part involves treating that other person in a pro-relationship manner, clearing the path and preparing the soil in which relationship might flourish. A pro-relationship manner consists of many specific skills, such as:

- Speaking respectfully
- Listening attentively
- Providing emotional support (emotional coaching)
- Showing warmth (unconditional positive attention)
- Being generous with praise and appreciation (conditional positive attention)
- Being considerate of the other's feelings and needs (showing sensitivity)
- Giving of yourself (attention, time, energy, resources)
- Setting limits and boundaries

Each of these skills must be fully developed by each person in a healthy relationship. In this section, we will explore ways of helping your children to acquire these skills. This will be one of the greatest gifts you give your children, because successful relationships are the basis of a successful life. Not only do you help your children to get along with you (something that is vital for their mental health), but you also help them get along with everyone they will ever encounter. Successful interpersonal relationships enhance mental and physical health and even contribute to job success and daily less-stress dealings with the world, but they're important far beyond these benefits: in the end, they are all that really matters.

Setting Limits and Boundaries

Oddly, it is the skill of setting limits and boundaries that allows us to teach all other relationship skills. As parents, we must first know how to set our own limits and boundaries. We have already explored one method of doing this in our examination of the 2x Rule. Now we will examine other important aspects of this skill.

I Give and Receive Respect

It is our job to treat others respectfully. We have another job as well: we must insist that they treat us the same way. This principle is especially crucial in parenting.

When we accept only respectful communications, we are sending the vital message that we consider ourselves to be worthy human beings, deserving of respectful treatment. By refusing to accept any other kind of treatment, we teach our children that they must interact respectfully with us if they want to interact with us at all. Training them in this way causes them to grow up *not knowing any other way. Being abusive won't be possible for them.*

To avoid dysfunctional ways of relating, live and teach The Relationship Rule: *I give and accept only respectful communication.* A corollary of this rule is: *I do not give, nor to I accept, any form of disrespectful communication (abuse).*

Teaching Respect

Your children will succeed at becoming respectful if you tell them exactly what you mean by "respect." Your description might include body language and behaviors. Here are some examples:

- "I don't make faces at you; please don't make faces at me."
- "I don't slam the door on you; please don't slam the door on me."
- "I don't hang up on you; please don't hang up on me."
- "I don't stop talking to you; please don't stop talking to me."
- "I don't roll my eyeballs at you; please don't roll your eyeballs at me."

These perfectly reasonable requests can, when necessary, be stated as Step 1 of the 2x Rule.

Showing Respect with Words

Your description of showing respect with words might include some of the following examples:

- "I don't yell at you; please don't yell at me."
- "I don't call you names; please don't call me names."
- "I don't insult you; please don't insult me."
- "I don't bark at you; please don't bark at me."
- "I don't order you around; please don't order me around."
- "I don't mutter under my breath at you; please don't mutter under your breath at me."

All disrespectful speech patterns can be eliminated by teaching a child the following two rules:

1. It is fine for a child to *ask* a parent; it is not okay for a child to *tell* a parent.
2. Always speak in a *pleasant tone of voice*, even when displeased.

Rule 1: Ask, Don't Tell

Since verbal respect is core in successful relationships, let's take a closer look at what's involved.

Look at the two simple rules of verbal respect stated above. They will help the child in many ways. The asking stance helps a child maintain a position of humility. It keeps him far from the arrogant, know-it-all attitude of pushy people. The *asking* stance helps a person to consider the feelings, wishes and status of another person. When a child learns to *ask* a parent, rather than *tell* the parent, he or she develops the lifelong habit of speaking respectfully to anyone, including, one day, his or her own spouse. Let's look at the results of learning Rule 1, *Ask, Don't Tell*.

- When wanting his dinner, the child learns to say, "Will dinner be ready soon?" rather than the less respectful, "I want to eat now." As a grownup, he or she will find the respectful version works just as well with a spouse as it did with a parent.
- When correcting a parent's error about what night is bath night, the child learns to say, "Is it possible that bath night is tomorrow, not tonight?" rather than the less respectful, "It's not tonight—it's tomorrow!" This strategy will save embarrassment to others throughout life.
- When dealing with a parent's accusation of breaking the kitchen scissors, the child learns to say, "Could I please explain?" rather than the less respectful "I did not!" This technique will help reduce automatic defensiveness in adulthood.

Now you might feel that the "less respectful" versions of speech in these examples were not all that disrespectful. After all, there was no name-calling, no swearing, no yelling. True. But there was also no respect for the feelings or dignity of the parent. When a parent is asked, rather than told, the parent feels in the right place. The parent, after all, is the "head" of the family in the sense of leadership and responsibility. When recognized and treated as such, the parent feels more positively toward the child and more inclined to want to please the child. Teaching your child this communication rule will be good for both of you.

Here's a little metaphor to help clarify the issue. Imagine that you live in a kingdom and you are one of the king's ministers. The king informs you that he has decided to send his army to the west. Thinking this is a dumb idea, you shout, "Your majesty! That's not a good idea! Send them to the east." The king orders you thrown in the dungeon for disrespect because you should have said it this way: "Your majesty, is it possible that sending them to the east might be more advisable?" By asking with deference, you would have maintained the status, honor and respect of the kingly position. Instead, by speaking in a "chummy" way, you have managed to effectively dethrone the royal personage.

Although most parents aren't kings or queens, all children can benefit from learning to speak to them as if they were! The way one would speak to royalty is the most respectful style of speech possible: considerate, sensitive, polite and deferential. By speaking in this manner to parents, children can acquire important character traits such as self-control, humility and sensitivity—traits that will serve them well in every relationship. Moreover, they can acquire the lifelong habit of being respectful in their communications to others. This will smooth their way, causing people to want to help them, support them and accompany them on life's journey.

Here is an example of a "chummy" parent-child dialogue, followed by a more respectful parent-child dialogue. Note the difference in tone:

Parent: *I'd like you to be home by 11 tonight.*
Teenager: *No way! The earliest I could get back is midnight.*

> Parent: *I'd like you to be home by 11 tonight.*
> Teenager: *Would you mind if I got back at midnight? I think
>   it'll be hard to be finished earlier.*

Parents are usually happy to work with respectful youngsters, glad to help them out. However, when parents feel pushed around, resentment inevitably builds up. Moreover, disrespect is a slippery slope. Teenagers don't wake up one morning swearing at their parents. Rather, disrespect of this kind develops slowly over time. At first, a little pushiness or insolence on the youngster's part is tolerated by the parents. The child's impertinent style then moves up a notch, and then another notch and then another. Eventually, the child is telling a parent off, speaking with utter disrespect. Teaching young children the rules of respectful speech prevents this unfortunate cycle by putting a protective fence around their communication style. It prevents them from becoming abusive, disrespectful or even insensitive. Will such formality distance children from their parents? No! Respectful speech is an emollient that keeps relationships running smoothly. Are husbands and wives "closer" to each other when they speak without regard for each other's feelings (i.e., when they speak "naturally")? Is a parent "closer" to a child when the parent is allowed to scream in the child's face? No. Disrespect creates distance because it is dehumanizing. It tramples other people's feelings, causing shame and pain. Respectful speech, on the other hand, fosters the growth of love, as it upholds the best in the speaker and listener.

Rule 2: Pleasant Tone of Voice

Ah, the challenge of a lifetime! A pleasant tone of voice is a defining characteristic of respect. Yelling is disrespectful in the extreme. We want to be able to say to our children, "I don't yell at you; please don't yell at me."

If you're not there yet, don't despair. Listen to your inner compassionate parent: "You're working on it—that's great! Why not make it a family project? You can tell the kids that everybody has to improve in this regard and that you'll help them and you want them to help you too. Everybody wins. Every day, you'll get better and better. If you keep working on it, you'll yell less and less often. You'll feel better and so will the kids. You're a great parent: I'm proud of you for trying!"

You don't have to be perfect in order to teach this rule to your children. You just have to show that you value the principle and that you are open to correction yourself. Teach your children to correct you *respectfully*, as in, "Daddy, is it possible that you are speaking very loudly right now?" or "Mom, that wasn't a raised voice just then, was it?"

Speaking in a pleasant tone of voice is not challenging for any of us when things are going our way. When a child asks Mom for a cookie and Mom gives her one, it will be very easy for the child to say "thank you" in a sweet tone of voice. When a youngster gets permission to stay out overnight, there's no problem with saying a pleasant "thanks." The challenge tends to arise when a parent must say "no."

Let's digress here for a bit, to explore a way to minimize the challenge presented by the word "no." It is helpful to reduce or soften the use of "no" whenever possible. Parents can often avoid direct use of the word "no." Say "yes" whenever possible; even when not possible, try to use the word "yes" in your answer. If that's not possible, still try to avoid the "no" word, while being careful to make a sympathetic, emotional comment in your response. Here are some examples:

Child: *Can I have a cookie?*
Parent: *Yes, for dessert.*

Child: *Can I have a two-wheeler bicycle?*
Parent: *Yes, when you turn 6.*

Child: *Can you buy me that "SugarSugar" cereal?*
Parent: *Oh, that looks really yummy, doesn't it? Too bad it's not good for our teeth.*

Teenager: *Can I borrow the car tonight?*
Parent: *Oh, I wish I could give it to you. Unfortunately, I need it for the auction.*

Why beat around the bush? Why not just say "no"? Well, try it out for yourself. Let's say you just thought of a great idea: you want to go out for dinner with your spouse. Which of the following two conversations would you like better?

You: *Honey, would you like to go out for dinner tonight?*
Spouse: *No.*

You: *Honey, would you like to go out for dinner tonight?*
Spouse: *Oh, that's such a nice offer! I'd love to, but I'm so tired. Could I take a rain check?*

Which of these conversations is a relationship builder? Which has the opposite effect? Remember, every communication we have with our spouse, and with our children, either strengthens or weakens the relationship. True, this "no" response is not such a terrible communication—it's not abusive or even disrespectful. But imagine if it occurred commonly in this marriage. Our negative words are like raindrops on stone, slowly wearing away what seemed to be solid. More divorces occur because of this sort of slow corrosion than for any other reason.

Our positive words, on the other hand, are nourishment for the soul, causing the heart to expand, healing ourselves and all those we touch. Positive words build, syllable by syllable, domestic peace and harmony. Even if it takes a few extra words to say a "yes-set" answer that really means "no," your extra effort will pay off in more loving relationships.

Despite the best efforts, however, a parent may find that her child clearly understands the implied "no" in the response and is decidedly displeased by it. Here is the parent's challenge and the child's. The parent wants to help the child deal with her disappointment, frustration and anger *respectfully*. This is essential for her long-term well-being, since she will encounter much more frustration and disappointment in life. Knowing how to process and express her feelings will keep her surrounded by love and support throughout life. Not having this skill will put her at significant emotional risk.

One of the great benefits of acquiring this skill is the tremendous growth in *self-control* that it yields. When children and parents can control their mouths in stressful moments, they have mastered the "wild child within." This particular inner child is a 2-year-old who cannot control her impulses. She screams, she rants, she raves. She can get us into trouble throughout life if we haven't developed a healthy relationship with her. There are fully grown men and women (you may know one or two) who throw fits—2-year-old tantrums—when things don't go their way at work, at home, on the road or wherever. These people have not learned how to help their inner 2-year-old, and they often suffer serious relationship problems as a result.

Working with your inner compassionate parent is one way to establish a healthy relationship with your "wild child within." Suppose your 6-year-old son absolutely refuses to go to bed. You've had a hard day at work and you haven't yet developed an effective parenting plan for this issue. As he runs around the house, you're feeling helpless, exhausted and furious. Your "wild child within" is about to let loose, when your inner compassionate parent comes to the rescue:

"Hey, sit down. Breathe slowly. Just relax. I'll make you some herbal tea in a moment. It's not an emergency. Let him stay up till 2 a.m.

tonight. You and I will create a parenting plan for this behavior and in about a week, we'll have him in bed every night at 8. Just ignore him for now and think about that book you wanted to read tonight. You can just go into your bedroom, shut the door and pull up your blankets. Put in your earplugs if his knocking bothers you. Just take care of yourself. We'll figure this out together. Just slow down and breathe."

Now that may help *you*, but what will help your children? You will help your children. By calming yourself down out loud when you're frustrated or upset, you are providing your children with a powerful demonstration of emotional control. In addition to your calm model, your lack of fear of their negative feelings and your firm, gentle education will help them to master their "wild child within." Each time that wild child bursts forth, you will work with it, taming it step by step. And, as they struggle with difficult feelings, you will provide them with emotional support and guidance. As a result of all this, *you will one day become their inner compassionate parent. It is your voice they'll hear in their heads as they go through life, your voice that will encourage and gently guide them.*

Let's look now at a process for teaching children self-control and the ability to speak respectfully, no matter what they're feeling.

How to Teach Respectful Speech

There are five steps in this process. They unfold, according to the child's rate of learning, over a period of weeks or, more commonly, months. They are then reinforced for the next 20 years. So take your time and go slowly. We're not after speed; we're after a lifelong skill. Remember, you yourself may also be just learning this skill. Be patient with everybody.

1. **Teach the two rules of respectful speech: "Ask, don't tell" and "Pleasant tone of voice."** Do this during a "teaching moment." A teaching moment is a moment in which both parent and child are calm, relaxed and fairly happy. It might be dinnertime, bedtime, story-time or any other quiet time.

It is the opposite of the kind of moment in which either parent or child is crying, hysterical, upset, angry, resentful, unhappy, enraged, very tired or very sick. Never attempt to teach anything at those kinds of moments.

During your lesson, be upbeat. Make the teaching fun and interesting, with lots of real-life examples and stories illustrating the correct and incorrect use of these rules. For young children, you might even use puppets, dolls or role-playing to illustrate your points. Always show the "right way" and the "wrong way" so that the child can clearly understand what's being asked for. For example, create a dialogue in which a parent gives a "no" answer to a child's request. "Daddy, will you please drive me to my friend's house?" "I'm sorry, honey. I've got work to do now." Have the child respond incorrectly (through puppets or storytelling techniques). "But I really need to go! You *have* to drive me!" and then have her respond correctly. "Daddy, this is really important to me. Is there any way at all that you could do this for me?" Ask your own child to give right and wrong types of responses to your simulated dialogues.

With older children and adolescents, go slowly and carefully. You can't suddenly spring new demands on this group. Present your information in a light, humorous way. Point out the benefits for everyone involved. If they're willing, engage them in role-play. If not, simply tell them that you, yourself, are going to try to follow these rules in speaking to them and you would appreciate their help.

2. Emotionally coach and then remind the child to use the rules. This strategy is used after you've completed teaching the two rules of respectful speech. It is employed at the actual time that the child is being disrespectful. Depending on the level of the child's upset, the sequence of your response could be *emotionally coach and then immediately remind the child of the rules,* or it might have to be *emotionally coach, wait until the child is calm (however many minutes or hours that takes), and then remind the child of the rules.*

For example, suppose your 7-year-old daughter wants to go outside to play, but you've told her it's too close to dinnertime now. She raises her voice, screaming that you never let her do anything she wants and that you're so mean! You respond with emotional coaching, saying something like, "You're mad at me for not letting you go—you don't like that at all and you feel that I'm being mean to you." Two things could happen at this point. The first one is that the child's feelings escalate, a common result of having feelings acknowledged. This is actually a good thing. The door has been opened, feelings have felt welcomed and now a flood of emotion might exit. This release prevents an unhealthy build-up of stress and resentment. If that happens when you acknowledge your child's upset feelings, just keep naming feelings until the child gets tired of expressing them. If the child stays enraged, end with telling her that you see that it's hard to get over this right now. Leave it that way for several hours if necessary. Later in the day, when the child is perfectly calm, return to this issue and *remind* her of the correct way to respond. Remind her of the examples you gave in the teaching sessions and remind her of the two rules. Then, ask her to say what she should have said earlier in the day. If she cooperates, offer generous praise and even reward.

The second thing that could happen after you name the original feeling is that the child quickly calms down. This often happens when feelings have been welcomed in your home for such a long time that there is no build-up of inner resentment. If this happens with your child, do the reminding step right then. Remind her about the examples and rules and show her how she might have replied when told "no." For example, it would have been fine for the young lady in the example on the previous page to say something like, "But Mommy, could I please go out if I come back as soon as you call me for dinner? I'll play right in front of the house so you can call me." Ask the child to say the words in the correct way. If she cooperates, lavish praise on her and tell her that since she said it so respectfully, you're going to let her go play after all. This is a powerful reward for speaking politely. In fact, I recommend that you give your child the "one-month-free introductory offer" for respectful speech. In this offer, any request that is spoken respectfully (except for one that is outrageous or simply impossible to comply with) receives a "yes" for the first month after learning the rules. This really gets them wanting to be respectful! Here are some further "reminding stage" dialogues.

> Child: *Don't help me with my book report; I'll do it myself.*
> Parent: *Oh, you'd rather do it on your own? Do you remember the rule we learned about asking, not telling? Could you please try expressing your wish in an asking way?*

> Child: *I'm not eating this!*
> Parent: *I see you're not thrilled with the broccoli. Do you remember how you're supposed to say that? Can you try it the "respectful way," please?*

> Child: *I'm not eating this!*
> Parent: *You're not? Do you remember how you're supposed to say that? Try it this way, "Mom, would you mind if I didn't eat the broccoli?"*

> Child: *That's not the way to do it, Daddy!*
> Parent: *Oh, Daddy got it wrong, did he? Do you remember how a little girl is supposed to tell her Daddy that he's doing something wrong? Remember . . . "Daddy, is it possible that you've made a mistake?" Could you say that, please?*

In all these examples, the parent offers understanding or coaching and then reminds the child of the rules. The parent then asks the child to say the statement in the respectful manner. It is very important for the child to actually practice the polite way of speaking. When the child has finished practicing the statement, the parent should give appropriate praise, label and, if possible, reward. It might sound like this, "Oh, that's great! You're sounding very respectful now! I think I'll just remove that broccoli for you." This is a version of the CLeaR Method.

Eventually, the "one-month-free introductory offer" will expire. At this point, the parent may not always please the child, even though the child has spoken politely. When an answer must be "no" it will be important to combine anti-arguing strategies along with the five steps for teaching respectful speech. The response of the parent to the child's disrespect will obviously depend on which step a parent is working on. In Step 2, "Reminding," a conversation might look like this:

Round 1

Child: *Can I please stay outside a little longer?*

Parent: *Hmm, let me think about that . . . No, sorry, Ben—it's time for bed; we've had too many late nights this week already.*

Round 2

Child: *NO-O-O-O! Everyone is still outside!*

Parent: *Oh, that's frustrating! Everyone is still outside and you have to come in. That's hard . . . Do you remember how to say that in a quiet voice with a question, like this, "Mommy, is it possible that everyone except me is still outside?" Would you please try it the polite way?*

Round 3

Child: *Mommy, is it possible that everyone except me is still outside?*

Parent: *You've said that beautifully, Ben! Yes, honey, I guess everyone is still outside. Unfortunately, I want you to come in for bedtime.*

If the child starts yelling again at this point, the parent would say nothing at all. The parent has already given criticism within the conversation (correcting the child's impolite speech) and cannot afford to be more negative. Moreover, ending the conversation after the second response is the standard in anti-arguing techniques. Finally, responding to the child's yelling may accidentally reinforce poor behavior. At this point, the child is gently ushered into the house. If the child actually refuses to come, however, then the parent can use the 2x Rule, entering on Step 2 (since a request—Step 1—has already been made). For the purposes of illustration, we'll continue the dialogue, showing the case of the uncooperative child:

Round 4
Child: *But I said it nicely! You said I could stay out longer if I said it nicely!*

Parent gives no response; holds door open for child.

Round 5
Child: *I'm not coming in! You said I could stay out longer if I said it nicely!*

Parent: *I'm counting to 5. If you are not in by 5, I'm going inside the house and you will not be allowed to play outside after school tomorrow.*

If the parent chooses to handle the situation this way, the child can now theoretically stay outside until midnight. The parent does not ask him to come in again. A parent who thought her child would actually do such a thing would not employ the 2x Rule in this way. Rather, the parent with such an out-of-control youngster would have to arrange to bring the child inside the house and then give the child a negative consequence for forcing her to have to do that. Depending on the age and size of the youngster, this might mean simply taking him by the hand, or stalling till Dad can carry him in, or waiting for other reinforcements.

Most often, conversations of this sort occur with fairly small children. However, the same style of conversation can occur with a teenager who has asked and been refused permission to take the car. The highly rebellious youngster could decide to take the car even though Mom has not given permission. Step 2 might sound something like, "If you take that car without my permission, I will confiscate your car keys for the summer." Here the parent is using a jail-level consequence because of the extreme disregard for authority exhibited by the adolescent.

3. Emotionally coach and then prompt. You may be able to start this step a week or two after the "reminding" step. When the child is making an error with choice of words or tone of voice, emotionally coach if there is upset and, if the child is calm enough, give a prompt. A prompt is a very short hint. Here's an example using the prompt phrase "tone of voice."

> The child is intensely refusing to go to his tutor. "I hate her! I hate her! I'm not going. There's no way I'm going!" The parent first coaches and problem-solves: "I hear you. You really don't like that lady and you really don't want to go. The trouble is, we have an appointment with her right now and we must leave. I could bring along a little treat, at least, so it won't be a totally bad experience. Would that help? It would? Good." Then the parent offers the prompt: "And Junior, remember 'tone of voice'? How about trying it again?" (Always ask the child to practice the correct way of speaking.)

At the prompting stage, the child is already familiar with the respectful way of speaking, since the parent has already spent some weeks in the "teaching" and "reminding" stages. Therefore, it may not always be necessary to emotionally coach at the prompting stage. Especially if the child's emotions are calm, the parent can try prompting without coaching. For example, suppose the child is standing with the fridge door open, complaining rather loudly, "There's never anything to eat in this house." If the child is mildly frustrated but not actually hysterical, the parent could leave out the coaching and just prompt: "What was the question, darling?" Hopefully, Junior answers, "Is it possible, Mother dear, that there is a shortage of food in the house?" Joyfully, the parent answers, "My, you asked that beautifully! Just for that, I'll buy you whatever you want—just name it!" (A little joking around is good for everyone.)

Here are some further dialogues at the coaching-plus-prompting stage. The first line is spoken by an irate child and the second by a calm, mature, amazing parent. The prompts are in bold type:

Child: *You don't know what I mean!*
Parent: *I can see you're getting really frustrated with me.* **Would you please just watch your tone of voice.**

Child: *I'm not going!*
Parent: *You really don't want to go.* **I think you forgot to phrase that as a question. Could you try it again?**

Child: *I want ketchup!*
Parent: *Oh, you'd like some of that yummy ketchup, would you?* **Try it this way, honey: "Mommy, could I please have some ketchup?"** (This is a modeling prompt, saying the exact words a child should use.)

Child: *I want ketchup!*
Parent: **Asking, not telling, please.**

Child: *I'm not going!*
Parent: **Tone of voice?**

Child: *NO-O-O! Everyone is still outside!*
Parent: **Was that a question?**

In these examples, you can see that a child may at times be breaking both rules of respectful speech—she may be both shouting and telling. Often, it is best to correct only one of the errors in the early stages of training. A few weeks later, when the child knows what is desired, it may be fine to use a general prompt that includes both errors:

- "Please say that more respectfully."
- "Respectful speech, please."
- "Please try that differently."
- "Politely?"
- "Can you try another way of saying that?"

4. Block. Emotional coaching-plus-prompting moves to prompting-without-coaching in its latter stages. In other words, after a few weeks, the parent may choose not to acknowledge the disappointment, frustration or other upset of the child and instead simply address the disrespectful speech pattern. This is a prelude to Step 4, "block." At Step 4, the parent does not emotionally coach, even if the child is upset. The child has been working on his ability to speak respectfully for a long time now—possibly several months—and he now knows what's expected of him. The parent can begin teaching the vital concept that no matter how upset a person may be, he is not allowed to behave disrespectfully to other people. Our fatigue, disappointment, anger, hard day, headache, stress, bad genes or anything else does not give us license to harm anyone emotionally. By blocking disrespectful communications, a parent teaches his child to be accountable. It is the child's own responsibility, from now on, to manage his mood successfully enough to remain polite. He must *think before he speaks*. This is what is meant by "self-control." No matter what he's feeling, he must remember who he is and to whom he is speaking. The "wild child within" is on a leash. It is essential, however, that Steps 1, 2 and 3 are successfully completed before working on Step 4. People who simply block disrespectful conversations with a child (or spouse!) without completing the first three steps are perceived to be shutting down communication. They are seen as uncaring and even cruel.

In Step 4, as soon as the child starts to speak disrespectfully, the parent blocks the communication with a blocking phrase. Here are some examples of blocking phrases:

- "Excuse me?"
- "I beg your pardon?"
- "Would you like to try that again in another tone of voice?"
- "Would you like to try asking that properly?"
- "Would you like to try that again?"
- "I'm sorry. I'd like to hear what you're trying to tell me. When you feel you can say it respectfully, please come get me. I'll be downstairs."

- "Are you talking to *me?*"
- "I'm sorry. I can't hear you when you're shouting."
- "I'm not going to respond to that until you've rephrased it."
- "I don't give or accept verbal abuse."
- "That's not how you ask."

Notice that the parent no longer explains the rules of polite speech, no longer attempts to understand the child's message or provide acknowledgment. At this point the parent has only one goal: to put an end to disrespectful speech.

5. Use the 2X Rule. Parents and children can get stuck at Step 4 for years on end. The child says it the wrong way, the parents say, "Excuse me?" and the child corrects himself. This is okay for a while, but not permanently. Our goal is that the child *does not say it disrespectfully at all*. After some weeks or months at Step 4, move on to Step 5—the 2x Rule. The parent says something like this:

"We've been working on speaking respectfully for a long time now. I know that you know what to say and how to say it. I'm really proud of your progress. Now, to walk you along the last mile of this work, I want to help you out with some gentle discipline. From now on, when you say something in a way that lacks respect, I want you to write an "action plan"—a short essay saying what you said, what was wrong about it, what you should have said and what you intend to do to help yourself be able to apply the rules in the future. It should only take you five minutes or so."

When using the 2x Rule, pick any consequence that is worth $100 to your child. The idea of an action plan is only one possible consequence. You could use writing out lines or essays, the withdrawal of "screens" (T.V., computer, video games, etc.), an earlier bedtime, a time-out in the corner or any other appropriate consequence.

In summary, there are five steps to reaching respectful speech:

Step 1	Teach the rules of respectful speech.
Step 2	Emotionally coach and remind.
Step 3	Emotionally coach and prompt.
Step 4	Block.
Step 5	The 2x Rule.

Why Use Such a Long, Drawn-Out Process to Teach Respectful Speech?

Some people feel we should skip all the warm-up stages and just go to the 2x Rule. The inner compassionate parent is the one who challenges this approach. Look at yourself, gently. Do you *always* speak respectfully, even when you're hurt, irritated, stressed, overwhelmed, on the brink, off the brink? . . . If you do, I bet your children are doing pretty well also. However, let's assume that, under enough pressure, your own "wild child within" sometimes escapes, causing you to speak louder than you should, in unpleasant tones, with unpleasant words. Do you think it's fair to give you a week or two to permanently clean up this lifelong habit? Besides being unfair, it's probably impossible to gain complete control that quickly. Sure, if you get an electric shock each time you speak poorly, it will speed things up. But that's not nice either. If you are teaching a very small child to speak respectfully, you can probably use just Step 1 and Step 5. That's because the child hasn't been talking long enough to develop any bad speech habits. But anyone past toddlerhood has already acquired deeply ingrained speech patterns. Go slowly and with love—it's worth the wait.

Other Pro-Relationship Skills to Teach Your Children

The Gift of Giving

A wonderful relationship-building skill to teach your children is how to give to others. By doing this, you are giving your children the gift of giving. It's a gift for them because they will experience the tremendous satisfaction that giving brings. If we parents do all the giving, claiming it is our pleasure, we are actually being selfish; we are depriving our children of the joy of giving to others.

In the parenting style of recent decades, we have been making the erroneous assumption that if we give our children everything, they will later turn around and give us everything as well. What happens, in fact, is that a child who is only given to, only learns to take.

He learns that it is his job to receive, your job to give. He will demand more and more and complain when you don't give him "enough"! And the fault will be yours. It is, after all, one of your parenting tasks to *teach* your child to give. It is not (for most people) an inborn skill. Teaching your child to give helps foster a strong parent-child relationship.

How to Teach Giving

Create opportunities for your child to give within the family setting, the extended family and even the community. Here are some ideas:

- Make sure your child participates in setting and clearing the dinner table from a young age—even 4-year-olds can manage some items. It is much easier to teach helpfulness to preschoolers than it is to teenagers. If you've never asked your teen for help before, be careful in introducing the concept now. Go slowly, patiently and kindly. Give generous praise and refrain from negative comments completely.
- Teach your child how to prepare food at a young age. You can work with fun foods like cookies and cakes, and real foods like toast, sandwiches, macaroni and scrambled eggs. Call the kids when potatoes need peeling and even teach them how to use the oven. Children should be able to make at least part of the main course, if not the whole meal, by age 12. Young cooks not only feel accomplished and competent (which boosts their self-esteem),

but they can also make a real contribution to the family.

- Teach your child to make or purchase gifts for every family member's birthday. Even 3-year-olds can scribble a card. Older children should use their allowance money.
- Teach your children to offer their seats (on a bus, at a party, etc.) to adults, and especially the elderly, pregnant women and the handicapped.
- Teach your children to offer to assist the elderly when the situation presents itself (cross the road, carry packages and so forth).
- Teach your children to interrupt their activities to greet a parent who enters the house.

Teaching Sensitivity

Another important pro-relationship skill to teach children is that of sensitivity. Parents try to be sensitive to their children's feelings, which means paying attention to those feelings and showing respect for them. Children need to be able to do this too. Some children are naturally tuned into the feelings of others and they know what is needed in a given situation. However, most children need help in this area. Emotional coaching is one way to provide that help. Research shows that children who are regularly emotionally coached show increased sensitivity to other people. Another tool parents can use is direct teaching.

Sensitivity training consists of talking to children about your own feelings and showing them how to respect those feelings. Here are some common situations:

- A parent is having a conversation with her friend. Her 5-year-old child keeps interrupting, asking for this and that. After the friend has departed, Mother tells the child that it's hard to enjoy her conversation with so many interruptions. (It is important to correct children privately so as not to embarrass them. This in itself is a model of sensitivity.) She teaches a sensitivity rule: *don't interrupt people who are speaking unless the matter is urgent.* She uses the training sequence of positive reinforcement, positive programming and rewards to help the child succeed in this area.

- Mom and Dad are having a discussion about a car they are thinking of purchasing. Dad likes one model, but Mom likes the other. Junior sides with Mom (although nobody asked his opinion). When Mom has gone, Dad takes Junior aside and explains to him that he feels badly when the kids side with Mom, and Mom feels badly when the kids side with Dad. He teaches the rule of sensitivity: *a child should not validate the opinion of one parent against the other.* This rule actually helps prevent the common dysfunctional family pattern of "triangulation," in which children side with and respect one parent while disrespecting the other.

- Mom has worked for hours to prepare a nutritious and delicious supper. As she's serving it, the children are starting to eat. By the time she sits down to her own meal, everyone has already finished eating! Mom explains to the children that this doesn't make her feel good. Instead of feeling like the "queen" in her home, she feels like an uncared-for servant. She teaches them the rule of sensitivity pertaining to eating with people: *guests should wait to eat until their hosts start to eat; children should wait until their parents have begun.*

- Now the family is eating together. Dad wants to tell about something interesting that he experienced today, but sees that the children have all left the table. Only Mom is still there. He calls the kids back and explains to them that he doesn't feel good when everybody just up and leaves like that. He teaches them the rule of sensitivity concerning children at their parents' table: *thank the cook and ask permission to be excused.* He helps them succeed in this new routine by focusing praise on those who remember to show sensitivity and appreciation.

- Dad is explaining how the new PDA works to his friend Michael. Junior notices that Dad's made an error. He says, rather politely he thinks, "Excuse me, Dad, but that isn't correct. The å function is for transferring data." Dad thanks Junior for the information. When Michael has left, Dad takes Junior aside. Dad explains that he felt a little foolish when Junior pointed out the error. He would have felt better if he had discovered it himself, which he would have in just a few minutes. He taught Junior the rule of sensitivity: *only correct a parent if the matter is very important, and even then, the correction should be put in a question form or a tentative statement rather than a straightforward correction, so as not to diminish the parent in any way.* If the information Junior had was crucial, for example, he could have put it this way: "Excuse me, Dad. I'm not sure about this, but I think I once learned that the å function is used for transferring data. Of course, I could be completely wrong." Such a self-effacing approach is the absolute height of sensitivity to the feelings of another person. A child who knows how to do this will be a diplomat wherever he or she goes in life.

The Benefits of Sensitivity Training

Parents who take the trouble to teach their children interpersonal skills are helping themselves, their children and the parent-child relationship. It will be impossible for children raised this way to swear at their parents or abuse them in any way. And such children will grow up to be people who are "naturally" respectful of everyone, enjoying the benefits that this will bring to their lives.

CHAPTER 10

Toddlers

Knowledge Is the Key

"The terrible twos" can be turned into "the terrific toddlers" when parents have the tools they need to guide them. Indeed, a little knowledge goes a long way, enabling adults to negotiate this phase of the parenting journey with pleasure, joy, competency and serenity—staying one step ahead of Junior all the way! In this section, we will look at parenting processes as they are practiced in the toddler years. Once these processes are acquired, parents can use them to negotiate any specific issue.

In the first three years of life, children present many behavioral and emotional challenges, including issues around eating, sleeping, exploration, emotional regulation, social behavior and much more. Parents can shape and guide both behavioral and emotional development by calling on the appropriate parenting process. For example, keeping in mind the primacy of the relationship, the importance of acknowledging feelings and the fact that positive attention reinforces behavior, a parent can appropriately solve a toddler's bedtime problem in any number of ways. The following scenarios illustrate that more than one approach is possible:

Nora really hates to sleep in her own room. She's only 2 1/2, and Jed and I think it's fine if she comes into our bed. So last night, after we found her sobbing hysterically in her bed, we told her that we understood how sad and scared she was and that it was okay to come sleep in our room. She quieted down immediately. Then we told her that because she settled down so nicely in (our) bed, she could sleep there whenever she wants. She felt great and so did we.

Jon and I have been exhausted lately because our 18-month-old son, Ezra, has been sleeping with us. No one is getting a good sleep. Last week we decided to insist that Ezra sleep in his own room. The first night was hard. When we finished tucking him in and started to leave his room, he protested really loudly. We told him that we could see that he was very upset; we let him know that we understood. We offered him whatever comforts we could—we even bought him a special stuffed bear. We told him we would be back to check on him every once in a while and he could call us if he needed us. Then we left the room. He was still crying but eventually stopped and went to sleep. He woke up a couple of times in the night, crying for us. We came in each time, tucked him in again, and left. In the morning we gave him tons of praise for sleeping in his own room. We repeated this whole routine almost every day last week. By the end of the week, Ezra finally began to settle better. He only cried for a moment when we left and also when we came in to him. I think we're on our way.

It's up to parents to decide how they want to solve the issues of toddlerhood: whether or not they will allow sweets, if and when a child is allowed in their bed, to have or not have a rule about eating only at the table. There is no single "right way." What matters most is that the parents use healthy parenting processes for raising their kids. Parenting processes begin at birth. Let's see how they unfold through the toddler years.

Baby Steps

Why do you think pregnancy lasts nine months? Wouldn't it be better to conceive one night and give birth the next day? No. Having to wait almost a year for the birth of a child allows expectant parents to slowly relinquish the idea of their carefree, self-oriented existence. As they peruse pregnancy books and baby stores, they begin to get the idea that life won't be the same—they will have to consider the needs of someone else *all the time*. Nine months allows this idea to sink in slowly—it gives parents time to adjust mentally to the life-changing event of a lifetime: becoming a parent.

Okay, so wouldn't it be better for children to be born as adults? Yes. That would save everyone the trouble of childrearing. But clearly, that was not the plan. Okay, perhaps children could be born as 5-year-olds instead of as infants. There would be distinct advantages: fewer sleepless nights and no diapers. However, think about the disadvantages: imagine what it would be like to give birth to a school-age child who doesn't listen, who tests parental limits, who talks back and who is old enough to get into serious trouble. How would parents cope with all of this on Day 1 of parenting?

Clearly, the task would be overwhelming. Even teachers facing their first class of kindergarten students have had at least three or four years of university preparation for the job, learning how to manage and educate small children. Parents, too, have at least four years of preparation for dealing with a 5-year-old: the child's first four years after birth! These years give the parents some time to climb the learning curve, an opportunity to ease into the skills involved in raising children.

Observing

The child's own development slowly introduces one major parenting skill at a time. In the earliest weeks of parenting, parents do not have to be familiar with ticket- and jail-level consequences, the five-step training program for respectful speech patterns and the 80-20 Rule—all at once! Rather, between birth and age 3—from infancy to toddlerhood—skills can be perfected slowly and one at a time.

The earliest skill required in parenting is observing. Observing forms the basis of all other, later parental interventions. For example, parents must use the skill of observing in order to do emotional coaching: they must observe the child's body language, facial expression, tone of voice and actual words. Observing is also required for reinforcing desirable behaviors later on in childhood: parents must observe that a desirable behavior is occurring so that they can strengthen it using the CLeaR Method. Parents will also be required to use observing for applying the 2x Rule: they must observe occasions of misbehavior and apply consequences as necessary.

Pregnancy introduces this basic skill to parents. Parents observe the baby moving within the mother's body. They are noticing what the child is doing as he or she rolls and kicks in the womb. There is nothing they can do to influence the child's behavior at this stage. Indeed, it is important to note that babies have a will of their own. Even as infants take their own sweet time to move down the birth canal and out into the world, parents learn that children are forces to contend with—they have their own agendas.

The baby at home presents similar opportunities to strengthen the skill of observing. Does the baby seem to be uncomfortable? Is he or she tired or hungry? Is the infant content? There is a great deal of observing that must be done in order to meet the needs of the child. Parents who succeed in closely observing the signals of the baby will be the most successful in soothing the child. They will be attuned to the child's nonverbal communication system. The willingness to look, listen and learn lays the foundation for an intimate bond between parent and child.

Kimberly sleeps in bed right beside me. When she wants to nurse, she starts to move her head around a little and makes puckering noises with her mouth. If I don't respond right away, she starts to make little whimpering sounds. Usually I don't wait until that stage, because I've learned her signals—I know what she wants. There's no point in ignoring her or waiting until she's screaming. Even in the daytime, I can read her small movements accurately enough that she rarely ends up having to cry out loud. People tell me she's a very quiet baby. I think I'm just a very observant and responsive mom.

Naming Feelings

Once the baby's state has been noted through observing, parents can begin the second basic parenting skill: *naming feelings*. Even though infants obviously don't understand words, they do understand tone of voice and body language. The parents' use of emotional coaching at this stage involves resonating emotionally with the infant and conveying their empathy through the non-verbal communications that accompany their words. In addition, even though a baby doesn't decode the words, it is good practice for parents to be putting their feelings into words; it trains the parent in one of the most important parenting skills that will be required throughout the 20-year process of childrearing.

Upon observing that the child is uncomfortable, a parent can—while tending to the baby's needs—name feelings: "You're not very happy, are you, sweetie? Let me change your position for you." Noting that the infant is smiling at a mobile, the parent can acknowledge, "You like that mobile!" Seeing that the baby seems to be tired, the parent can state, "You've had enough for now, haven't you? You want to have a rest."

Indeed, parents often talk to babies almost instinctively. As the baby becomes a toddler, however, naming feelings often gets pushed aside in favor of instructions, corrections, reprimands and direct teaching. This is a mistake. *Naming feelings* always precedes other parenting interventions and should be used generously throughout all the years of parenting.

Wrong way:
Parent: *No! Don't throw your food around!*

Right way:
Parent: *I see you like to throw your food around. It's fun, isn't it? The trouble is that it has to be all cleaned up and Mommy doesn't want to have to do that. Please leave your food right here on the dish.*

As always, emotional coaching brings parent and child closer together, whereas instructions given without this technique often end up feeling like a battle of wills.

Wrong way:
Parent: *It's time to put your toys away.*

Right way:
Parent: *I see you're having fun with your blocks. You can play again later; right now, it's time to put the toys away.*

These conversations will grow up along with the child:

Wrong way:
Parent: *When I tell you that 1 a.m. is your curfew, I expect to see you here at 1 a.m.—not 1:30.*

Right way:
Parent: *I know when you're out having a good time with your friends, it isn't always easy to pull away to get home on time. It can be inconvenient or embarrassing or awkward—I remember that from being a teenager myself. However, I want you to find a way to work it out, because when I say that 1 a.m. is your curfew, I really want to see you here at 1 a.m.—not 1:30.*

Naming feelings takes more time, patience and skill than just telling a child what to do or not do. However, the extra effort is rewarded tenfold! Besides all the practical benefits resulting from emotional coaching (emotionally coached children have better health, academic performance, behavior, social skills and so forth), parents who coach their kids enjoy the intangible but invaluable benefit of having a good relationship with them. That benefit may endure a lifetime—a large reward for a small effort. The habit of naming feelings may not be natural at first, but the many months of babyhood give parents the time they need to develop expertise in this area. The toddler years are a time of integration of this skill along with other parenting interventions.

Introducing the 80-20 Rule

Infants are designed to elicit positive attention from adults. Perfect strangers feel compelled to make cooing noises and happy faces at small babies, and even parents find their own offspring generally irresistible. Babies who lie around drooling and smiling will generally receive high doses of good-feeling attention from parents, such as smiling, talking, praising ("you're so cute!"), hugging, kissing, holding and playing. Parents will also find themselves naturally offering conditional positive attention to their babies, using both words and body language to reinforce desirable infant behaviors such as eating "nicely," sleeping "nicely," accomplishing physical feats such as holding up the head, sitting, looking clever, playing with toys, smiling and showing any other "signs of life." Many parents will easily give an 80% or higher ratio of positive to negative attention to their "cooperative" babies. Shows of parental fatigue, frustration or irritation (for example, in response to having to clean up a baby's regurgitated mess), along with simple nonresponding (e.g., ignoring a baby's cries for a while), will constitute the 20% bad-feeling allotment.

Unfortunately, not all babies are cooperative. This has serious ramifications for the 80-20 Rule, since unhappy babies tend to provoke unhappy adult responses. People often become ill-tempered and overwhelmed when trying to console an inconsolable infant. Colicky babies, for instance, are at risk of jeopardizing that 80% good-feeling attention diet from their parents. Indeed, their parents may become depressed and anxious, as well as angry; they may withdraw from the baby emotionally or dislike her actively. Some will directly express their displeasure.

I know it's ridiculous, but I get so frustrated with Caitlin's incessant screaming that I sometimes start screaming myself! I just yell at her to stop making such a racket. Sometimes she looks up at me in shock— silent for a moment—and then she starts screaming even louder. I guess I scare her when I do that—it sure doesn't get her to calm down.

Unfortunately, babies don't seem to "benefit" from bad-feeling interventions. Yelling, telling them to change their ways or threatening them with punishment just doesn't work at all. For the first 15 months or so, the primary interventions used to shape a child's behavior are *good-feeling ones*, since infants, babies and toddlers do respond to positive reinforcement such as smiling, talking in a pleased tone and other good-feeling signs of pleasure. Toddlers on the way into trouble can frequently be turned around with the good-feeling strategy of *distraction*. Distraction redirects a youngster to an acceptable activity that can be praised or attended to in some other way.

Ned has just begun to cruise around the furniture. This means he sometimes tries to touch things he shouldn't. Rather than scare him with a loud "no," we usually try to get him to look at something on the other side of the room while someone runs over to remove the untouchable object. Ned is none the wiser and has been spared a reprimand. We figure there will be enough reprimands when he really starts to crawl around!

Parents of an unhappy baby, like those of an unhappy older child, will have to work hard to overcome their natural tendencies in order to give the child what it needs: 80% good-feeling attention. Even though the baby may be distressed, genetically or temperamentally challenged, in pain or otherwise miserable, he or she still needs to feel loved. In fact, any signs of parental rejection will only worsen the baby's condition. Parents can take comfort in knowing that their baby actually absorbs the soothing warmth of positive parental actions and words, even when the infant is incapable of showing pleasure in the moment.

Whether it is easy to be positive or whether it is difficult, the need for parents to give 80% positive attention begins at the child's birth. Parents have many months to practice this skill before their children become mobile and old enough to actually require negative attention.

Introducing the CLeaR Method

The process of a child's education starts on the first day of birth. The way the baby is handled, the environment around him and the emotional tone of the home all teach the infant about the world he's just entered. Some active educational interventions are used by parents even in the first months of a baby's life—if we consider "praise" to be an active intervention ("that was a good burp!"). Moreover, even in the first months and years, babies are exposed to the world of limitations. Sucking at the breast is great for a nursing toddler; biting is not acceptable. Playing with the pots and pans is a fine project; playing with the knives is not. Crawling around the family room is okay, but exploring the bathroom is not allowed.

Certainly, as soon as babies can get around on their own, specific educational interventions become a necessity in every home. The baby now has to learn that he or she cannot touch everything, go everywhere, or do everything—destructive or dangerous activities must be curtailed. At first, parents can solve the problem by simply lifting the baby and moving her elsewhere. However, this is a very short-term solution! The active baby must somehow be persuaded to avoid problematic activities and encouraged to engage in safe and positive ones.

Persuading children to engage in appropriate behaviors and refrain from inappropriate ones is called "discipline"—meaning guidance, education and socialization. Even 1-year-olds are responsive to some forms of guidance. Although a child's language skills may be insufficient for processing instructions and reasons, his or her emotional skills have been powerful instruments for learning from the first days of life. Parents can employ these emotions for constructive education.

A careful use of the "pleasure principle" provides much of the education that this young group requires. The CLeaR Method is a form of guidance that uses the pleasure principle to shape a child's behavior. It is the first actual discipline skill that parents will practice. All desirable behaviors can be reinforced by attending to them with the first two steps of the CLeaR Method: commenting and labeling. The parent must use observing to identify when a desirable behavior is occurring. Then the parent can give an appropriate comment and label—and perhaps even a reward. For babies who do not yet understand the words, the accompanying emotional information conveyed through tone of voice, pitch, facial expression and other forms of body language serves to convey pleasure. Moreover, even small babies can be "rewarded" with a hug and kiss or an excited clapping of hands. All of this positive attention causes the child to engage in the desirable behavior more often.

Very little attention should be given to the undesirable behaviors. Lack of attention tends to extinguish behavior in people of any age, including even infants. Purposeful failure to attend can therefore be employed as a gentle intervention that discourages harmless undesirable behaviors. (It is in no way to be confused with unhealthy or abusive forms of "ignoring" in which a parent actually punishes a child with lack of attention.) Reduction in attention, rather than lack of attention, is used when the behavior must be tended to for reasons of safety or other concerns: the parent then intervenes in a very quiet manner, using as few words and actions as possible. Desirable behaviors, on the other hand, are acknowledged with positive fanfare. In this way, toddlers learn that certain behaviors are better sources of attention than others. They will engage in those behaviors more frequently. A common error of the untrained parent is to give loud, dramatic, intense attention to undesirable behaviors. Unfortunately, the intensity of attention rather than the quality of attention seems to be most important to young children. Thus intense negative attention can be very reinforcing, causing young children to repeat negative behaviors just for their attention value!

Wrong way:
Parent: *NO! DON'T TOUCH THOSE KNIVES! THEY'RE SHARP!*

Right way:
Parent: *Those knives are interesting, aren't they? They're too sharp to play with. Let's play with these pots and pans—aren't they great? GOOD FOR YOU! YOU'RE PLAYING SO NICELY WITH THE POTS AND PANS! WHAT A GREAT SOUND YOU CAN MAKE—YOU ARE A TALENTED MUSICIAN! I think you deserve a chance to play with Mommy's new wooden spoon today!*

In the "wrong" scenario above, the child gets excited parental attention for *doing the wrong thing*. Since the child is not redirected, there is no possibility of using the CLeaR Method to reinforce the desirable alternative behavior.

In the "right" scenario, the parent uses quiet and brief emotional coaching to bond with the child. Then the parent redirects the child to an alternative desirable behavior, using a louder, more excited voice. Once the child is engaged in the desirable behavior, the parent employs the CLeaR Method, enthusiastically praising and labeling and, in this case, also rewarding the appropriate behavior. Obviously, the parent must suppress the very natural inclination to be dramatic when the child is engaged in dangerous activity. Instinct must be pushed aside so that the parent *unnaturally* speaks in a normal tone of voice about the undesirable behavior and speaks in a louder tone about the desirable one. It helps to keep in mind that the "natural" way can actually harm the child.

Until the child is around 3 years old, the CLeaR Method is the discipline method of choice. In these toddler years, it involves redirecting a child from an undesirable behavior to a desirable behavior, and then applying part or all of the CLeaR Method. Undesirable behaviors must receive minimal acknowledgment, even when they are dangerous or destructive. Intense attention reinforces behavior, even if that attention is bad-feeling. Therefore, intense attention is saved for use with desirable behaviors only.

When Lynda was 2, she'd hug and kiss the newborn—and then she'd start smacking him! I know she had mixed feelings about his arrival; it was definitely a love-hate relationship. I couldn't let her hurt him and I was frankly panicked by her behavior. The first few times she did that, I instinctively screamed at her to stop doing it! However, the more I screamed, the more she seemed to do it, so I tried another method instead. When she hit the baby, I didn't say a word—I just took her hand and moved it in a gentle stroking motion up and down his arm, saying to her really loudly, "You're stroking the baby so gently! What a wonderful sister you are! I think the baby is smiling at you because he likes you so much!" She seemed to really like that. She started calling me over to see her "stroke the baby so gently"—she found a good way to get some nice attention from me and I found a good way to keep the baby safe!

At 18 months, Sammy is really into exploring. He particularly likes to climb—the higher the better, it seems. Of course, Marla and I get very unnerved finding him up on a counter or other high place. Somehow he managed to get on top of the refrigerator last week— you can imagine how scared we were! But we both decided that hysterics on our part wasn't the way to go. We'd have to be yelling at him all day if that's the technique we wanted to use. This is the way we do it: when he's up on a table or someplace he shouldn't be, we pick him up and say "no," firmly but quietly. Then we put him down on the floor and say really loudly, "Sammy's playing on the floor! Sammy is a safe baby!" And then we try to reward him with a big kiss or a special toy that we set aside for the purpose, or sometimes a favorite food. Several times a day, when we see him crawling around the floor, we do the same routine. We don't want him to think that we only get excited after he's climbed on something—he's a smart little guy and if we only gave him treats after he climbed up high, then he'd climb up high just to get the ball rolling on the treats! That's why we make sure he understands that we're happy any time we see him safely playing on the floor. We want him to know that the floor is a good place to be. Sammy isn't completely cured of climbing yet, but he has improved since we started doing this and he's a lot better than our next door neighbor's baby of the same age. When that little guy climbs, his parents shout really loudly. They want to show him how serious this misbehavior is. The trouble is that their little boy just laughs and tries to run away from them; then he climbs some more, like it's some sort of game of hide-and-seek—we've been at their house when he does this routine. Their method obviously isn't working very well.

Bad-feeling Attention for Toddlers

Some bad-feeling attention must occur in parenting. As stated earlier, all instructions are slightly bad-feeling. Therefore, when a parent tells a toddler to move away from the electrical socket, this must be counted in the 20% negative-stroke allowance. The word "no" is bad-feeling, even when said in a patient, sweet tone of voice. However, it must be used at times. The trick with toddlers is *not to use it constantly*. Parents of toddlers need to continue to use the good-feeling techniques of earlier months, even as the baby begins to get into mischief. All negative-feeling interventions must be restricted to their small place in the parenting dialogue.

Shows of parental anger are intensely bad-feeling. Consequently, angry communications should, as always, be severely limited—although it is possible to feign anger on very rare occasions for the child's own benefit. For example, a parent who is worried about the child's safety may use a very strict voice and facial expression to reprimand a dangerous activity, even though the parent is more anxious than furious. When used *rarely*, intense parental disapproval of this sort can be an effective teaching tool.

However, the routine use of anger with toddlers is not recommended. When shouted at, toddlers tend to laugh or cry, depending on the inborn nature of the child. The thick-skinned variety are not particularly bothered by parental disapproval. They can see the humor in an adult's total loss of control because—let's face it—an angry adult is often being sort of ridiculous. However, children who are timid and sensitive by nature totally fail to see the humor in a tantrumming adult. They can be fearful to the point of tears. If children laugh, there will be no learning. They have not suffered an educational negative consequence from the raised voice, since they did not perceive it to be negative. It didn't feel bad to them. If they cry, there may still be no learning because the young child does not always understand what it is that is causing the parents to shout or what it is that is wanted of her. There is also the possibility that the child understands full well and that learning will occur. However, in this case, the parents are also simultaneously teaching that forceful intimidation is a valid form of communication—a lesson that even young toddlers can begin to make practical use of. Moreover, frequent use of loud negative interventions can cause developmental and relationship disturbances in toddlers. Excessive shouting at an infant or toddler can cause the child to feel rejected and fearful. The response can be withdrawal, refusal to cooperate, emotional deadening or reactive rebellion. For this reason alone, it is best to avoid the use of anger as a teaching tool.

Can parents use disapproval as a tool instead of actual anger? *Disapproval*, when conveyed infrequently, is not as harmful or rejecting as anger. From the child's point of view, it is more likely to convey displeasure than hatred. The angry adult, seen through the eyes of a tiny toddler, appears as an enormous, terrifying monster (try to catch yourself really angry on video or camera some time, then blow up the image very, very large: this is how you look to your small child). The disapproving adult, while not a pretty sight, is not as overwhelming.

Due to temperamental differences, there is no standard effect of disapproval. A stern look may deter one youngster from throwing the block across the room, while another child experiences the look as an irresistible invitation to misbehave. However, many children at this age are keenly affected by a parent's displeasure or temporary loss of affection. Thus, expressing these emotions when a child is behaving inappropriately can often deter these youngsters from those behaviors. For those who will learn from it, disapproval in the form of a displeased look or a curt, businesslike "no" can be used in the parent's 20% allotment for bad-feeling interventions.

> *Simon is very sensitive. We only have to give him a disapproving "look" and he'll immediately stop doing whatever he is doing. The other day, he started to reach for Dan's glass of tea that was on the coffee table and I just gave him that "look"—he put his hand down right away and got involved in something else. I don't even have to say "no" to him—so I don't bother. I treat "no" as a rare commodity, not to be squandered.*

> *I've improved my technique lately. I used to say "no" to Belinda in a very long, singsong style, like "No-o-o-o-o-o-o-o-o, Belinda." She obviously thought I was playing around. She'd look at me and smile, then continue doing whatever she was doing. I now find I'm much more effective using a smart, cold "no." It sounds really businesslike. I don't make any threats along with it but it sort of sounds threatening on its own. She almost always stops whatever she was doing when I use it.*

Related to disapproval, but less intense, is *indifference*. Indifference is a withdrawal of attention that is experienced as negative from the child's point of view. A toddler's tantrum can be treated with indifference. The parent simply carries on with his or her regular activities while the child screams and cries. Even the violent, foaming-at-the-mouth, clutching-onto-the-parent's-ankles variety of tantrumming toddler can be treated with indifference: the parent, without saying a word, leads or carries (or, in really bad cases, gently drags) the child to his room (or a different room that is less destructible) and leaves him there for the duration of the tantrum, with the instructions to "come out when you've

stopped crying." Rather than hold the door shut (which actually satis-
fies the child's need for attention), it is preferable to deposit the child
and quickly get as far away from the room as possible. If the child comes
out, the parent should return him to the room again and again, still
demonstrating indifference (ideally while talking to someone else at the
same time, either in person or on the phone). If the parent gets impatient or has other things to do, a severely disapproving look and tone
can accompany the very firm instruction to "stay in your room until
you are finished crying." Most children will comply if the tone is serious enough. However, there are always some who fearlessly defy their
parents, following them around the house screaming at the top of their
lungs. Although it is understandably tempting to turn around and scream
in the child's face when this happens, parents should avoid doing that.
Rather, they should show as much indifference as possible, by putting
on earplugs if necessary and carrying on with their activities.

If, when put in a room, a toddler "trashes" it (emptying the drawers
and throwing the bedding onto the floor, etc.), parents should again
show indifference. After the tantrum, it is preferable for the parent to
simply leave the mess there without comment. The bed isn't made nicely
for bedtime, nor are the clothes tidied up for the next day. At some
point later in the week, the parent can put away a few things at a time
until the room has gradually returned to normal. Since the child generally trashes a room for effect (i.e., to upset the parent), lack of upset
usually extinguishes the behavior fairly soon. If indifference doesn't
reduce the frequency of room-trashing over a month or two, it may be
possible to use the toddler-modified 2x Rule (see next page).

Whether inside a room or out, the tantrumming child eventually
runs out of steam (thank goodness). Parental indifference should be
continued for another quarter of an hour past this point. Parents who
cuddle their toddler immediately after a tantrum are actually reinforcing tantrumming by giving good-feeling attention to inappropriate behavior. They often discover that the child continues to have
frequent tantrums (surprise, surprise) despite their loving reassurance
technique. Parents, insecure after their child's fit, frequently feel that

they need to reassure a child that she is loved after she has been so upset. Parents who are, in general, giving the child 80% positive attention *do not* need to remind the child of their love; the child will already be feeling quite secure in that regard. Disinterest shows the child that the parents are not interested in tantrums. Indeed, no specific hugging or cuddling should be given to the child for quite a while after a tantrum, even when the parent has returned to a normal, "interested" state. Rather, the parent should gradually show more pleasure and warmth toward the child, simply coming back to the "normal" position. Intense affection should be reserved for particularly happy moments a little later in the hour.

The 2X-Rule (Modified for Toddlers)

In general, toddlers are not candidates for the standard form of the 2x Rule. Their ability to understand the concept that negative consequences will occur at some future point in time is limited. They can, however, understand consequences that will happen almost immediately. For this reason, Grandma's Rule can be introduced to toddlers.

> *I get Lisa to tidy up by using Grandma's Rule. I say, "as soon as you put away your toys, I'll read you a story." Then she runs to put away the toys.*

A modified use of the 2x Rule, using only immediate consequences, can also be very useful with toddlers. When a parent finds that neither *disapproving* nor *indifference* deters a child, he or she can employ the modified 2x Rule. The parent warns the toddler that a specific consequence will occur immediately, unless the child complies with the parent's wishes.

> *When Lenny holds the ball up, ready to throw it across the living room, I give him a disapproving look and tell him that if he throws*

it, I'm taking it away. I've had to take it away a few times and now he knows I mean business. When I tell him I'm going to take it away, he puts it down immediately.

Sharon never wanted to go to bed. We used to put her down for the night and two minutes later she'd be up and running all over the place. It was Eddy's idea to use the modified 2x Rule and, boy, has it worked! Now we tuck her in and tell her that if she gets out of bed we're going to put her back right away and take away the bear she likes to sleep with. She loves that bear, so we only had to take it away once—after that, I guess she understood that we really meant it.

Parents would not remove a toy that the child actually *needs* to sleep with. Thus, pacifiers, bottles, security blankets or other transitional toys are not to be used as negative consequences. Toys that the child likes, but can live without, make appropriate consequences. The modified 2x Rule for toddlers only employs immediate consequences. Sometimes the child is old enough to comprehend the parent's warning; in these cases the parent can give the child the choice to cooperate or to face a negative consequence. When the child's language skills are not sufficiently developed, parents do not describe rules in words, but rather use consistent actions to help form a rule in the child's mind. Here's an example:

Jenny liked to throw food off her tray. She thought it was pretty funny. I didn't. I made a rule in my own mind: "From now on, when Jenny throws food, her meal is over and I will give Jenny the cold shoulder." Of course, there was no point in telling Jenny the rule because she wouldn't understand. Instead, I simply started applying it. Whenever she threw food, I immediately took her out of her chair and withdrew my attention for a few minutes—just enough that she could see I was displeased. After about a week of following this process, Jenny's mealtime behavior started to improve.

As is true for older children, bad-feeling consequences for toddlers must fit into the 20% allotment for negative interactions. Negative consequences for this age group usually involve removal of a desired object or privilege. The toddler loses her toy for a few minutes because she has been throwing it, or she is not allowed to play with the baby for a while because she is being rough with him. Some children between the ages of 2 and 3 will be ready to use a "thinking chair" version of time-out, but some are not. Again, temperamental differences determine which toddlers will just sit in the chair because their parents tell them to, and which ones will actually need jail-level consequences to train them to sit in the chair.

> We're trying to train Marnie not to bite people. Though she's only 2, her language skills are great and she understands us perfectly. So we've told her that when she bites, she'll have to sit in the thinking chair. Since she doesn't tell time yet, we say "you have to sit here until we tell you to get up." We give her a two-minute time-out. Marnie takes us very seriously and will never get off the chair until we tell her that her time is up.

> We tried putting Philip in a thinking chair. Philip is almost 3, so we thought there would be no problem. Boy, were we wrong! We made a rule for him that whenever he stuck his tongue out at someone (a current favorite activity of his), he'd have to sit in a chair for three minutes. Not only wouldn't he sit there for three minutes, we couldn't even get him near a chair! He ran all over the house! So we had to come up with a "jail-level" consequence for him. We told him that if he didn't sit down and stay down, then he wouldn't have his chocolate milk for a snack. Philip is addicted to chocolate milk. Naturally, he didn't believe us at first. He stuck his tongue out at the nanny, so we told him to go to the chair. He wouldn't go, so we told him that if he didn't get there right away, he would lose his chocolate milk. Well, he lost his chocolate milk for that day and that was it—from that time on, he went to the chair when we asked him to.

Toddlers are often easy to educate when parents are firm and willing to carry through. In fact, it is ideal to introduce small bits of discipline at this early age. It helps children be accepting of adult authority and guidance, which helps adults do their job. Toddlers who are under the impression that they are in charge are at risk of provoking intense parental rejection. Adults who cannot direct their 2-year-olds feel overwhelmed, resentful and angry; it is better for the child when the adult is in his or her rightful "in charge" position.

Of course, due to those old temperamental and genetic differences, there are some toddlers who do not gracefully accept the modified 2x Rule or any form of direct instruction. Inflexible, uncooperative and/or willful, these little guys and gals can bring full-grown adults to their knees. Stay-at-home moms can spend their days in tears, as they utterly fail to control or direct this child's behavior. Marriages can crumble under the strain of a tiny tyrant. When the situation is intense, professional psychological counseling can provide much-needed relief. These children should be considered "special needs" kids and given the help they require to develop in a healthy way. Naturopathic interventions can also be helpful.

Anti-Arguing Strategies

Verbally competent toddlers will test their parents. They want to know what techniques of persuasion will be effective. Does whining work? Will endless requests be effective? How about ranting and raving? Toddlers will try it all, with the goal of discovering the limits of their influence and power.

Thus, a toddler who wants a candy will ask for it, then whine for it, then beg for it and then scream for it. Parents who follow anti-arguing strategies, refusing to reply more than twice, help curtail the socially unacceptable behavior of their toddlers. However, it is not always easy to be firm with toddlers. More irresistible even than a child's anger is his or her fear. When a toddler asks a parent to do something to make him feel safe, parents will often comply even when the demand is ridiculous. For example, a toddler might ask the parent for a kiss goodnight. *Fair enough*. Then the child wants just one more. *Okay, can't resist*. Then a third. *Oh, all right*. Then a fourth. *Okay, just this last one*. Soon the parent is involved in giving the toddler 10 kisses a night. Then it's 15.

It is often challenging to distinguish between a toddler's normal ritualistic behavior and the development of a true anxiety disorder. However, the use of sound anti-arguing strategies can help in both cases. When ritualistic behavior is driven by anxiety, engaging in the ritual causes the anxiety to spread. In just the way that 10 kisses becomes 15, the child's need for the parent to "say good night" can soon become, "say good night and I love you," and from there it can become, "say good night, I love you and I'll see you in the morning," etc. When the parent follows the 2x Rule in anti-arguing strategies, the parent does not allow for the escalation of rituals. Even if the child cries and fusses, the parent does not expand upon the ritual. In this way, anxiety disorders can be treated in their very beginning stages. Professional psychological intervention and/or naturopathic interventions can also be helpful for toddlers who exhibit excessive fear or anxiety.

Toddler: *Look under my bed for monsters, Mommy.*
Parent: *Okay, I don't see any monsters.*
Toddler: *Now look in the cupboard.*
Parent: *This is the last place I'm looking. Nope—no monsters in the cupboard. Good night, sweetie.*
Toddler: *Just look behind the rocking chair.*
Parent: *No more looking. It's time for bed. Good night.*
Toddler: *Look behind the rocking chair!!!*
Parent has left the room.

Will this sequence traumatize the toddler? Certainly the child will be unhappy and even anxious for a little while. However, surviving temporary anxiety helps the child overcome long-term anxiety. When parents stop the anxiety temporarily by engaging in a ritual, the anxiety is never overcome. Rather, the ritual becomes a necessary tool for the child, preventing the experience of anxious feelings. The child never gets to learn that the anxiety will end by itself. Of course, the parent must possess the ability to tolerate a child's temporary unhappiness and anxiety in order to help the child. Chapter 13 looks at the parent's own anxiety in detail. Parents need their own emotional intelligence in order to help their children tolerate and heal painful emotions.

Graduating from the Toddler Years

When parents have graduated from the toddler years, they are fully prepared to raise a school-age child. They know how to be observant, name feelings, maintain an 80-20 ratio, employ the CLeaR Method of positive discipline, use appropriate bad-feeling interventions to provide education and guidance, introduce the 2x Rule and avoid arguments. They've had four solid years to hone all of these skills. Now all they have to do is maintain their skill level for another 15 years, and most of their parenting work will be done!

Teenagers

The Teenager

Whether a parent is just learning skills or whether he or she has been practicing them for a decade, applying them to the teenage population will be challenging. This is because teenagers are challenging. On the one hand, these youngsters still enjoy the freedom of childhood, the ability to "play" with their friends, the opportunity to be a student. They're still being financially supported and, usually, they are "looked after" by their parents, provided with meals, cleaning services, comforts and "extras" like computer access, car and phone privileges and more. At the same time, this age group is beginning to move into the adult mode, spending more time away from home, developing intimate relationships, discovering sexuality, experimenting with leisure and work-related activities.

All of this is challenging for the youngster at a time of rapid physical change, hormonal flux, identity crisis, changing body image and emotional instability. Overriding everything is a natural, urgent drive to grow up and become independent, to function without parental supervision or limitation. However, the adolescent's lack of life experience, combined with youthful enthusiasm, overconfidence, fearlessness and impulsivity can lead to reckless behaviors. Naiveté, short-sightedness and immaturity form a terrifying trio, often ushering teenagers into harm's way. It is not surprising that parents of this age group often feel fearful, anxious and overwhelmed. It is also easy to see how these emotions can lead to angry outbursts, as parents desperately try to gain back some control. Obviously, skill is required to negotiate this stage of development successfully and happily. By the end of this chapter, that skill can be yours!

In this section, we will revisit the parenting process to see how it can be applied to raising adolescents. Again, the process allows parents to teach values within their own belief systems. Whether a parent endorses or discourages sexual activity for teenagers, for example, doesn't matter in this model. What matters is that parents handle all issues with sound parenting techniques in mind: taking care to nurture the relationship, set boundaries and show and demand respect. Here are some examples of how parents with different values handled the issue of drug use:

> *Elizabeth told us that she regularly uses marijuana to relax. She said that it's really the same as alcohol and probably even safer. She also said that she prefers to invite friends to our house to use the drug—she feels most comfortable at home. We're really glad that she feels she can talk openly to us and, in fact, we told her to do so. We said she's welcome to do whatever she wants in our home—we know she's smart and that she'll make good decisions—we let her know that we trust her. Elizabeth has earned our trust over the years; she's never shown really poor judgment. Our belief is that she'll form her own conclusion about drugs based on her experiences, just like we all do. Our task is to support her.*

> *Ray told us that he uses marijuana regularly just for pleasure. He explained that it's really a harmless drug, legal in some countries and certainly better than hard drugs or alcohol. I think he even put coffee into that list! In any event, Marie and I told him that we're glad he talks openly to us. We also let him know that we appreciated his thoughts on the subject and we know that lots of people share his view. We did let him know, however, that we are not among them! We told him that we think that people should be able to have a perfectly good time when they're not stoned and we also expressed our*

concerns about the long-term use of marijuana based on research we've seen. We clearly told him that we preferred that he didn't use the drug at all and, in any event, we definitely didn't want him using it at home. We expressed our hope that he would trust our thoughts on this matter but we also acknowledged that we knew he was free to do whatever he wanted to do (we don't follow him around outside the house!). We let him know where we stand, but we threw the ball back to him in the end. I think the conversation went very well. Ray said he heard where we're coming from.

Joe told us that he uses marijuana regularly to help him study. He says it relaxes his brain and allows the information to "just slide in." We've noticed, however, that it doesn't slide out too well, so Joe's grades are pretty poor. We let Joe know we appreciated his honesty about this. Then we asked him if he minded if we shared some of our thoughts. He gave us the go-ahead. So we told him that we thought he needed a clear head for studying and told him there are other ways to get a relaxed mind and that we're willing to take him to a professional who can show him a variety of techniques and so on and so forth. Joe is a good kid but he has a few challenges—some learning issues, social issues and stuff like that. To tell you the truth, he lacks maturity and sound judgment. Of course, we're not going to tell him that! We just try to guide him the best we can and we're careful to keep things positive with him. So we ended the conversation by telling him that we'd rather he didn't use marijuana on weekdays and certainly not for schoolwork. He accepted this. Now if we find him stoned during the week, we'll move into the 2x Rule with him and take it from there.

As you can see, there are many different ways that parents can handle individual issues and situations. There is no "one-size-fits-all" parenting kit. Parents will direct their children according to their own values and each child's individual requirements. The job for parents is to keep the big picture in mind and use a healthy process.

The Finished Product

Parents are almost finished their task of childrearing by the time a teenager ends his or her 19th year. Hopefully, the "finished product" is one who is competent to step out into the world. When parents keep the goal of competency in front of their eyes for the whole second decade of parenting, the chances are increased that it will be achieved.

What competencies should parents be aiming for? To begin with, somewhere between age 19 and 25, an adult child should be able to form healthy relationships. Self-control, anger management, stress management, emotional sensitivity, respectfulness, consideration, the ability to give and other pro-relationships skills should be well established. Moreover, marriage readiness skills should also be in place, such as the ability to take care of one's health (e.g., not be regularly stoned or drunk), to get out of bed independently, to carry out one's own work and study-related responsibilities without outside supervision, to manage money responsibly, and to be flexible and compromising.

Every young adult should be competent in the domestic arena, knowing how to cook (at least the basics), shop (for one's own personal articles, clothing, food), clean (at least one's own room and belongings, contribute to the cleanliness of shared spaces in the home), and do one's own ironing and laundry. In today's world of working couples, both genders will need to be competent at both breadwinning and domestic skills. Thus, adolescents need to be developing functional skills for the world of employment. They will need to be organized and independent, able to carry out their own research (how to get a job, make travel plans, find a specific educational program), and be competent in setting and achieving goals. Now is the time to learn to drive, sew on a button, unblock the toilet, manage personal finances, arrange for a passport, as well as the time to develop interests and talents that can inspire a lifetime of accomplishment, satisfaction and meaningful activity.

In other words, the "finished adolescent" is a person whose parents don't do much for him or her anymore, other than provide love, encouragement and money. The process of achieving such competency is obviously a gradual one. Starting from the tender age of 4 or 5, a child can be assigned increasing levels of responsibility. In the beginning, for example, a child can be shown how to tidy her toys and make her bed. A little later on, the child can be taught to set and/or clear the table. Over the next years, more tasks will be added and more support withdrawn. Mom and Dad will eventually stop waking the kids up, stop reminding them to do their homework, stop doing their banking, stop running little errands for them. Eventually, the child is expected to make his or her own breakfasts, and then lunches. Soon, the youngster can be asked to make part or all of a meal for the family. Slowly, step by step, more and more skills are introduced, covering broader areas of function, until—one day—a young, independent adult, ready to leave home, stands in the place of the child.

The process of becoming competent is actually a pleasurable one for children. It feels good to be able to do things. By adolescence, competency is associated with independence—the coveted goal. When parents start the child's education in competency at a very early age, the task is easier, since younger children are eager to learn, deriving great satisfaction from accomplishment and contribution. However, if the parents suddenly decide when the child is 16 that responsibility is in order, the teenager may be resentful rather than excited to participate. If, for some reason, parents have neglected the education of their children until such an age, it is preferable to introduce tasks and responsibilities very slowly—with much praise and appreciation. It is not the child's fault that no demands were put upon her earlier. Indeed, by accidental negligence, the parent who has waited so long has inadvertently created an unnecessary challenge for the adolescent.

By using their imaginations, parents can better understand how difficult it will be for older teenagers to suddenly be called upon to do activities from which they have thus far been exempt. All that is required is for the parent to think of an area of activity that he or she "doesn't do." For instance, some people "don't do" dishes, some "don't fix anything under the hood of a car" and some "don't barbecue." There are some who "don't do" anything on the computer or "don't do" the family accounting. Although anyone can learn anything at any time, those who have failed to acquire the habit of doing a skill can notice how resistant they might be to taking it on at a later date. This is how it is for a teenager whose habitual way of functioning is now well entrenched. Nonetheless, it is better for a parent to undertake late training than no training at all. In this case, however, lower initial standards and more parental sensitivity and patience will be required.

Raising Teenagers

The question, of course, is how does one guide one's teenage offspring through the turbulent decade preceding adulthood? How does one place increasing demands for competency? The answer is: cautiously!

The techniques that parents employ for their child's education during this phase must be primarily good-feeling ones. The results of excessive bad-feeling parent-child interactions in the first decade of the child's life are not manifest until the second decade. Children under 10 years of age may act out by being uncooperative, angry or disrespectful. However, they are too dependent on their parents to completely dissociate themselves from them. In the second decade of life, this is no longer the case. The child still needs room and board, but little else of a practical nature from his or her parents. If the feeling of being loved is unavailable, adolescents will seek it from their peer group. Children who don't like their parents at this point can now stop interacting with them and/or stop cooperating with them. Although it is possible for parents to repair damage done to the relationship earlier on, damage perpetrated during the second decade of their children's lives can sometimes have enduring effects. When parents know how to heal old wounds and prevent new ones, when they can successfully convey love and provide healthy guidance to their teenagers, their families will flourish during this phase of life.

Staying Positive

The secret to success is in the *ratio*. The proportion of positive feelings to negative ones for younger children (the 80-20 Rule) must be increased for the adolescent. The new ratio is 90-10. The adolescent is more like an adult (at least in his or her imagination!) and now is less tolerant of correction. Adults generally prefer a ratio of 100% good-feeling interactions to 0% bad-feeling ones. Ask any adult: "How much bad-feeling attention do you want from your spouse each day?" Virtually everyone answers: "Zero." Adults have had enough criticism and complaint in childhood to last them a lifetime! Similarly, adolescents feel that they've had enough disapproval, correction and reprimand—they now want only good-feeling interactions. Unfortunately for them, they will still need some bad-feeling communications such as instructions ("Would you please take your dishes off the table?"), criticisms ("Please don't speak to me in that tone of voice") and consequences ("From now on, if you don't get your linen ready for the laundry on Wednesdays, I won't be washing it for you—you can take care of it yourself.") Therefore, parents have a 10% allotment for such communications. However, even within that 10%, care must be exercised. Since *intensely negative* communications can destroy hundreds or thousands of positive strokes, all of the bad-feeling interactions should be only mildly negative. This means that there cannot be any name-calling, insulting, swearing, yelling or other forms of abuse on the parent's part. (Abuse on the child's part, of course, will be a disciplinary concern.)

Positive interactions include both conditional (earned) and unconditional (free) forms of attention. As with younger children, giving gifts, joking, sharing, offering acts of helpfulness or kindness, engaging in quality-time activities and providing emotional coaching are all valuable forms of unconditional good-feeling attention. Praise, appreciation, acknowledgment, compensation and gifts can be offered as conditional forms of good-feeling attention. These kinds of interactions must constitute almost the entirety of the relationship between parent and child if the relationship is to be experienced as a positive one by the adolescent.

Particularly valuable is the gift of emotional coaching. The ability to listen attentively and name feelings shows understanding, acceptance and compassion. It creates intimacy. A person who receives emotional coaching feels seen, acknowledged and valuable—the very opposite of one who is ignored or discounted or, worse yet, corrected or mocked. When parents name an adolescent's feelings, they are also helping to build the child's emotional intelligence, which, as we've seen earlier, leads to benefits such as improved emotional regulation, social competence, better health, higher academic performance, more cooperation and overall higher levels of functioning.

The 90-10 Rule not only keeps things "pleasant" between parent and teenager, but also enables the parent to maintain a position of mentorship, leadership and authority. When the relationship feels good, young people care about their parents' feelings, trying not to aggravate or hurt them; they care about their thoughts as well, being willing to hear them, discuss them and possibly integrate them into their own lives. In other words, the positive relationship allows adolescents to take their parents seriously out of both respect and love. Parents of teenagers need to recognize the truth that their *only* source of power is the power to influence and motivate. They must create an atmosphere in which the teenager *wants* to listen and learn, and *wants* to comply or cooperate. Their own behavior as adults must be *admirable* as well as loveable, so that the adolescent will look up to them and accept their influence and even their model.

Naturally, parents who try to use "strong arm" methods of direct criticism, hostile communications, threats and heavy-duty punishments only succeed in pushing their teenagers away. Instead of gaining power, such parents lose power completely. Showing the child "who is boss" completely alienates the youngster, leaving the "boss" with no one to boss! Almost-adult children look at raging parents with contempt and disrespect. The grownup acts like an out-of-control child. Even when the teenager acts no better, the youngster is looking to the parent to show the superior way, looking to the adult for a model and for direction. When there apparently is no adult, the teenager is left thrashing on his or her own without support, guidance or inspiration.

Criticism itself, even when not offered in an insulting or abusive manner, is always intensely negative. In order to minimize its potentially destructive effect, parents should limit its use even within the allotted 10% bad-feeling attention department. Teenagers, like adults, respond so poorly to criticism that the ideal amount of it would be close to "zero." So-called constructive criticism is as painful as any other kind, and since one would never be using "destructive criticism" (at least, not on purpose!), it is actually the only permitted form for parents to employ. Why criticize at all if it is not meant to be constructive for the teenager? Unfortunately, criticism is rarely constructive in any event; it is more often discouraging and debilitating. Humans progress from strength to strength, and regress from failure to failure. Highlighting what is "wrong," therefore, is both generally ineffective as a teaching tool and specifically destructive as a relationship tool. Thus, as with younger children, the use of anger and criticism should be severely curtailed. However, because the teenager's response to these bad-feeling techniques is often more immediate, dramatic and negative than it is for younger kids, parents will suffer more with this age group if they insist on using such interventions. Out of self-interest alone, parents may want to develop expertise in the good-feeling strategies—it will be easier on them during this decade of parenting!

> *I don't know why Leslie hates me so much—I do absolutely everything for her. If she needs her bracelet repaired, I run it to the jeweler's for her; if she wants pizza for dinner, I order it; if she wants to have a party, I run all over town picking up snacks and stuff—whatever that kid needs, I provide it. And do you think she ever says "thank you"? Never! She doesn't help out, she doesn't clean her room, she doesn't get up in the morning. Even if she uses a plate to make a sandwich, she just leaves everything on the counter for me to clean*

up. She is so irresponsible! Schoolwork? Forget it—she never picks up a book. I tell her over and over that she better pick those grades up but it falls on deaf ears. And do you see the way she dresses? How she can go out of the house looking like that, I have no idea! And she doesn't listen to a word I say—even though I'm just telling her for her own good that if she doesn't get her act together, she's going to ruin her life. If her mother doesn't tell her these things, who will?

Most parents criticize out of love and helplessness. They want their teenager to be healthy and successful. However, instead of strategizing toward that end, they simply speak their anxieties out loud in the form of destructive criticisms. This form of education can completely destroy parenting power through destroying the relationship. Heavily criticized teenagers fail to feel the love in their parents' hearts. They only experience the rejection.

The costs of failing to successfully convey love are more than emotional. There are long-term behavioral consequences as well, due to loss of parental power. The emotionally abandoned teenager is left to struggle through adolescence relying on peer support and experimentation. He or she cannot access a loving guide and role model. This may result in an increase in dangerous, unhealthy and otherwise risky behaviors. To avoid this scenario, it is essential for parents to be able to show love to their teenagers. The 90-10 Rule moves the parents' love out of their hearts and into their youngsters' souls—where it belongs. The result is a happier home during the adolescent years, a healthier parent-child relationship and a healthier developmental outcome for the child.

Loving Guidance

When guidance is necessary during the teen years, it needs to be carried out with respect. The overall relationship must always be kept in mind—no particular lapse in an adolescent's behavior is worth the destruction of parental power through anger or abuse. As always, the preferred form of guidance and discipline is the use of the CLeaR Method—a purely good-feeling form of discipline. The CLeaR Method can be used with adults as well as children, so it is certainly fine to use with teenagers.

Roy has a short fuse; he gets irritated really easily. Sometimes I forget that I already asked him to do something so I end up asking him a second time. In the past when this happened, he would almost snap my head off screaming things like, "You asked me before, and I already told you I would do it after lunch!" Every time he did that, I automatically said something like, "Don't raise your voice to me, young man!" However, it finally dawned on me that no matter how many times I was complaining about his tone, he was still using it! I thought I should try something different.

I decided to use the CLeaR Method, even though I didn't think it could work. But, having nothing to lose (since my technique obviously wasn't working), I began commenting positively when Roy spoke nicely to me. Then, I started adding a label and, finally, I starting mentioning various privileges "coincidentally" right at the end of these little conversations. For instance, let's say I left some laundry on Roy's bed and he complained about it saying, "Can you please not put the laundry on my bed?" I would say, "Sorry about that. Yeah, I'll be more careful. And thanks, honey, for using a pleasant tone when you asked." (I'd say that as long as he wasn't actually yelling.) "That was considerate of you. By the way, I'm not using the car tonight so if you need it for something, you can take it." I'd really look for opportunities to use the comment, label, reward strategy. By the end of a month, I could definitely say that Roy's level of respectful communication toward me improved significantly. And to top it off, our relationship feels better as well—less tense.

The second step of the CLeaR Method–labeling–is particularly important to employ. Although thanking the child, praising her or showing interest are all positive forms of reinforcement, it is the label that contributes to the teenager's forming identity. The label helps the adolescent to develop a sense of herself as considerate, smart, attractive, funny, creative, responsible, helpful and so on—whatever traits the parent highlights. Once a teenager's identity is bound up with positive labels, the young person increases the strength of those traits through the power of the self-fulfilling prophecy. "I think I can, therefore I can; I think I am, therefore I am." The parental use of positive labels empowers the adolescent to discover and utilize his or her strengths and talents.

Firm Guidance

Consistent use of the 80-20 Rule in the first decade of a child's life, followed by consistent use of the 90-10 Rule in the second decade, increases the chances that an adolescent will be a mature, considerate and well-behaved person—not in need of real discipline. However, due to those genes we've been talking about, good parenting is not a guarantee of a "good" child. Certainly, troubled parenting always makes everything worse—that *is* a guarantee! But healthy parenting is not sufficient to produce a healthy child. Hereditarily established disorders of mood, temperament and behavior can cause children and adolescents to be explosive, rigid, intense, dramatic, rebellious, uncooperative, unmotivated, anxious and/or otherwise disturbed or dysfunctional—in other words, "difficult" to raise.

Even adolescents without genetic challenges sometimes need extra guidance during the second decade. Sometimes, earlier parenting lapses such as a failure to establish adequate boundaries or discipline, or a failure to convey sufficient positive attention, result in more challenging adolescent behavior. Sometimes, the child's exposure to a difficult peer group or his own personal challenges (social, academic, physical, etc.) are at the root of behavioral issues manifesting on the home front. Whatever the cause, inappropriate behavior that is unresponsive to positive interventions still requires formal discipline during the adolescent years.

Hence, the Upgraded 2x Rule.

The Upgraded 2X Rule

The 2x Rule for teenagers shares a lot of the characteristics of its forerunner, the 2x Rule for children 12 years old and under. For example, it is to be used only *rarely*. Parents need to carefully consider its use because, although powerfully educational, it is a truly bad-feeling intervention that has negative side-effects for the relationship. However, when parents do decide to use it, they follow the earlier procedure of making a request or giving information, in a normal tone of voice (Step 1). Step 2 involves repeating the request and offering the teenager the choice to fulfill it or face a negative consequence ("ticket"), or, in the case of a repetitive misbehavior, naming a rule and offering the teenager the choice to follow it or face a negative consequence. As in the original 2x Rule, there is no raised voice, hysteria, verbal abuse or other drama. Here are a couple of examples:

A Single-Occasion Request
Step 1: *Would you please get out of bed now?*
Step 2: *I asked you to get out of bed. If you're not out when I come by in three minutes, you will not be borrowing my car this evening.*

A Repetitive Misbehavior
Step 1: *Sleeping in on school mornings is not acceptable because you have a responsibility to be in school and functioning properly. Please get up when I ask you to do so in the morning.*

Step 2: *I told you yesterday that it is not acceptable to sleep in on school mornings because you have a responsibility to be in school and functioning properly. From now on, when you don't get up after I call you, you will not be allowed to use the computer past 9 p.m. on that evening.*

Consequences—or "tickets"—for teenagers are modified. Removal of possessions (cellphone, car keys) and removal of privileges (use of the car, computer, video and other electronic media, ability to sleep out, have friends over, go out, receive an allowance, use the phone) can be extended from 24 hours up to 48 hours if necessary. It is still preferable to keep negative consequences to as little time as possible. One evening's loss of possessions or privileges is better than two. At this age, there is no "time-out" ticket. The consequence of "grounding" is actually the removal of the privilege to leave the house and can be used for up to 48 hours, as described above. With younger adolescents, writing out lines may still be used, but the only kind of writing appropriate for the older teenager might be an action plan (a statement of what went wrong and what is going to be done to remedy the situation in the future) or a letter of explanation and/or apology. With all age groups, addition of work is a possibility. For example, a teenager who repeatedly leaves his bike in the driveway or her dish on the table can be asked to do 15 minutes of clean-up work as a consequence. Over-learning (practicing the skill that needs improvement) is inappropriate for this age group.

In summary, then, appropriate "tickets" for teenagers involve removal of possessions, removal of privileges, some kinds of written work, and addition of work. Teenagers 15 years old and under are the prime candidates for negative consequences. Hopefully, the older adolescent will have outgrown the need for discipline. However, some adolescents in the 16- to 19-year-old range will still need the occasional consequence. It is best to use natural and logical consequences whenever possible with all teenagers, but particularly with the older group.

Natural consequences are those that occur without the parent's intervention. For example, an adolescent who wakes up late for the car pool has to take the bus to school on his own (Mom doesn't drive him even if she is technically available to do so). A teenager who leaves her assignment to the last minute must find her own way of getting it done (Dad doesn't stay up all night to help her hand it in on time). A teenager who forgets his appointment with the psychologist must pay for his missed session (Mom and Dad don't pay for him). A teenager who doesn't put her clothes in the laundry hamper doesn't have clean clothes to wear. When allowing natural consequences to be the instructor, it's crucial that parents not lecture, reprimand or criticize ("It's your own fault and I'm certainly not going to bail you out!"). Rather, parents should maintain a neutral, even slightly sympathetic position ("I know it's frustrating. Unfortunately, it's not a good idea for me to take care of it for you.")

Logical consequences are "punishments that fit the crime." They make sense in light of the transgression. Unlike natural consequences that occur on their own, logical consequences are constructed by parents.

Here are some Step 2 scenarios involving logical negative consequences:

- *"From now on, when you spend all of your money, you'll just have to find a way to earn more—I won't be covering your loss anymore."*

- *"From now on, when you misplace your car keys, you'll have to stay homeor take the bus. I won't be lending you mine."*

- *"From now on, when your cellphone bill is too high, I will disconnect your service for the next month so that I can recoup the loss."*

- *"From now on, when you get a parking ticket, you'll have to pay for it yourself."*

- *"From now on, when you raise your voice to me, I will end the conversation right at that point and not resume it until you apologize."*

- *"When you consistently ignore my requests to help around the house, I feel resentful. After a while, I don't feel like extending myself for you by running around town to get things that you need or lending you my car or giving you a few extra dollars. If that's the kind of relationship you want, I guess that's the kind we'll have."*

- *"When you speak to me so unpleasantly it hurts my feelings. After a while, I don't even feel like interacting with you. I'm not sure why you want to talk to me like that—please tell me if there's some reason for it—but as long as you do speak that way, I won't feel so friendly toward you. I personally think it's a lot better if you and I get along and treat each other nicely—I like doing things for you and helping you in whatever ways I can. But if, for some reason, you think it's better this way, then this is the way it will be until you change your mind."*

The last two consequences are particularly suitable for older teenagers and young adults.

A troubled relationship is the actual consequence of one person's consistently poor behavior. The parent is simply pointing that out. This consequence is most useful when it is clear that the parent is not the one with the problem (i.e., the parent has, in fact, been using the 90-10 Rule). In such a case, the loss of, or injury to, the relationship is an actual negative consequence. When the relationship isn't good to begin with (i.e., the parent is highly critical or otherwise negative), losing it may be more of a relief than a punishment!

The 2x Rule is meant to completely replace yelling and other hostile or abusive parental activities. It can only do this if parents use it exactly as designed. Nothing is said more than twice. After the second time, a reasonable consequence is applied. If the teenager fails to comply with the reasonable consequence ("ticket"), a much harsher consequence will be employed ("jail"). The consequences do the teaching. No parental anger is employed.

Jail-level consequences for teenagers follow the same rules as those for younger children. "Jail" is earned by failing to pay a ticket, committing a heinous crime (something very destructive or very dangerous) or for showing disrespect to parents (e.g., swearing, name-calling, threatening, etc.). For jail-level consequences, the usual time limits (48 hours) for loss of possessions and privileges can be extended to days and weeks. Again, the shortest period that will be effective is the one that should be used. Thus, a computer addict can lose the privilege of computer usage for one week or three weeks—parents would select the shortest period that would effectively educate the child. Writing assignments can be prolonged from the number of minutes of the approximate age of the teenager (e.g., a 14-year-old gets a 10- to 15-minute writing assignment) to twice or three times that long (e.g., a 14-year-old gets a 20- to 30-minute writing assignment).

> *Howie was really upset with me when I told him he couldn't take a week off school to go down to Texas with his best friend to visit the young man's cousins. Howie's grades aren't that great and I didn't think he could afford to lose all that time. When he started yelling at me—in front of his friend, no less—I didn't say a word. But as soon as his friend left, I told him that if he ever did anything like that again, I would remove the computer from his room for three months. Howie can't live without the computer so I know that he would think twice about mistreating me in the future. And he knows that I would do it if I had to.*

Howie trusts his parents to carry out their threats because they have taken care to carry through with their promises in the past decade. Even if they only started carrying through in the past year, however, their track record would be sufficient to earn them his trust.

> *I asked Marianne to clean up the kitchen while I was out. When I got back, everything was just as I left it. That was no surprise, because the same thing had already happened a couple of times this past month. I told her that the next time it happens, she'll owe me half*

an hour of "slave labor" after school the next day. Well, it happened again on Monday, so I told her to come straight home after school to help me do the ironing. When she didn't turn up until 7 p.m., claiming that she had to stay for her drama club meeting, I told her to start the ironing right away and be forewarned that missing her "appointment" with me would, from now on, result in her losing a month's worth of spending money.

Teenagers must be forewarned about jail-level consequences, just as they are with ticket-level consequences. The first time that an adolescent doesn't cooperate with her negative consequence, she is told that future lack of cooperation (not paying the ticket) will result in a jail-level consequence. Thus the jail-level consequence cannot occur until the second time the teenager fails to cooperate with a negative consequence.

An Anger-Reduced, Stress-Reduced Decade

The 2x Rule is only effective when it is utilized within the context of the 90-10 Rule. Thus, the relationship *must* be a positive one in order for adolescents to be affected by parental disapproval, reprimand or punishment. *When the relationship is not warm and loving, all energy must be spent to bring it to that point.* Negative consequences should not be used until the relationship is in good shape. At that point, parents will be able to use tickets and even jail, in the correct non-hostile tone. If Mr. Jones has ruined his credit rating by acquiring too much debt, the bank manager *regretfully* informs him that a loan cannot be arranged (a logical, negative consequence of overspending). Similarly, parents applying the 2x Rule, in the context of a loving relationship, *regretfully* shut down the computer, remove the allowance or disconnect the cellphone. There is no anger, no lecture, no screaming match. Adults stay adult, providing an excellent model. Teenagers, themselves, can appreciate the fairness of the situation; this helps them to accept responsibility for their own behavior. Most importantly, the relationship stays healthy, increasing the likelihood of achieving a lifelong positive bond. The benefits can extend down into the next generation as loving parents become loving grandparents, continuing to be a source of positive influence and love to their children and grandchildren. The 90-10 Rule, combined with appropriate boundary setting, is the key to a successful second decade of parenting.

CHAPTER 12

Marriage as a Parenting Tool

Teaching Relationship Skills

Your relationship with your spouse, partner or ex-spouse (all of whom will be referred to as "your partner" in this chapter) is a primary parenting tool. Through this relationship you are teaching your kids how to express and receive love and how to negotiate long-term intimate relationships. You teach them how to create healthy boundaries, handle conflict, share space, manage resources and cooperate. In fact, your personal model of partnering will be a hard-to-erase blueprint for your youngsters to emulate. Both consciously and subconsciously, your kids will absorb the relationship lessons you impart. Therefore, you will want to ensure that the lessons you are passing on are ones that will serve them well.

While many modern parents take care to communicate well with their youngsters, far fewer make the same effort with their partners. Parents take classes, read books, go on-line and spare no effort to learn how to build respectful, loving relationships with their kids. At the same time, however, they may be fighting ferociously with their adult partners. When half of all marriages are failing, we can only hope that partners are being nicer to their kids than they are being to each other! The goal is for adults to be as respectful and loving toward their children as they are toward their partners.

Your child learns about love both from the way you treat him and from the way he sees you and your partner treat each other. Although you can't control the behavior of your partner, you can certainly control your own—offering your child at least one healthy relationship model. In fact, the healthier your own relationship behavior, the better "behaved" your partner is likely to be in any event—much the same thing that occurs when your healthy parenting behavior produces a better-behaved child. This can be a benefit both for you and your child.

Healthy Models of Love

It is easier than you might think to provide a healthy model of love. Do you recall how the 80-20 Rule conveys love from parent to child? Eighty percent of communication must feel good to the child in order for the youngster to *feel* loved. Twenty percent can consist of instructions, teaching and limit setting. Correction, reprimand and criticism can constitute a tiny proportion of this twenty percent. When these ratios are maintained, a child not only feels securely loved, but she also loves her parent. A strong bond is created that invites cooperation, trust, respect and caring.

The 80-20 Rule becomes the 90-10 Rule for teenagers. This age group, as we saw earlier, has less tolerance for instruction and correction than younger children. While the younger kids must be told to brush their teeth, get ready for bed, do their homework and so many more things, older kids want to enjoy more autonomy and less direction. For this reason, we try to limit our bad-feeling communications even more.

Guess what the ratio is in marriage? Ask any adult how much negativity he or she wants from a partner each day and you will receive a predictable answer: none! Adults want the 100-0 Rule! However, it is necessary to make requests of partners and sometimes to set limits and boundaries, and for this reason we make the adult love ration 95-5. That is A LOT of positive communication and EXTREMELY LITTLE bad-feeling communication. If you look at your current, typical minute-by-minute communication with your partner, what ratio do you seem to be applying?

Does it make any sense to give your children 80 or 90% good-feeling communication while giving your partner only 10% of the same? What would your child conclude? One possible conclusion could be "Children receive love but adults don't. Don't have an adult partnership." Or, perhaps the child sees you as a Dr. Jeykll and Mr./Mrs.Hyde: sometimes loving and sometimes nasty. Whatever the conclusion, it must be confusing and disheartening. Instead of offering a consistent and reliable model of loving, many parents are sending very mixed messages.

See if you can raise your ratio with your partner. Aim toward 95-5. After awhile, you'll notice a change in your children. Increased relationship harmony usually spills over to the children as the entire family experiences greater security and stability. The benefits of your new ratio will be experienced by every family member, both short term and far into the future.

Healthy Boundary Setting

Parenting techniques work wonderfully on partners. There is no need to yell at children (as we've seen) and similarly no need to yell at partners! Indeed, witnessing parental relationship anger is just as toxic to children as being victims of parental rage themselves. A screaming adult is a screaming adult—a scary, out-of-control model of abusive communication. It doesn't really matter who the adult is screaming at. The Relationship Rule—"*I give and I accept only respectful communication*"— applies to the whole family, not just the parent-child dyad. Parents who scream at their partners are teaching their kids one of the very worst communication strategies. This particular strategy, absorbed directly into their neural pathways in an osmosis-like way, will bring them nothing but relationship misery throughout their own lives. This is not something loving parents want to gift their kids with.

On the other hand, setting boundaries with your partner the less-stress way provides a model your kids can safely and healthfully emulate. By establishing the 95-5 Rule and using techniques like the CLeaR Method, Emotional Coaching and the 2X-Rule, you can accomplish all sorts of behavioral changes with your partner. (You may be surprised at the inclusion of the 2X-Rule in this list. However, applying it replaces all forms of anger, lecturing and nagging. Consequences for adults are different than those for kids, but you can use your imagination to come up with appropriate "tickets" for your partner. For instance, a person can warn a spouse as follows: "It's important to pick up the kids on time. However, if you can't do it then I'll have to arrange for them to go on the bus and this will cost us money that we'd like to be saving for that new Jeep....").

Relationship Skills

Your marriage teaches children how to conduct themselves in family life. Do you make your own intimate relationship an obvious priority? Do you set aside "adult time" so that you can actually have an adult relationship and so that your children can see that this relationship is an important part of your life? If not, your children may get the erroneous impression that good relationships can thrive without nurturing. They need to see that good relationships, like good marks in school, generally require some time and effort. While the occasional genius can get away without studying and the occasional couple can thrive without spending much time alone, most students and most couples really have to apply themselves in a more purposeful way. Even if your kids protest that they want you to stay home with them, it is essential to show them that YOU want to go out with your PARTNER and that you need to spend time together in order to nurture your companionship. Despite tears and complaints, children are happiest knowing that their parents want to spend time with each other.

There are many important relationship skills that your marriage can teach your kids. Handling responsibility is one example. Are you trying to teach your kids to do their homework, come home on time, put gas in the car? Hopefully, you relate in similarly responsible ways toward your partner so that you child has an excellent model to emulate. You get up in the morning by yourself, you take out the garbage, fulfil your work and/or home responsibilities, clean up after yourself, manage money appropriately and generally function in an independent, responsible way. No one has to beg you to do what you're supposed to be doing. Your child sees in you a model of caring, thoughtful, respectful and responsible behavior. Growing up to conduct himself like you will bring peace to his own adult partnerships.

Intentional Relationships

Relate to your partner with your kids in mind. Give them a model that will bring them relationship success because relationship success is at the core of a successful life. Even if your partner has been and/or is being badly behaved, you can show your kids how you would want *them* to cope with trying situations, severe disappointment and hurt. Would you want your kids to become angry and bitter? Would you want them to be chronically depressed if they found themselves dealing with a very imperfect partner? Or would you want them to carry on in the best way possible, holding on to their own right to be happy, optimistic, kind, thoughtful, loving and so on? Real relationships are challenging. Intimate partnerships are difficult on so many levels. How do you want your kids to face those stresses when they meet up with them? Your own way of handling these difficulties may very well become their way too. Seeking counselling, reading books, taking classes and doing all the things you've done to become an excellent parent can also be done to become an excellent partner. Just showing kids that relationships are a work in progress and that you are working toward a goal is a healthy model in itself.

Your marriage is a parenting tool whether it is happy, troubled, intact or not. How you conduct your intimate relationship and how you interact with the parent of your children provides serious lessons to your kids. Their eyes are on you. Show them the way.

CHAPTER 13

Parenting: The Inside Story

Parenting from the Inside Out

A variety of tools and strategies has been presented that can help bring out the best in children while simultaneously reducing parental stress. If, after reading them over, parents could use these tools on a daily basis, their family lives would run much more smoothly and success-fully. However, there are two impediments to things working out just this way: 1) there is a lot to learn and assimilate and 2) the emotional world of the parent gets in the way.

The first problem can be solved by patience and perseverance. Re-reading the material on a regular basis can be helpful. Creating a par-enting group that reviews the material together is even better. It takes time and practice to incorporate new behaviors into one's repertoire. Concentrating on one skill at a time (e.g., picking one skill to focus on for the month) can make success more likely. Even after achieving mastery, re-examining the material again every few months or years is beneficial because the changing parental landscape requires constant refreshment of skills.

The second problem—the emotional world of the parent—creates a greater challenge. Clearly, *knowing* what to do after reading this book does not automatically translate into being able to do it. Very few people will simply read about the dangers of the raised voice and then pro-ceed to parent without raising their voice ever again! Indeed, many parents who have read parenting books and attended parenting classes still find themselves unable to use all that they've learned when they are at home in the heat of the battle. This is because the "heat" sets off smoke detectors in the emotional section of their brains. Logical information is processed in the frontal cortex of the brain. This area can be thought of as the corporate affairs section—the place where knowledge is translated into plans and strategies. Emotional information, however, is processed and stored elsewhere—in the "furnace room" of the brain, deep inside and lower down. As long as the furnace is functioning well and is not overheated, the corporate affairs section upstairs will also function well and maintain control. However, if the furnace is overheated, the alarms start ringing and the corporate affairs department must temporarily shut down. The emergency crew is called in to put out the fire, using whatever desperate measures may be necessary. Hence, the screaming of sirens and the flooding of emotion. When the fire is out, the corporate affairs section can assess the damage and begin the process of repair and future planning.

The problem is that parenting emergencies can occur frequently throughout the years and even the days of parenting, disconnecting the logical and knowledgeable sections of the brain while the fire department takes control. The result is an emergency-based parenting style that employs primitive and often desperate measures (such as yelling) instead of the reasoned strategies (i.e., the information in this book!) learned and deposited in the frontal cortex.

What are all these fires about? Parenting is a deeply emotional experience. Helplessness, confusion, frustration, fear, hurt and rage are constantly triggering explosions on the *inside*. Different parents are vulnerable to different emotional situations: some are easily angered, some are easily frightened and some are easily saddened. All are emotionally challenged. There are many surprises, problems, struggles and disappointments in the course of raising children, each one forcing the parent inward to face, examine and process the deepest aspects of his or her personality. Parents are thrust both backward to their own childhood programming and forward to their fears for the future. Parenting seems to shine a heartless light into the soul, exposing limitations, blocks, insecurities and weaknesses—forcing an unnerving encounter with personal vulnerabilities. Besides being painful, these intense emotions can severely compromise parenting decisions and actions. They can and do interfere with the parent's *intention* to act or speak kindly, patiently and reasonably. When the furnace overheats—and emotions bubble over in unforeseen ways—parents are left feeling guilty, helpless and inadequate—more painful emotions!

This section examines some of the common emotional challenges faced by parents. By becoming familiar with "the enemy," parents can begin the process of taking back control. As we have seen in earlier chapters, all emotions are acceptable, whereas not all behaviors can be embraced. Emotions are only called "enemies" when they attack one's children. When they are allowed to control the parent's mouth and actions, they can cause real harm. However, these same emotions can be safely settled *inside*, where they belong. In their appropriate location (i.e., not in control), they can be comforted, soothed and released—in other words, healed.

During the stage of transition, between "temporary insanity" and "enlightenment" (the parent's journey), some disturbed emotions may not be so easily settled. At these moments, it's okay to pretend. In fact, it's a must. Parents can act normal even when they are feeling disturbed. Many terrified parents, for example, comfort their children on airplane trips even though their own fear is greater than their child's! It is an act of maturity and love to pretend for the sake of the child's well-being and protection. Just imagine that you are someone you admire, someone who knows how to parent, someone who is in control. Think of your favorite actor or actress or character from a book. Act the part. Eventually, you will learn how to soothe whatever feelings lie between you and actually being that parent. One day, you will both act the part and feel it.

Meanwhile, listen to your inner compassionate parent: "I'm so proud of you for doing the right thing for the children even though you have parts that feel so upset. You take care of the children and I'll take care of you. Let's read these chapters together and find ways to soothe the troubled feelings."

In the next three chapters we will look at three intense but common feelings in parenting: feelings of inadequacy, fear and despair. Each of these feelings has many sources and many flavors. Each can trigger a raised voice and other displays of "irrational" behavior. By befriending these emotions and taking the time to heal them, parents can prevent many potentially destructive interactions and also reduce the need to control themselves with anger-management strategies. In fact, once disturbing emotions are released, parents will have more personal happiness, health and energy—a wonderful side effect of improving one's parenting profile. Let's begin!

Inadequacy

Feeling competent is a wonderful, strong, powerful sensation. Most parents have plenty of experiences of feeling competent. Unfortunately, feelings of inadequacy are also bound to occur at times during the parenting journey. As we shall see, every normal parent will experience this disheartening emotion at some point, or even at many points. The difficulties we have with our youngsters are shared by millions of parents around the world. It only *seems* to us that everyone else's child is well adjusted, yet as King Solomon so aptly put it: "There is nothing new under the sun." Our child's bizarre behavior is neither truly bizarre nor even rare. Our inability to cope with it is just as common. Moreover, many causes of parental feelings of inadequacy have nothing at all to do with the behavior of children. Much of it has its roots in the personal coping mechanisms of the adult.

In this chapter we will examine some of the many causes of inadequacy as well as preventative measures and remedial strategies. For our children's sake as well as our own, it is important that we face, heal and prevent feelings of inadequacy. By becoming more aware of the impact of these feelings, parents will be better equipped to deal with the more intense and challenging aspects of childrearing.

Feelings of Inadequacy Interfere with Parenting

When parents lose themselves in the mire of painful feelings of inadequacy, they also lose the ability to parent appropriately. There are many synonyms for "inadequate." It can imply any of the following: deficient, inferior, unacceptable, inept, incompetent, incapable, unskilled, ineffective, unfit, unqualified, unworthy, failing, weak, found wanting, mediocre, not good enough. Whatever the particular shade, this feeling leaves a parent in an uncomfortable, child-like state, a position from which it is difficult to take charge.

> *Deena came home from school obviously very upset. Her eyes were red and puffy—I could see she had been crying. When I asked her what was wrong, she said, 'nothing.' Why wouldn't she tell me? I thought we were so close. I thought she trusted me. Had I let her down? Was this the beginning of the end of our relationship? I got really upset. I asked her over and over again why she didn't trust me. I knew it was wrong but I couldn't stop myself. She made me feel like a failure.*

This mom was derailed by her feelings of inadequacy. Her daughter needed space and time but received neither. Instead of being able to assess and meet the needs of a youngster, parents suffering from inadequacy are busy wringing their hands and berating themselves. Their feelings of inadequacy cause them to take the child's behavior personally; at a time when they should be addressing the child's needs, the parents are worrying about their own. They end up challenging their children: "How can you do this to us?" and "Why do you always get into trouble? What have we done that's so terrible?"

Often, parents in this state emotionally abuse their children, instilling in their youngsters the same sense of failure they themselves feel for not measuring up: "What's wrong with you? Why can't you be like other people? Why do you always have to mess up like this?"

Discovering problems of adjustment in one's children can cause parents to blame themselves and to imagine that the world is joining them in this process. All fingers point accusingly toward the "guilty" parent—at least in the overactive imaginations of some. For example, when Miriam found out that her daughter Talia was binge eating, she was beside herself: "I am a horrible mother! This is all my fault! I've made my daughter sick. The shrinks will blame me and will scrutinize all of my parenting mistakes. . ."

In other words, Miriam could only think of herself and how her daughter's behavior and illness would reflect on her as a mother. Miriam's approach to her daughter, shaped by the critical, self-blaming process that Miriam was experiencing, was less than supportive. "Couldn't you have come to me with your problems? Couldn't you have even given me a chance?" Miriam simply could not give her daughter the sympathy and understanding that the youngster so badly needed. A parent's own feelings of inadequacy can take front and center, completely pushing aside empathy and compassion for a child's pain and difficulties.

Helplessness Leads to Feelings of Inadequacy

Poor parenting, arising out of inadequacy, often occurs during "helpless" moments. For example, a parent who feels helpless to gain a child's cooperation is often overwhelmed by inadequacy. "What kind of parent am I if I can't get my kids to listen?" Helplessness is triggered by not being able to make our children be what we want them to be or do what we want them to do. Helpless inadequacy often causes many parents to resort to angry temper tantrums and other abusive behaviors. They try these heavy-handed, inappropriate tactics in order to gain back the control they seem to be losing. Under the influence of feelings of inadequacy, they forget the primary rule of parenting: angry interactions weaken (and can utterly destroy) parental power. The only power we have is the power of relationship—the child's *desire* to please us and accept our direction. When we cannot make the child do what we want her to do, we must back off. We may need to take time to build and strengthen the relationship and then think carefully about quiet discipline strategies that may be helpful. Handling our feelings of inadequacy by becoming angry will only increase our helplessness.

> *No matter how many times I asked Jason to keep his curfew, he ignored me. Finally, I had it out with him. When he arrived at 3 a.m. I was all ready at the door: I started ranting and raving and ranting some more. That was four weeks ago and he hasn't kept his curfew or talked to me since then.*

Doing a Good Job and Feeling Inadequate

Feelings of inadequacy can occur even when a parent is being perfectly competent. This is because parental competency does not predict any particular parenting outcome. Children can be thought of as "wild cards": you never quite know what you're getting when you raise a human being. In other areas of life, we can achieve at least the illusion of having some control: if we follow Steps A, B and C, the cake will be baked, the bank account opened, the computer will compute and so forth. However, parenting is not like that at all. It is a much greater adventure, involving unexpected curves and turns, inconsistencies and surprises—not all of which are pleasant.

There is, for instance, the parent who reads books diligently to a toddler, only to be frustrated that the child shows no interest in literature—ever. There is the parent who values emotional sensitivity who finds herself living with an aggressive, bullying grade-schooler. There are the parents who carefully feed their children only the best and the healthiest diet who discover that their offspring are candy thieves and sugar-holics.

In other words, try as they might, parents *cannot always get the results they are aiming for.* Whereas doing things the right way has generally led to positive outcomes in other areas of their lives, doing things "correctly" in parenting may lead to the desired results, may not lead to the desired results or may lead to the exact opposite of the desired results. The consequence for parents can be a feeling of inadequacy. If parenting is one's main occupation and/or main source of self-esteem, the threat to one's mental health can be significant.

I quit my lucrative job to stay home. I spent all my time with my kids—I took them to lessons, I put them in the best programs, I did everything for them—and look what I got: Daniel is underachieving, Eli is into drugs and Melissa suffers from anxiety. What was the point? I probably should have pursued my career.

Parenting is not the kind of occupation that necessarily feeds one's ego. On the contrary, it can lead to deep feelings of inadequacy even if one has truly applied oneself to the job. There are so many factors out of one's control and so many challenges to face during the extremely long maturation period for humans. Parenting is not the career of choice for the faint of heart!

Doing a Poor Job and Feeling Inadequate

Feelings of inadequacy that are triggered by actual bad parenting can be even more painful. For example, most parents would not pat themselves on the back for yelling insults at their child. (If you do pat yourself on the back for that, please re-read Chapter 5!) It's not that we *want* to be abusive; it sometimes just seems to "happen." Some parents find themselves struggling for 20 years of childrearing, promising themselves each morning to be "better" and finding themselves falling repeatedly into the same old destructive rut.

There are parents who are not home enough, who are always promising to make a change but somehow never finding a permanent solution. Somewhere in the back (or front) of their minds they are aware of not being very good parents. Then there are the negative parents who know they're uptight and whose children may openly rate them as failures (*"you're the worst mother in the world"* or *"I wish you were like Josh's dad"*). This group, too, feels the stinging truth of the accusation.

There are parents suffering from stress, illness and/or depression who know that their mental, physical and emotional absence is not a good thing, but who simply do not currently have the ability to do better. They know they're being inadequate parents even if it is not their fault at all. Indeed, all adults who know they are doing a poor parenting job—generally, or in a specific area, or even for a specific moment in time—suffer the discomforts of inadequacy.

> *By the time I get the kids out the door in the morning, I'm a wreck. First they don't want to get out of bed. Then they don't like the clothes I picked out. Then they dawdle and fight with each other instead of getting ready. Then they won't eat breakfast. Of course, I'm screaming through all of this. In fact, everybody is screaming. When they're finally gone, I feel like such a failure.*

Being Uncertain and Feeling Inadequate

Not knowing what to do—being confused and uncertain—is another cause of feelings of inadequacy in parenting.

> *Marla headed the marketing division of a huge corporation. She was responsible for staff management as well as marketing operations. People respected her competent and professional manner; she was highly successful in her job. At the end of the day, however, it was a different story for Marla. She simply couldn't get her two little boys into bed at night—the youngsters ran circles around her. Marla felt helpless and incompetent in the parenting arena. Whenever her in-laws made comments about her parenting style (i.e., her lack of control over the kids), Marla felt humiliated. She couldn't defend herself because what they said was true—she was out of her element.*

Indeed, many working parents find it easier to succeed at the office than they do on the home front. Some moms actually return to work earlier than necessary because they miss the feelings of success and accomplishment that they enjoy at work. For some it is more intense than that: the feelings of being overwhelmed, incompetent and inadequate at home drive them out of the house. Inability to calm a relentlessly colicky baby, tame an out-of-control toddler and/or entertain a high-needs preschooler produces uncomfortable feelings of inadequacy. Many parents naturally want to escape. Those who don't hold down jobs may become involved in out-of-the-house community and personal activities, leaving the child care mostly to a nanny or day care. It is not always boredom or lack of fulfillment that leads parents away from their small children—rather, it is often the extremely unpleasant sensation of being inadequate to the task. We enjoy and pursue those activities that we're good at, and dislike and avoid those that leave us feeling inadequate. No one can completely avoid doing parenting once they have children, but many people certainly try to minimize the amount of hands-on parenting they must do. Some hand the task over to spouses, some to the hired help and some to institutions, therapists, relatives or others. Inadequacy is the culprit behind many such disappearing acts.

Lack of Control Leads to Feelings of Inadequacy

> *My 6-year-old refuses to eat—she just nibbles. I can't get her to eat a meal or even small amounts of protein. Everyone else's kids eat— why won't she? I feel like such a bad mother.*

> *I thought I had a very good relationship with my 16-year-old daughter. One night she went out with her friend Janice and accidentally left her cellphone at home. I needed to reach her to tell her that my schedule had changed and I wanted her to come home a little earlier. I decided to call Janice's mother to see if Janice had a phone with her. Janice's mother told me that Janice was out of town! When my daughter showed up a couple of hours later, I asked her who she had spent the evening with. She said, "I told you before—Janice." When I told her what Janice's mom had said, my daughter said, "Oh. Then it wasn't Janice." I was flabbergasted! I couldn't believe she would lie to me! She knew how I felt about dishonesty, how disgusted I was with people who weren't truthful. How could she do this after all I had taught her? What was wrong with our relationship that I didn't even know about?*

One universally shared difficulty in parenting is the experience of lacking control over a child's behavior. Nonetheless, despite the commonality of the problem, lacking control seems to leave the average parent feeling terribly inadequate. It is so hard to acknowledge to ourselves that we can't really make a 6-year-old eat. Nor can we make a 10-year-old do homework, a 12-year-old choose appropriate friends or a 15-year-old talk respectfully. (Review the lists in Chapter 2 of what we can and can't do in parenting.) We may be able to provide encouragement and motivation, but we cannot force them. When we come up against the limits of our parenting power, we often feel inadequate, helpless and out of control.

Being Overwhelmed Leads to Feelings of Inadequacy

The limits of our parenting power are experienced in more ways than just loss of control. Sometimes we come up against our very human limits of endurance, patience, strength, capability and energy. This state is called "overwhelm."

> When tax season arrives, my husband's career as an accountant makes me a single parent for two months. He works late every night and leaves early every morning. That leaves me with three children to take care of on my own—the baby, the toddler and the preschooler. I'm exhausted! Getting them dressed and fed in the morning is impossible. Taking them with me on errands is a nightmare. Putting them to bed at night is a joke. By 8 p.m. I'm lying on the floor pulling my hair out. I just can't do it and I resent my husband and the kids and I hate myself for feeling this way. I'm obviously such a baby. My mother raised four of us without any help from Dad and I never heard her complain.

Feeling overwhelmed is bad enough. However, blaming ourselves for being deficient adds salt to the wound. We often imagine that we should be able to handle everything the way some idealized "Super

Person" would be doing it, despite the fact that our own unique personal history and genetic make-up create obvious disadvantages. Sometimes we blame ourselves for that as well!

> *I had such a busy day today at work and I knew that I was already tired and irritable the minute I walked in the door. Wanting so badly to be a "good" mother, I promised myself that I would talk nicely to everyone the whole evening, despite how worn out I was feeling. A couple of hours went by and I was true to my word; I was pretty pleased with myself. "You deserve an award," I was thinking. But then Ruby wanted to talk to me while I was trying to look something up on the computer. I asked her to give me 10 minutes but she refused to leave the room. I was getting all messed up—I needed some important information quickly and she was distracting me. I asked her nicely several more times to please leave but she wouldn't budge. Finally, I screamed at her to get out! Then I felt like a miserable failure. I knew that all she would remember of the night was the furious face of her mother.*

Knowing what good parenting looks like can actually compound feelings of inadequacy. Parents who take their job seriously, by reading parenting books, attending parenting classes and working on themselves, can be particularly devastated by their occasional errors and normal human limitations. Unfortunately, when parents are overwhelmed with responsibilities, they will find it harder to parent appropriately.

Emotional Abuse that Causes Feelings of Inadequacy

Some people feel inadequate as parents because of the critical, unkind and/or abusive things other people say to them. A spouse can erode the parenting confidence of his or her partner by direct put-downs: "You haven't got any brains. You don't know how to make a simple decision." "You're too hard on the children—they're going to hate you." "Don't give him that to wear—it looks ridiculous." A spouse can also erode a partner's confidence by aligning with the children against the partner: "Don't make him go to bed now that he wants to stay up a little longer—let the kid have some fun."

Abusive children can also erode a parent's confidence. In families without a protocol for teaching respectful behavior (see Chapter 9), children may be allowed to say horrible and hurtful things to their parents. From the little one's *"I hate you! You're so mean!"* to the bigger one's profanity-ridden curses, children have the ability to cut deeply into their parents, leaving the adults feeling both wounded and inadequate. Teenage and adult children who have cut themselves off completely from a parent also deliver a severe non-verbal insult: "You are just too horrible to associate with." Some parents receive this message with bowed head, knowing that they lacked important parenting skills during their children's critical developmental years. The guilt in no way minimizes the assault on their self-esteem; in fact, it can intensify existing feelings of inadequacy. Other parents are truly confused, at a loss to account for their child's withdrawal and rejection. However, as they witness the warm relationships enjoyed between their peers and their offspring, intense feelings of inadequacy can be triggered.

There are still others who can fuel feelings of parental inadequacy. Grandparents and other in-laws seem to have a particular talent for this. "She's awfully skinny; do you think she's eating properly?" "Why do you criticize him so much? He's okay." "How much did you spend on that? You should have gone to BabyWorld—they have a better one for much less!" "I don't think you should let him out of the house looking like that." "Didn't you teach her to say thank you?" Members of the older generation have not always been fortunate enough to be able to heal the wounds of their own childhood experience. As a result, they may use a "helpful" style of parenting their adult children that is full of criticism and negativity. The result is a free lunch of inadequacy.

Chronic Inadequacy

Unremitting feelings of inadequacy during the childrearing years—despite a plethora of parenting successes—may particularly plague the chronically insecure parent. This parent may bring a personal history of inadequacy to the parenting task. Perhaps this adult's own parents were critical and fault-finding, leaving him with a damaged self-concept. People who are unsure of their own self-worth can find the emotional challenges of parenting overwhelming. They will find endless ways to fail in parenthood. Their children won't seem to be (at least, in their own opinion) as well behaved as other people's children, or as accomplished, or as popular, beautiful, successful or admirable. And since children do not grow in a straight line upward, but rather follow a bumpy curve of successes and setbacks, there will be plenty of opportunity for insecure parents to find what is wrong and failing. When their child is sent home from play group for biting another toddler, these parents feel like outcasts and failures. "What is wrong with my child? What kind of terrible parent am I for having a child like this?" Similarly, when the teacher or principal calls home with a complaint, when the child is not invited to the right party, when the report card is lacking, when the child gets into trouble with the law for teenage mischief or worse, these parents blame themselves and their inadequacies. The worse the child's "crime," the greater will be the pain of inadequacy. The child's imperfect behavior or imperfect social standing or imperfect emotional health or imperfect physical health—indeed, any kind of imperfection at all—is a serious threat to the parents' own identities, rendering them "failures." They are unable to see themselves as competent, successful parents as long as their child is less than perfect. Since no one at any age is perfect, insecure parents will always feel inadequate.

*My sister's kids are perfect. They're all excellent students, extremely pop-
ular and into all kinds of extracurricular activities. They do everything right—they even keep their rooms clean. My kids seem to spend
their lives in detention and they're not on any teams or anything. I'm
just a lousy parent.*

Living with Inevitable Inadequacy

We have seen that feelings of inadequacy—sporadic or chronic—are
a natural part of parenting, just as they are a natural part of life. We
have also seen that they can interfere with our ability to make healthy
choices in parenting. Inadequacy-driven actions can rob our children
of the nurturing they need, or even harm their development. Let's look
at some ways to minimize our experience of inadequacy and its negative effect on our parenting.

Accept and Heal Feelings of Inadequacy

Each child, each stage of life and each situation is different—there will
be times when a parent is faced with something new, something that
he or she just doesn't know how to handle or just can't cope with. There
are times when each parent will feel, and actually be, inadequate.

One way—a graceful way—to deal with this fact is to simply
acknowledge and accept its inevitability. When confronted with overwhelming or overtaxing situations, be willing to say out loud to your
kids something like, "I don't know what to do right now. I'm taking a
time-out (to think about it/consult with the other parent/consult with
professionals/consult with religious advisors/consult with others) and
I'll let you know what I've decided." Seeking emotional support from
friends, family and professionals can be as valuable as seeking their practical advice. Inadequacy is a sad feeling that appreciates a sympathetic
and supportive listener.

Ilana was dumbfounded when she walked in on her 14-year-old holding a cigarette in his hand. After all the "health" education she had given him? How was this possible? Was he insane? Ilana looked her son in the eye: "I don't know what to say, Michael. I'm going to think about it and get back to you."

Ilana's "thinking" included a good cry on her husband's shoulder, a chat with a fellow comrade-in-parenting and a call to the school's guidance counselor for direction. By the time she approached her son, she was no longer incapacitated by feelings of inadequacy.

Some people will need more than this when challenged by intense feelings of inadequacy. Apparent over-reactions to a child's age-appropriate misbehaviors can signal a need for personal counseling. Signs that this may be the case include an inability to "get over" the issue at hand, a feeling of complete overwhelm, loss of appetite or loss of sleep (or an excess of either), or symptoms of depression or anxiety. Sometimes parenting stress is the straw that breaks the camel's back—the last thing that a parent can handle in an emotional pressure cooker. When this is the case, psychotherapy can provide more than parenting relief—it can initiate a complete emotional make-over. The parenting challenge is then a gift in disguise.

Lower the Bar

We don't have to know everything and we certainly don't have to have all the answers right away. We have 20 years to parent—that gives us some time to think! Simply giving ourselves this permission to be lacking—in skills, information, energy, experience or whatever—can provide an antidote to burdensome feelings of inadequacy. Feeling inadequate means we have set our bar too high; we cannot meet our own unforgiving standard. Lowering the bar to something more humane and more reasonable allows us to breathe easier in parenting. It lets us enjoy the journey more. It also expands our compassion for ourselves, others and even our children, allowing for a more realistic and optimistic approach to life.

Lowering our standards to something doable, something that allows for human frailties and failings, does not mean that we will be content to do a terrible job of parenting. Parents never want to do a terrible job of parenting! The lowered bar simply allows us to recover from our errors, limitations and oversights more quickly and gracefully, to get on with the job. More compassionate standards allow us to be permanent students, ever willing to learn and improve our parenting skills. "I see where I went wrong. I'll try again." Less energy will be wasted on self-flagellation and more can be directed toward moving forward. Looking at ourselves with gentle eyes is also a good model for our children. "Yes, I remember when I used to yell at you guys when you were small. I really regret that now. I know how much that hurt you and scared you. I've learned that a parent doesn't have to abuse a kid in order to discipline him. I'm sorry that I didn't know that earlier." Without diminishing the impact of our erroneous ways, we can show our children that our mistakes don't cripple us. Rather, they can be reflected upon and gained from. We're still intact. We'll still okay. This powerful model—used in conjunction with a similarly gracious acceptance of children's errors—helps youngsters to be kind to themselves throughout their own journeys, able to reflect and grow rather than be stunted by harsh self-rebuke.

Moreover, the lowered bar makes it easier to accept things that are out of our control. A parent can decide, "I'll be responsible for what I do and I'll be a guide to my child." This is a far cry from "I'll be responsible for what I do and what my child does." Taking too much on leads to feelings of failure, as we have already seen. We're not running the world or other people's lives (much as we might wish to). Keeping our task limited and realistic can lead to feelings of contentment and accomplishment.

Listen to the voice of your inner compassionate parent: "What's really wonderful about you is that you are reading this book and trying to do your best. There's no parent in the world who says and does everything perfectly. To err is human. You're showing your kids a real person and that's a good thing."

Focus on Your Parenting Strengths

Keeping perspective can be helpful. There are so many joyous and happy aspects of the parenting journey and so many areas in which our strengths will shine through. Fortunately, areas of competency and success can mitigate feelings of inadequacy in parenting. No one is inadequate all day, every day, for 20 years of parenting! Bad parenting days can be offset with good ones, just as bad parenting moments can be balanced with more positive ones. There is much to be proud of and pleased with throughout most parenting days. It is essential to pay attention to these moments—to highlight them, in fact. It is easier to feel like a "good enough" parent when we scan the whole picture instead of zeroing in on particularly disastrous episodes in our day, week, year or decade. Just like a photo album makes everything look happy and positive (because of all the smiling people), a written journal of our own good parenting news can help us view the journey and ourselves in a more positive light. "The kids loved the dinner I made tonight." "Danny thanked me for helping him with his project." "Tara won the poetry contest." "I used emotional coaching with Alex and it really worked wonders!" "I played cards with the kids tonight—we had a blast." "I finally had the courage to give a consequence to Derek." In this journal, only the upbeat, good news is recorded—no bad news. Reading the journal every once in a while can remind us of our adequacy. It can save us from a narrow focus on the negative.

Another strategy uses a mirror. Standing in front of a mirror every evening, the parent looks herself in the eye and commends herself on specific parenting actions taken during the day. "Good work, Gertrude! You got the kids out the door this morning in an upbeat manner. I like the way you found time to make appointments for their annual check-ups. It was great how you greeted them when they came in from school. I like the little jokes you made at dinner. And speaking of dinner, that was a very healthy and delicious meal you prepared today—good for you!"

Developing the habit of paying attention to the positive is an important tool for rewiring the critical tendency. Most people focus on their mistakes and weak moments. Talking out loud to themselves in a positive way on a regular basis can heal this tendency.

Indeed, during the two decades of parenting, there is plenty of room for each parent to excel. Someone who is "terrible with the baby stage" of child care may recover competency with the older child. Someone who is at a loss with a challenging, explosive child may shine with another easier, more cooperative youngster in the family. Someone who lacks skills for the teenage period may be able to build a successful relationship with a child who has left home for good. Someone who had trouble raising the first three children may do marvelously with the younger two. (Of course, having more than one child provides a wider range of opportunities for feelings of both success and inadequacy.)

When your internal critic starts listing your faults and failures—making you feel terrible—call your compassionate inner parent for help. Listen carefully to the supportive, kind words: "Parenting is a hard job. You handle so much of it really well. I'm proud of you!"

Enjoy the Growth of Adequacy

We can feel more and more adequate as we learn to gain perspective. This means coming to appreciate that the parenting journey must include—for everyone—experiences of loss of control, incompetence, failure to achieve desired outcomes, helplessness and other frustrating elements. Seeing all of this as normal and necessary helps to maintain our self-esteem.

Moreover, parenting is meant to be a growth experience for adults. Therefore, we can take pleasure in the growth we achieve, and include it in our "adequate" self-concept. "Okay, I didn't say that very nicely to my son, but at least I didn't go on and on about it. I'm learning to avoid the lecturing routine and I'm pleased with my success in that area." In other words, we can work with our parenting errors. We can get better and better with our skills, so that by the time the child is 20, we're excellent! Of course this means that we all make our major parenting mistakes in the early years of our children's lives, when they will have the most destructive impact. But take comfort: this is true for every person and it has obviously been set up that way for a purpose. The goal of parenting is not to raise a perfect child. The goal is to perfect ourselves and to help our children step onto the path of growth. It seems to be part of the divine order that each child must work on herself throughout her lifespan—maturity is not handed to anyone on a golden platter. We all have to work for it on our own.

Diversify

Perhaps your oldest child is under a year and has been a very easy, cooperative baby who has not yet challenged your feelings of adequacy. That's nice. However, if you hang in there for the whole ride, you—like the rest of us—will experience moments or days or years of that nagging inadequate sensation. During those times of pain, it is helpful to have relief.

A good way to help yourself is to diversify. Always keep up those activities and interests that feed your sense of adequacy. Surround yourself with at least some people who foster your sense of competence. Your children will sometimes be great fans, whose positive feedback nurtures your soul; however, many times during their developing years they will be unable to appreciate you. Rare is the 6-year-old who can say, "I like the way you disciplined me, Dad. Your patience is incredible. Where did you learn those great techniques?" On the contrary, after Dad executes a top-notch educational strategy, Junior may be screaming and crying in utter misery. Mom might be asking unsupportively, "What did you do to Junior?" And the other children might be cowering in the corner.

Hopefully Dad will at least be able to sing his own praises to himself: "I did it just like the book said: no yelling, no insults, no anger. It was a perfect job and I'm proud of myself." Nonetheless, it will also be good for him if he happens to be meeting his friends in the near future for business or pleasure. It helps to be able to get out of the domestic realm sometimes, to a place that provides affirmation, appreciation, accomplishment and obvious opportunities to shine.

People can find areas of success in their work, their extended family, their circle of friends, their religious communities, their hobbies, their exercise routines and in any number of other venues. The important point for parents is *to seriously access* these places of accomplishment while in the throes of raising children. If parenting is the only valued activity, the parent's emotional well-being is threatened. Parents must take care of their mental health not only for their own sakes, but also in order to do a good job of parenting. So get out there and feel good!

Resolving Unremitting Feelings of Inadequacy

We've looked at several ways of dealing with parental feelings of inadequacy. However, a purely cognitive understanding of the problematic feeling and its solutions is not always enough. When feelings of inadequacy or any of its cousins (overwhelm, incompetence, helplessness, etc.) are chronic, depressing and/or debilitating, professional help can provide much-needed relief. Counseling professionals are trained in a variety of techniques that can uproot and heal deep-seated feelings of inadequacy, giving parents a new lease on life as well as more energy for parenting. Sometimes, emotionally based self-help techniques are sufficient for treating feelings in need of soothing and healing. One such technique is offered to you for experimentation in Appendix A. It can often effect a deep healing for feelings of inadequacy or any of the troubling emotions that you or your family members feel. It can be tried before accessing professional psychological support or used along with psychotherapy for at-home, on-the-spot relief.

CHAPTER 14

Anxiety in Parenting

Cause for Concern

Anxiety starts, for most parents, before the child is even born. "Will the baby be healthy? Will I be able to cope? Will the other kids in the family adjust well?"

Anxiety is a constant companion for many on the parenting journey. Others will experience only moments or short periods of anxiety. No matter how often or how rarely we experience it, however, it is important to learn how to make it work for the family rather than against it.

Anxiety is an important emotion for its signal value. As with all emotional signals—such as fear, anger or sadness—anxiety delivers the message "pay attention." Anxiety specifically asks us to pay attention to some potentially dangerous or troublesome situation (in the real world or within our psyche) and to take steps to prevent harm. If we listen to its call and tend to whatever needs tending to, the anxiety will diminish and eventually disappear. This is true in cases where anxiety is a temporary, normal response to a real world anxiety-provoking situation (e.g., walking alone in the dark); where it is caused by an internal psychic trauma due to a long-ago incident (such as being robbed several years back) or chronic childhood abuse; where it results from a genetic tendency or from childhood programming by anxious parents. In other words, no matter what is causing the anxiety, the treatment will be the same: pay attention to it and address the need it is expressing. Sometimes this process requires professional assistance and sometimes it can be accomplished with self-help tools. We will look at both strategies later in this chapter.

Parents who have not yet acknowledged their anxiety may "act it out" during parenting. Intense anger can sometimes be a cover-up for underlying anxiety (take the case, for example, of parents who rage at their children for coming home late). It can also happen in parents who admit they are anxious but who have not yet addressed and healed that anxiety. We will look at common triggers for parental anxiety, parenting problems caused by anxiety and techniques for reducing anxiety.

Anxiety Interferes with Parenting

Anxiety in large doses can erode the pleasure of parenting. Like other negative emotions, it can also interfere with rational parenting. Decisions made out of anxiety may not be the wisest. Parental actions that are anxiety-driven may be harsh, loud and inappropriate.

> *My friends' babies all started talking by 14 months old. Jeremy doesn't say a word. I'm beginning to wonder if something is wrong—maybe he needs some kind of therapy or maybe he has some kind of disability. Even though Dr. Brown told me everything is normal, I can't relax. What does Dr. Brown really know?*

> *When Kevin gets that maniacal look in his eyes, I panic. Doug's brother, who suffers from bipolar disorder, gets that look when he's angry—and he gets very angry. I know the disorder is genetic and that's why I get so scared when Kevin gets that look; I think maybe he's developing the illness. The problem is my reaction to him is totally crazy—I literally scream at Kevin to get that look off his face! There's probably nothing at all wrong with Kevin—he just looks like that because he knows it makes me upset.*

In anxious moments, it is not uncommon for parents to over-react or react with undue harshness. A parent may impulsively assign an excessively harsh punishment for an anxiety-provoking crime committed by a youngster, instead of taking time to think out the best educational intervention. Moreover, when anxiety intensifies to the point where fight-or-flight chemistry is released into the body, the rational brain is short-circuited completely and we operate on "automatic pilot." Whatever is biologically or environmentally programmed overrides logical thought processes (i.e., the ability to make a good parenting plan).

> *When Carly ran into the road, I was frightened out of my wits. I chased her and—please don't report me to Family Services—I actually smacked her. It must have been instinctive; I know that's how my parents used to handle me if I did something really dangerous. I wish I could have just brought her to safety, then calmed myself down to think about the best way to handle this. Maybe the smack "worked," but I get frightened over a lot of things she does and I don't want to be smacking her all day!*

Anxiety also interferes with parents' ability to guide and support their children. When a child's behavior or emotion frightens a parent, the parent goes into "survival mode," offering a panic-driven response meant to quell the parent's anxiety rather than help the child.

> Child to divorced parent: *If you remarry, I'm going to run away from home.*
>
> Parent: *Don't worry—I'm not going to remarry until you're ready.*

Naturally, a divorced parent is already intensely concerned about his or her child's mental health—threats of intense emotion or behavior can raise anxiety in anyone and certainly in someone who is already worrying. But making rash promises not only gives the child a false sense of security (the parent could, after all, renege on a decision to marry only when the child is "ready"); it also robs the child of what he or she needs most during such conversations: emotional coaching. When a child speaks about desperate emotions, the parent's job is to help the child process that pain, as we have seen in Chapter 5. Unfortunately, when parental anxiety enters the picture, emotional coaching becomes impossible. Rather, the parent rushes to solve a problem or provide reassurance, or even to try to stop the child's feelings directly. A parent is ideally a "midwife" to a child's pain, someone who helps the child process difficult, painful and confusing emotions. The parent must set his or her own anxiety temporarily to the side in order to be present for the child. The following example illustrates the possibilities when a parent can focus on the child instead of on his or her own discomfort:

Child: *If you remarry, I'll run away.*

Parent: *Wow! You sound really upset about the idea of me getting married!*

Child: *Yes—no one is going to come in the house and take the place of Daddy.*

Parent: *You're horrified at the thought that someone would try to take Daddy's place.*

Child: *Yes—and I don't need another father. No one is going to tell me what to do!*

Parent: *You wouldn't want anyone bossing you around, acting as if they were your father—you already have a father.*

Child: *That's right. So you better not get married.*

Parent: *You really don't want me to get married.*

Child: *And I don't want any more changes. Everything's changed enough already.*

Parent: *I see. You've already had too much change and the idea of even more change is overwhelming—just too much.*

Child: *Right. So don't even think of it.*

Parent: *I can see how worried you are about this, how scary the idea is for you, and how much you just don't want me to do it.*

Child: *Yeah, so you better not.*

The emotionally present parent can listen compassionately—even when every sentence is a personal threat. In order to do this, a parent must master the management of anxious feelings. This emotional coaching can be followed by the giving of information and/or the solving of problems. The coaching provides a "hook-up" to the child, allowing this information to be heard and utilized. In this way, a parent can be a truly effective guide and teacher. For example, the divorcee in the previous example may, after emotional coaching, begin to talk about remarriage and the way that the child's fears and concerns could be addressed. This part of the discussion might occur in the same conversation or later in the week or even after several weeks—depending on the needs of the child and of the situation.

Anxious Parents Raise Anxious Children

Anxiety-based parenting may contribute to the development of anxiety in children. Children will inevitably learn to worry like their parents do. Anxiety tends to run in families, both by nature and by nurture. It is not clear how much is genetically programmed and how much is learned, but it seems clear that both factors are operating. Anxious parents may be over-protective, sheltering their kids from normal childhood experiences and thereby preventing them from experiencing their own ability to deal with risk.

> I don't care if other people let their children go to camp. The counselors are just kids themselves—they can't possibly be responsible for a group of children. I'm not exposing my children to that kind of risk.

Chronically anxious parents teach their children that the world is a scary place and life is threatening and/or overwhelming. Danger lurks behind every corner. It's not that they are wrong, of course; it is simply that this kind of truth causes suffering and struggle. Phobias, for example, are also rooted in truthful assessments: spiders can be dangerous, heights can lead to deadly accidents, airplanes do crash. Indeed, no one has a phobia for completely harmless objects—for example, no one has a phobia of carpets or erasers. (A person can form a traumatic associa-tion to any object, but that is different from a phobia.) The problem with phobias—as with anxiety in general—is that the likelihood of dan-ger is overestimated. The extremely small chance of getting fatally trapped in an elevator needn't cause us to make a daily trek up 20 flights of stairs to our office. The very rare possibility of being in a plane crash should not stop us from traveling abroad. Anxiety about these kinds of things will not make us safer, thereby prolonging our lives indefinitely; instead, it will create constant limitation and difficulty during our lifetimes. Anxiety is not the gift we want to pass on to our children.

Even when parents have anxious genes, there are many steps they can take to help themselves and their children minimize their impact. We will examine helpful strategies that anyone can use—whether they are suffering from an anxiety disorder or whether they are simply hav-ing an anxious moment.

Everyday Anxiety

Inevitably, some measure of anxiety affects all parents because of their lack of experience. Parents are not fully experienced until they have raised many children all the way to adulthood—therefore, they are inex-perienced for most of their parenting years! All new frontiers are anxiety-provoking for normal people, and entering the realm of the unknown always arouses caution, if not outright fear. Parenting offers new frontiers daily—particularly in the case of raising a first-born.

> We're leaving Jason with a babysitter for the first time tonight. I'm really nervous. I'm afraid he won't like her. I'll feel just awful if he screams the whole time we're out. What if he vomits? I hope she can handle everything. I'm leaving her my mom's number just in case, and my next-door neighbor's number and Dr. Joe's number, of course, and the emergency number and—do you think I should give her my sister-in-law's number too?

It's unsettling when we don't know what to expect. As we become "old hands" at parenting, some of this kind of anxiety lessens. Nonetheless, even organizing our first wedding for our eldest child can be anxiety-inducing, along with all other "first-time" experiences.

Indeed, everyday parenting throws up all kinds of opportunities for anxiety. Parents feel weighty responsibility for their children's physical, mental, emotional and spiritual well-being; they are constantly on the lookout for anything that could jeopardize optimal development. Devoted parents with vivid imaginations and anxious tendencies can be "on edge" for 20 years straight.

> *Brenda is going to Europe with her friends this summer. It's her first big trip. She's all excited but I'm a wreck. I can't stop thinking about everything that could go wrong. What if she needs us? What if they get lost? What if her friends get busted for taking drugs or doing something crazy? How do I know she'll make smart choices—what if they run into a bad crowd? I know she's always been a good girl, but there's a first time for everything, isn't there? What if she gets into trouble?*

Worries About the Future

One arena that provokes a lot of anxiety for parents is their child's *future*. What does it hold? Will the child be okay? After all, parents are trying to raise an infant successfully to adulthood, hoping that the child will be able to stand on his or her own two feet to lead a productive, positive life. It is only natural that parents should think ahead, even as they are raising their youngsters. This future-looking tendency can have a downside, however. Sometimes a child's small setbacks or failures cause parents to generate terrifying future scenarios. "Catastrophizing" is, in fact, a common hobby of parents. A child gets a poor grade on her science test and her parents paint a dismal picture of adulthood: the child will never graduate from elementary school, will never find a job and will finally end up living as a beggar in the streets.

This vivid imagery would be amusing except for one serious negative consequence: the parents proceed to parent as if their anxieties have true value. Reviewing the test results with their youngster, they shriek hysterically, "Don't you want to get into university one day? Well, performance like this sure won't get you there! Are you trying to destroy your life? You need to put a lot more effort into this, Young Lady!"

> *I became very anxious whenever Randy—who was 19 when this all started—would tell me that he had done well at the casino. I knew this could cause him to make gambling a serious pastime or even a full-time career. He'd come home all pleased with himself for making some money and I'd start yelling at him that he would ruin his life. I couldn't talk to him about it rationally. I was just terrified.*

Parental anxiety can lead to a toxic, fear-based style of parenting. Worst-case scenarios thrown in the child's face to motivate him simply program his brain with fear and negativity. He becomes debilitated by his own crippling anxiety. "Helping" children by filling their head with fears is not really help at all; it is a curse that the child may need to struggle against for a lifetime.

> *My father's way of "encouraging" me was to throw insults in my face. When I brought home bad grades he'd tell me I'd never amount to anything. He told me that so many times, I came to believe it and, as you can see, I never did amount to much. But now that I'm older, I think he spoke to me like that because he was genuinely worried about me. I think that was his way of handling his anxiety.*

When children have trouble making friends, parents worry about their present happiness and future relationships. When children have physical health issues, parents worry about their current functioning and their future well-being. When children don't perform well academically, parents worry about their school placement and career prospects. Some children do indeed have serious handicaps, and their parents worry greatly about both their current and future happiness and health. But parents can worry even when there is nothing apparent to worry about. They worry just because they are so invested in their children. They worry more if they have been genetically or environmentally primed to do so.

Anxiety About Health

Parents are responsible for their young children's physical health; they often continue to feel that responsibility well into the teenage years. That's why they work so hard to get their youngsters to eat and sleep well, why they slather them with suntan lotion and why they insist on warm clothing in cold weather. Anxiety increases when their child is unwell.

An infant's fever, a toddler's fall, a 6-year-old's inexplicable rash or a 15-year-old's unremitting exhaustion are legitimate causes of worry. The uncomfortable emotion prompts parents to consult books on child health, do Internet research, call their parents or friends and/or make an appointment with a health practitioner. Mild anxiety and worry are signals to take precautions and to take action. They are valuable emotions.

However, many parents have difficulty turning the signal off, even after they have attended to the matter. Their days and/or nights may be plagued with anxious thoughts. Some parents are quite frightened by physical symptoms—stomachaches, headaches, lumps, pains, coughs and so forth—afraid that each one points to a life-threatening disease. Since children experience so many health concerns during two decades of growth, these parents suffer considerably.

> *Mitchell has been suffering from headaches recently and I can't help but think the worst. The doctor said it is probably just stress from school, but Mitchell has had plenty of stress before and he never got headaches. We've scheduled an MRI just to be sure everything is okay but that isn't going to happen until next month—meanwhile, all*

these terrible thoughts keep going through my mind. What if it's a tumor? I don't think I can wait a month to find out. I'm suffering from dizziness and palpitations. I don't think I can take it. Ironically, Mitchell isn't concerned at all—he's much better than I am about it.

Although all parents will feel anxiety about their child's health at some point, some parents are chronically anxious about health issues. This kind of worry is usually as unpleasant for the parents as it is for the child. It can cause parents to fuss and fret over their kids' minor sniffles, nag their children incessantly to take their vitamins or eat their meals, or drag children to numerous (often unnecessary) medical appointments. Taking legitimate concerns to a level higher, anxious parents can worry themselves and their children about contaminated water and beef, deadly insects, viruses and bacteria—to the point where the joy of living is dampened by the constant fear of dying.

In addition, anxious parents may give their children more attention when they are ill than when they are well, inadvertently reinforcing a tendency to express stress physically. In fact, many families are more comfortable expressing unhappiness with a stomachache, fear of failing with a headache or feelings of pressure with a cold. Illness—even when surrounded by fear and worry—can be less scary to some people than talking about unpleasant emotions. Worry and concern around illness can actually communicate love and care in families that lack an emotional vocabulary. Indeed, for some parents, active worrying about a child's health is equivalent to showing love. Often, they have learned this equation from their own parents. However, aligning worry with love is dangerous; chronic worry can cause health problems for the parent—the last thing a child needs! True love involves taking good care of oneself as well as one's child. Moreover, the ability to give true emotional support (see Chapter 5 on emotional coaching) can actually help reduce the occurrence of stress-related physical illness in every member of the family.

Anxiety About Safety Issues

Who *isn't* anxious about safety in today's world? Terrorism is a very real threat in every country. War is a threat in some places. Robbers, thieves, child predators, rapists and other violent citizens trouble almost every neighborhood. Even school can be a dangerous environment. How can parents protect their youngsters? How do they feel when they know they can't?

> *My daughter Dana's class left on their year-end outing yesterday to visit the capital. They took one of those coach buses. To tell you the truth, I'm really worried. How many times do we hear of those buses turning over on the highway? I won't be able to sleep till she gets back.*

Tragedies do happen. There are legitimate safety concerns. The problem is that we really lack control. Much as we may wish to tie our children to the bedpost to keep them safe, it is against the law to do so! We must let them leave our watchful eyes and travel the streets to their various destinations. We have to let them go.

> *Lenny just got his driver's license. Every time he pulls out of the driveway, I get a sickening feeling in my heart. Do you have any idea how many teenagers get into car accidents every year?*

> *Every morning when Paul rides off to school on his bike, I wave goodbye and try to look cheery. Actually, I'm always wondering if he's going to make it there safely.*

> *Elise is furious with me for insisting on accompanying her to school every day. I know a lot of parents around here let their kids walk alone, but I just don't feel it's safe. An adult needs to be there.*

Not only do parents worry about what might happen to their children, but they also worry terribly about what might happen to themselves. Personal safety is a major concern for many who travel for work or pleasure.

> *I have a serious fear of flying without my children. If I leave them at home and the plane crashes, who will raise them? Their lives will be ruined. On the other hand, if they're with me when the plane crashes, at least we'll all be together in Heaven.*

Parental anxiety about safety issues can have the same negative consequences for parenting as all other forms of anxiety. Parents can place unreasonable limits on permitted activities for their youngsters ("No, you can't ever use a computer—there are dangerous magnetic energies that can cause epilepsy!") or display hysterical anger and upset over safety-related mistakes made by their children ("You *what*?! You told that man on the phone that Daddy isn't home?? Didn't I tell you to *never* tell anyone that Daddy isn't home? Do you want that man to come over here and kill us all?"). Anxiety of all kinds is driven by the fight-or-flight chemistry that re-routes logical processing. The result is an irrational parent whose desperate search for safety and security actually erodes every trace of it in the child's world. Anxious parents frighten their children.

Anxiety About Friends

Many parents worry about their children's friends. They worry if their youngsters don't have friends, since this might lead to loneliness, sadness and other kinds of emotional pain. They worry if they do have friends because the friends may be bad influences. They worry if they spend too much time with friends because they may be "up to no good." When teenagers start to date, parents worry about their sexual behavior. When they're older, they worry about the child's choice of marital partner or lack of marital partner. In-between, they worry about their sexual orientation.

> *I don't like the look of Tammy's new circle of friends. They're not nice kids like the ones from her old school. These kids look tough. They're probably involved with some gang or something, and I'm sure they're seriously into drugs. I told her what I thought and she swore up and down that they're the nicest people and really good to her. There's no point forbidding her to see them—they all go to school together. That's fine. But she better not come to me to get bailed out of jail.*

Childhood social relationships can leave lifelong scars. Most of us have some of these, so we know only too well how our children may be suffering. However, we are helpless to prevent the social hurts that occur to all children in the course of growing up. Children get bullied. They get left out, uninvited and rejected. They have no one to play with or visit or date. They sometimes have poor social skills, make poor social decisions or act in ways that are inappropriate and embarrassing. Since a positive social life is an important aspect of a happy life, parents are often very anxious about their children's ability to fit in, make good friends and be well liked by others.

> *Max isn't invited for play dates. He's got a reputation for being wild—the other moms are afraid to have him over. I think it got around that he had a temper tantrum at the birthday party last month. I'm really worried about him—what if he doesn't grow out of this? What if he never makes friends?*

> *It really bothers me to see Sandi sitting around by herself every weekend. I keep telling her to pick up the phone and invite someone over or make an arrangement to go out. She makes a thousand excuses! Last Sunday I got so frustrated I started screaming at her to call someone, but even that made no difference. I hate fighting with her about it*

but I'm really worried—she doesn't seem to realize the importance of cultivating friendships.

Adult insecurities can be heightened by their children's social failures. Some parents have not recovered from their own social traumas—painful experiences of rejection or isolation. The trauma is then freshly triggered by a child's interpersonal difficulties or social habits. Triggered trauma may create panic attacks, which, in parenting, often lead to attacks of anger as well.

Morrie has one friend—Tim. Now if I had just one friend, I'd be sure to treat him really well, but Morrie doesn't take care of this friendship at all. I hear them on the phone: Tim calls to make a social arrangement and Morrie mumbles "not tonight." He's not even nice about it, and half the time he's not doing anything else anyway—he could have gone out with Tim. I'm always on his case, telling him to treat Tim better and to value the friendship properly. Of course Morrie just continues doing what he wants to do. I actually lose sleep over the whole thing because I can't stop worrying about it.

Sometimes children are alone because they prefer it that way; introverts enjoy activities and their own company more than hanging out with other people. They are happy on their own rather than disheartened. Introverted parents understand this whereas more socially inclined adults may be anxious about their introverted child's lack of friends.

Living with Anxiety in Parenting

As we've seen, there are so many occasions for anxious feelings to occur in parenting. Parents who are anxious by nature will suffer more than others, but every parent will experience anxiety on numerous occasions. Some situations just are, by definition, anxiety-provoking.

Whatever the cause, parents' worries are limited only by their imaginations. Unfortunately, because worrying takes up a lot of brain space and energy—and operates both day and night—it tends to be exhausting. We have already seen that it erodes more than parental peace of mind, however. Anxiety tends to spill over into stressful parent-child interactions. When parents can soothe their anxious tendencies, everyone in the house benefits. Much of parental anxiety can be minimized or even avoided by using various self-help techniques.

Healing the Tendency to Worry

When anxiety occurs to the point that it interferes with sound parenting or causes the parent distress, it can be treated with various self-help tools. Anxiety that persists in the face of these tools may be better treated by a professional psychologist. Professional psychologists use a variety of effective counseling procedures and interventions to heal anxious processes; a short course of personal therapy may significantly improve two decades of parenting. Increased joy in living is just one of the positive "side effects" of therapy!

In addition, there are some body-mind treatments in the alternative health field that are excellent for the relief of anxiety (acupressure, homeopathy, herbal medicine and aromatherapy are just a few examples). Each discipline licenses its own practitioners. Naturopaths are general practitioners who may also have expertise in one or more of the alternative health disciplines.

For serious, unremitting anxiety that has been unresponsive to other interventions, medical treatment is also an option. Accessing such treatment when necessary can be a gift to oneself and one's family.

For now, we will explore some tools that many parents find sufficient for healing typical parental anxiety.

Self-Help Tool #1: Changing Mental Images. Worry involves the imagination, as we have noted before. The worrier imagines—pictures and thinks about—a negative scenario. The worrying parent has developed a habit of making such images, and therefore has well-formed pathways in the brain ("neural pathways") for this behavior. This is similar to knowing how to drive a car or even walk; once a person has practiced many times, he or she can perform almost automatically because of the well-formed neural pathways. When learning a new song, a pianist must go slowly and carefully at first. With many repetitions, a new neural pathway is formed and this song can then be played without active thought. Worrying parents have scary images in their brains, ready to download for every occasion: pictures of disaster, violence, catastrophe, death, failure, harm and every other sort of emotional and physical torture. Contrary to popular belief, worrying does *not* keep our children safe. In fact, some scientists and proponents of quantum physics suggest that negative thought patterns can actually attract negative events! Whether or not our thoughts affect our destinies, however, it is clear that positive thinking reduces stress and improves functioning. Moreover, positive thinking generates better brain chemistry, causing a person to feel happier and calmer.

The treatment: the worrying parent must flood his or her mind with positive images—pictures and thoughts of safe, happy outcomes. When faced with a future scenario, the parent should notice his or her original, alarming thought images. Then the parent should purposefully create positive alternative images. Verbalizing, writing, imagining and drawing the happy outcome are all helpful approaches. For example, when a child is about to take a cross-country trip, the anxious parent might first notice thoughts of accidents, natural disasters, molestation, robbery and so forth. Then the parent would intentionally imagine the child leaving home and arriving safely at his or her destination. In-between pictures of the young person enjoying beautiful sunsets, good friends, laughter and other delights can be generated as well. If sketches of these images can be drawn in a little pocket notebook, the parent can flip through those drawings a few times a day to reinforce the new neural pathways.

At first, creating positive images will be a laborious exercise, feeling artificial and inauthentic. After many repetitions, however, the brain will be able to regularly follow the new road to a calmer, more positive set of images. When challenged by an uncertain outcome in parenting, the parent will (eventually) automatically generate a positive scenario.

Self-Help Tool #2: Restructuring Thoughts. In addition to negative imagining, people engage in negative thinking and worrisome thought processes. Another form of flooding the mind employs words rather than images. Many people find that affirmations—short, positive thoughts— repeated throughout the day eventually reprogram the brain. This repetition can occur while one is engaged in otherwise mindless tasks like washing dishes or chopping vegetables, sitting on the bus, standing in line or listening to one's mother-in-law on the phone (just kidding about that last one). Again, the initial efforts may seem awkward and feel false. However, frequent, repetitive use of affirmations can wear away the old pathways much as water drops can wear away stone. There are endless books that offer affirmations as a central part of their anxiety-reducing strategy. Louise Hay's beautiful work of art, a book called *You Can Heal Your Life*, is one among thousands of such resources. In addition, parents can certainly write out and say their own affirmations to suit the needs of their situations. For example, a parent can repeat any of the following kinds of thoughts: "My child is able to find his own solutions," "God is in charge" and "The most likely outcome is a positive one."

Self-Help Tool #3: Relaxing Deeply. Deep relaxation not only feels amazingly pleasant, it also has a way of lowering the anxiety thermostat. When people relax deeply at least once a day, they become calmer mentally, emotionally and physically. The calmness builds day by day so that "regular relaxers" have a much lower level of anxiety than the average person. The mind cannot produce anxiety in the presence of the chemistry of relaxation. There are several different ways to achieve the level of relaxation that will be effective. One method for busy people (like mothers of young children!) is to use a one-minute deep-breathing technique four or five times during the day. Although there is an endless number of breathing techniques that can be used for the one-minute breath, two popular breathing styles are Dr. Herbert Benson's

Relaxation Response (breathe in normally and think "one" on the breath out) and any breath which takes twice as long on the exhale as it does on the inhale. For those who would like to enjoy all of the mental, physical, emotional and even spiritual benefits of meditation—described at length in the medical, psychological and spiritual literature—10 or 20 minutes of this technique used daily provides all this and a greatly reduced tendency toward anxiety. In addition to the regular use of deep relaxation techniques, daily stretching and exercising enhances all other forms of treatment for worry and anxiety.

Self-Help Tool #4: Bach Flower Therapy. This is a naturopathic treatment for distressed emotions, including intense states of anxiety. It can be used effectively as a self-help tool. If results are partial or non-existent, however, a consultation with a professional Bach Flower Practitioner can be helpful. Mechteld Scheffer's outstanding book, *The Encyclopedia of Bach Flower Therapy*, provides in-depth information on this modality for those who are interested in self-treatment. There are many other books on the market as well.

Instructions as to how to prepare and use flower essences (it's simple to do) are available at health food stores, online and in books on the subject. The treatment is taken until the anxiety clears up. Parents might consider the following essences:

> *Red chestnut*—for the tendency to worry about loved ones
> such as one's children or spouse
> *White chestnut*—for obsessive worrying (i.e., constant thinking)
> *Mimulus*—for worrying about unpleasant scenarios (such as
> dangers, problems, difficulties)

There are 38 different Bach flowers, used for every kind of stressful emotion. Although the three suggested here for parental anxiety may be helpful, there are actually many others that can treat different "flavors" of anxiety. You can learn about them on your own from books, Internet resources or a professional practitioner.

Those who would like to experiment with this self-help tool should be aware that there is insufficient medical research in North America to establish the clinical effectiveness of Bach Flower Therapy at this time.

Self-Help Tool # 5: Energy Psychology. This is a rapid, novel intervention for removing anxious thoughts and feelings. Parents can treat both themselves and their children. This amazing technique may resolve both isolated episodes of worry and the chronic tendency to worry. For those who would like to learn it, Energy Psychology is described in detail in Appendix A.

CHAPTER 15

From Despair to Renewal: Intense Emotions in Parenting

Intense Feelings in Parenting

Parenting can be intensely joyful. The moment of birth, for example, can be a moment of ecstasy. Sleeping children of all ages are breathtaking to gaze upon, simply for the miracle of their existence and the sweet innocence of their resting souls. There are so many wonderful experiences in parenting—a baby's first words and steps, a toddler's joyful exploration of the world, a schoolchild's proud accomplishment, an older child's foray into the world of work and relationships and so much more—so many occasions of success, humor, pride and delight.

This chapter, however, is not about the joyous side of parenting. As we delve into the darker underside of the parenting journey, it will be helpful to reflect upon the words of King Solomon inscribed upon the ring he always wore, "This, too, shall pass." King Solomon was reminding himself, and all generations after him, to take time to appreciate every good moment, for it is time-limited. In parenting, this means that we should be grateful for every healthy day, every normal misbehavior, every giggle, every hug, every task involved in a child's care, every shared moment in time. We should relish the positive side of parenting.

King Solomon's motto also helps us to survive challenging times, knowing that these, too, will pass. Specific troubles have resolution, critical states of illness end, ongoing sickness and dysfunction fluctuate, individual crises resolve, chronically painful situations are interspersed with happier times and even trauma has an end-point (although professional help may be needed in order to find that end-point and heal sufficiently to access joyful emotions once more). All things change. King Solomon helps us to track the ebb and flow of suffering in parenting, as in all other areas of life.

Depending on the nature and characteristics of the individual child and family, there can be more or less of this unhappy side of parenting. Some people live relatively undisturbed lives, spared from harsh challenges. Others, however—perhaps the majority—face severe trials along the way. For instance, some parents are living with serious illness—their own, their spouse's, their parents' or their child's. Serious illness brings intense stress, anxiety, anger and sadness into the family. Some families are dealing with mental illness, others with severe financial limitations, many with separation and divorce, some with death or abandonment, most with marital difficulties. All of these, and the myriad other real-life stressors that parents face, invite negative emotions into the home. These emotions have lifelong impact on the children who are growing up in their midst. Children's own feelings of fear and grief help shape their destiny, but the parental model of coping with intense stress also leaves its mark.

Do parents fall apart under stress? Do they become ill or depressed? Do they rage or act out? Do they turn to addiction for solace? Do they flee? Do they seek help or do they isolate themselves? Do they gracefully rise to the occasion? Do they face their tests with courage and faith? Any parental response is a form of education for the watchful students of life sitting at the kitchen table year after year. The children are learning, both consciously and unconsciously, how to deal with the hard side of life.

Parents want to do the best for their kids, even when under tremendous stress. Their response to severe stress, however, may be less than ideal, shaped not so much by their good intentions as by their life histories, family histories, genetic profiles and other factors. For example, one person might sail through a nasty divorce with relative good humor and energy. Another might be bowled over by feelings of helplessness and overwhelm. Even the same emotions can be expressed differently by different people. Thus, in one person, helplessness and overwhelm lead to withdrawal from appropriate parenting activities like nurturing or disciplining. In another person, helplessness and overwhelm lead to excessively controlling behaviors like criticism, anger or even abuse.

The good news is that once parents have recognized that their own "natural" style of expressing stress is somehow harmful for their children, they can consciously work on themselves to change it. Through self-help and/or professional help, adults can dramatically change both their emotional and behavioral response to stress. In this way, they can provide a good model and a healthy home environment for their kids.

Because intense parental stress will have direct consequences for child development, we will examine the full range of negative emotions that real parents experience under real stress. By addressing and healing the stressful emotions that underlie inappropriate parenting actions, it is possible to interrupt the generational legacy of family dysfunction and introduce healthy new models for the future.

Adult Problems

We will examine two sources of intense stress. The first one, adult stress, will be explored briefly, to study its impact on parenting. The second one, parenting stress, will be explored in detail, with a focus on understanding and healing the troubled emotions that can interfere with healthy parenting. Both kinds of stress occur to the nicest people; they are part of the human condition.

Let us begin, then, with adult stress. Parents can sink into the mire of desperate emotions because of issues in their own lives, quite apart from childrearing. For example, the discovery of a spouse's infidelity often provokes a full range of trauma-like responses, including shock, grief, fury, insomnia, panic attacks, depression, obsessive rumination and hypersensitivity. Needless to say, the parent who is in such a state will find it almost impossible to be "present" for his or her children.

So much energy is being consumed by the adult's inner processing that there is barely anything left for the kids. Moreover, the nerves of people in the throes of trauma are drawn taut, resulting in quick tempers, zero patience and frequent over-reactivity. They are not fun to live with and they don't make the best parents.

Trauma and its fallout is not a rare phenomenon; it is a routine part of the human experience. Although full-blown post-traumatic stress disorder is considered to be the product of extraordinary, life-threatening events (such as witnessing or being a victim of an assault or car accident, escaping a house fire or tsunami, being a victim of war or terrorist attack, being a survivor of childhood abuse), people regularly experience partial trauma syndromes from the routine traumas of life. Watching a loved one die, undergoing major surgery or dental work, going through a divorce, experiencing family violence, having a complicated childbirth, becoming unemployed, moving away from one's family of origin, suffering a miscarriage and so on and so forth—all are examples of life events that can trigger traumatic fallout in vulnerable adults. Nor do such events wait politely until one has finished raising one's children; they occur throughout the lifespan, including the decades of childrearing. This means that many parents will be severely on-edge (and/or deeply disturbed) at some points during their children's development.

Moreover, trauma-related stress is not the only kind of stress that normal parents experience. Having in-laws move into town or into the house can be unsettling (to say the least). Moving to another city to start life anew can take a heavy toll. Experiencing a severe financial loss or change in job status is always hard. Giving birth, though a happy stress, is a stress nonetheless. Having twins, triplets or other multiples is, of course, more stressful. Suffering from injury or illness makes everyday functioning difficult. Enduring marital stress can be depleting. Pursuing education and training can be taxing. Even creating a family celebration can be hard. Although these kinds of stressful events do not lead to deep emotional pain, they do wear parents down. They form the backdrop against which other, more serious stressors can "break the camel's back." An accumulation of normal life stress, topped by the birth of a handicapped child, for instance, may be too much for a particular parent to bear.

> *We've moved six times in the last eight years. It's been really hard. But I was coping—till the illness of my dad. It's not just that we're in different cities now—which is bad enough—but I can't stand knowing that he is in pain. I find myself crying throughout the day; I really feel like I'm falling apart. And I feel terrible if Beth catches me in tears—what do I say to her?*

Some people are under the erroneous impression that childhood is supposed to be an innocent, carefree and stress-free period of life. Since children live with parents and parents are, as we have just seen, subject to intense stress in the normal course of life, children will almost always be living with stress. In addition, children have their own personal stresses brought about by schoolwork, peer relationships, teachers, extracurricular activities, siblings, parents and so on. It is obvious, then, that children lead stressful lives; this is both normal and beneficial.

You might be wondering how childhood stress can be "beneficial." Think of it this way: childhood is a time of training and preparation for adulthood; adulthood is a time of achieving one's potential. Difficult adult experiences actually push people into their highest gear, bringing out their latent attributes and skills in order to survive and thrive under challenging circumstances. During childhood, youngsters practice handling their own problems as they watch parents handle theirs. The type of parents who can model the journey from darkness to light are able to instill in children a deep sense of hope, faith and courage for their own lives. On the other hand, the type of parents who collapse in the face of life's deepest difficulties often scare their children. "If my own parents can't handle life's challenges, how can I ever hope to do so?"

Since we are powerless to protect our children from experiencing painful life events, the best protection we can offer them is support and guidance and a healthy model for handling those events. Understanding our own very normal feelings under circumstances of intense stress is critical to our ability to carry out this support and guidance. It enables us to be emotionally honest with our kids ("I'm crying because I'm sad about Granddad's illness—crying makes me feel better for a while") and it helps us to be effective emotional coaches for them as well ("You look like you're worried about Mommy—are you upset to see Mommy cry?"). Moreover, being aware of our feelings helps us to meet our own needs more effectively—needs for rest, support, release, nurturing or whatever. Meeting our needs helps us to maintain "a full tank"; instead of trying to parent "on empty," we can actually have the necessary reserves to do a good job.

Personal stress and parenting stress can challenge adults to the hilt. Both can interfere with parenting. Let's look now at the kinds of intense stress that parenting itself can generate in adults.

Parenting Can Trigger Deep Wells of Pain

Parenting can trigger deep pain. At its worst, it can provoke feelings of overwhelming confusion, stark terror, blinding rage and heartbreaking agony—some of the most powerful negative emotions experienced in life's journey. Fortunately, these emotions are not the daily fare of parenting; however, they can and do afflict most parents at some point in their two or three decades of childrearing.

Not all of this pain is caused by the child. Much of it—most of it, in fact—is only triggered by the child and is actually caused by the parent's life history and genetic make-up. What is the difference between pain "caused" by the child and pain "triggered" by the child? In the former case, the child's situation is fully responsible for the suffering of the parent. For example, when a child's life—Heaven forbid—is threatened by illness, the child "causes" a certain amount of parental pain. If we were to measure that pain on a 10-point scale, where 10 is the highest level, this kind of event is typically a 10. In the case of triggered pain, however, the child's actual situation may objectively rate only 1 to 6 on the parental pain scale, but the parent subjectively experiences this pain as an 8 to 10. For example, consider this mother's reaction to her daughter's social difficulties:

> *When Kaitlin told me that she stands all alone in the schoolyard at recess, my heart nearly broke. I also had trouble making friends when I was in school and I know what she's feeling. This is the last thing I want for my child. I want her to be popular, to have lots of friends— not suffer like I did. I feel completely devastated.*

This mother has a very intense reaction to her daughter's difficult experience—perhaps an 8 or 9 on a 10-point scale. And yet, outsiders (such as a spouse, for example!) may be quick to point out that the child's experience is "not so terrible." As so commonly happens, the child's pain triggers or reminds this parent of her own unhealed wounds. Indeed, if parents have not completely resolved the pain of their own traumatic incidents and painful childhood events (through self-help or professional psychotherapy), they have "minefields" just waiting to be triggered by their children's personal challenges. An overweight child can trigger deep feelings of helplessness and humiliation in a parent who—despite being normal weight as an adult—has never recovered from the hurts endured in the experience of childhood obesity. A child who does poorly in school can trigger old feelings of paralyzing inferiority in an adult who still harbors painful memories of repeated academic failure. Indeed, all of a parent's unresolved issues create potential hazards in parenting, often rendering the parent emotionally incapable of properly helping the child negotiate the difficulty. Almost always, pain that a parent would rate as 5 or more on a 10-point scale is triggered pain—pain and anguish that stems more from the parent's personal issues than from the child's personal challenge. Overcoming triggers is an important task, since only when parents are not triggered can they maintain emotional stability in the face of their child's pain. This stability enables them to be effective emotional coaches and problem solvers.

Jordan's been in pretty bad shape ever since he found out that he failed his first year of law school. I'd say he is depressed—and I can't blame him; he worked so hard, day and night, and then…this. But I know he'll get through it. He'll need some time, but I know he'll rally and try again. I'm sure he'll do better next year. Meanwhile, I'm just trying to be there for him. He knows he can talk to me.

The triggered parent would probably be more depressed than Jordan, co-dependently feeling all of Jordan's pain and rushing to cheer him up with promises of a brighter future. However, the untriggered parent maintains patience, confidence and optimism, even in the face of great trials. Like a midwife attending a hysterical woman in labor, this parent holds a calm, objective perspective and a helpful set of skills. There are ways for parents to reach this place of emotional equanimity. The road begins with awareness. Let's heighten our awareness, then, by examining some of the common, intensely negative feelings experienced in parenting, both those that are caused and those that are triggered by one's children.

Shame

Shame can occur for many reasons in parenting. As we saw earlier, feelings of inadequacy can lead to shame. When a principal reprimands a parent for having an out-of-control child, the parent may feel helpless, inadequate and ashamed. Of course, the reprimand can be a simple as, "Mrs. Jones, I have to tell you that your son has skipped six classes this week," spoken in a disapproving tone. Had the principal said the same statement in a sympathetic tone, as in, "It's so hard being a parent sometimes, isn't it?" the parent might actually feel supported rather than reprimanded. However, since principals sometimes speak to parents as if they were directly responsible for a child's bad behavior, parents often do feel real shame. Moreover, principals are quite likely triggering a parent's childhood memories or fears of being in trouble at school—the parent feels small again, talking to a principal.

Out of the shame, induced by the communication with the school, can come the parental shriek: "Your principal called again today and I'm getting absolutely SICK of it, do you understand?" Shame has an odd way of reducing emotionally intelligent parenting.

Shame also occurs when a child has any sort of "invisible" disability. In some cases, such disability remains the family secret; in other cases, the child's inadequate functioning at school reveals an "inexplicable" condition. Since the child looks normal, why is he or she under-functioning? For example, a child who appears perfectly normal may have ADHD (attention deficit/hyperactivity disorder), OCD (obsessive-compulsive disorder), Asperger's Syndrome or any other mental health challenge. For some reason, people accept physical disabilities as part of life and don't blame parents for creating handicapped or challenged offspring. However, others—including some professionals in the mental health field—seem to point a finger at parents whose children have emotionally based disorders. Modern research indicates that genetics may play a role in all such syndromes, but environment has also been implicated in the development and maintenance of mental health issues. Consequently, parents may feel shame when their child has been diagnosed with a mental health issue. Having to see a child psychologist or family therapist can be stigmatizing, despite the fact that the experience can be one of the most positive growth events in a parent's life. While parents wait for society to become enlightened regarding mental health problems and their solutions, they may harbor resentment toward the child for being unwell. Moreover, they often carry the burden of shame during the course of the child's development.

> My friends' kids are all graduating from high school this year and moving on to college. Steve has to make up about 10 credits in order to get his diploma and he doesn't show any signs of wanting to do it. He spends a lot of time sleeping, staying out late at night and doing nothing. We feel he's too young to leave home, but he isn't applying himself to his schoolwork and he's not looking for a job. I'm sure he's lost, maybe even depressed, but when we try to speak to him about

*what's going on, he won't open up. We honestly don't know what to
do with him. He probably feels terrible, watching his friends move
forward and, to tell you the truth, it's really hard for us to face our
own friends when they ask what university he's going to next year.*

Shame can occur whenever one's child doesn't look right or act appropriately. The child is seen as an extension of oneself—an uncontrollable extension. It can be mortifying for parents to expose their child to the judging eyes of the community.

*Carly is 40 pounds overweight at just 10 years old. I know she's teased
by the kids at school and I feel terrible for her. But when I have to go
out with her in public I also feel tormented. I feel like people are pointing the finger at me, blaming me for not being able to control my
child's eating habits. I feel so much shame and then I feel shame for
feeling shame—after all, she is my own daughter. And of course, all
I try to do is control her eating—so much so that our relationship is
scarred by all the "help" I give her.*

*I always looked forward to being a parent, but since Elliot was born
my life has been one big mess. He screamed non-stop for the first nine
months; he just would not be soothed by either Michael or me. I'd see
everyone else holding a cooing little babe in their arms, and there
would be Elliot, purple in the face, foaming at the mouth and totally
inconsolable. I felt like a terrible mother. But that's nothing compared
to how I feel since Elliot started daycare. The other parents drop their
kids off, wave good-bye and that's it. Not us! We have to peel him off
our shirts while he screams at the top of his lungs every single morning. We get such looks from the other parents! Michael and I are both
mortified. And I'm actually afraid that the neighbors will call the child
abuse hot line because of all the screaming that goes on at home in the
evening around bedtime—I'm sure they think we're beating him. I
can't look anyone in the eye when we meet in the street.*

Feelings of shame can cause parents to over-react to their kids. Catching her obese daughter munching on corn chips after returning from a shopping expedition can cause Mom to "lose it" completely: "I can't believe you're eating that after our shopping trip! Didn't you see how hard it is to find clothes for you? Do you want it to be that hard for the rest of your life? You need to go on a serious diet—not stuff your face with junk food!"

This parent's "educational" speech is driven by shame and helplessness. It is likely to be more harmful than helpful to her daughter's long-term eating patterns. Healing shameful emotions helps prevent destructive parenting outbursts; techniques for doing so will be explored in this chapter and in Appendix A.

Guilt

Guilt is a parental favorite.

Guilt is actually the feeling induced by an internal voice—the internal "critic." This part of the personality reprimands other parts, causing them to feel guilty. For example, the internal dialogue might sound something like this:

> "I": *I feel very annoyed at Leslie.*
> Internal critic: *You shouldn't feel annoyed at him—he's just a little boy and can't help making messes, beating up his sister and calling you names.*
> "I": *Yes, you're right. I'm really a bad parent for being annoyed.*

Internal dialogues like this one happen covertly, just below our conscious awareness. However, they cause very real feelings—like guilt. It is possible to "turn the volume up" on these inside conversations by purposely trying to induce guilt. Just talk to yourself out loud, with the intention of making yourself feel really guilty. Use the word "you" when addressing yourself. ("You are mean to your children! You are a bad parent!") The process involved in doing that will mirror the process that is actually going on inside. (Once the process is noted, it can be changed, as we will see in a moment.)

The guilt-inducing process can be triggered by so many parenting experiences—some within the parent's control and some outside of it. Parents can blame themselves for almost anything! They can blame themselves for giving birth to a challenged child—whether that challenge is a major physical, mental or emotional disability or a common challenge like attention deficit disorder, learning disabilities, chronic negativity, pervasive fearfulness or any other difficulty in functioning or feeling. They feel that they themselves have somehow created the genetic and temperamental templates of their offspring, and have done a bad job of it! When a child is deeply challenged by life, parents can feel crushing guilt for bringing the youngster into this world.

Parents can also feel guilty for actions taken by their children. For example, parents can feel guilty because their older child chooses not to marry or have children, or because their teenager is struggling with sexual orientation, or because their young child "hates" his siblings. Parents often blame themselves when their children fail to measure up in some way, thinking that their poor parenting is the cause of the failure. (Review the concept of inadequacy in Chapter 12.) The child's choices, feelings and actions are somehow experienced as being the parent's fault.

Although the child's genetic profile and personal behavior are both factors that are obviously beyond a parent's control, words spoken and actions performed by the parent are relegated to the domain of real personal responsibility. This is the area in which parents act badly or wrongly *of their own free will*. There are factors that influence poor parenting episodes, such as being exhausted, overwhelmed, stressed, emotionally aroused, uninformed, unsupported and, of course, being badly programmed by one's own parents, but the bottom line is that a parent can "blow it." Upon reflection, the parent can see that an error has been made. This awareness often opens the door to guilty feelings, triggered by the guilt-inducing process. The inner dialogue may sound like this: "Why did I say that? Why didn't I just walk out of the room? Why do I let myself get out of control?"

In addition to suffering over errors made in the parenting moment, parents can blame themselves for choosing the life they live. For example, they can blame themselves for marrying the person they married, for staying married, for getting divorced, for making bad choices, for living where they live, for moving too many times, for having too many children, for not having enough children and for any number of other parenting "crimes."

Since life is just one large learning experience, it is characterized by constant experimentation and error. Adults, like kids, make mistakes regularly; some are avoidable, some unavoidable, some are fixable and some permanent, some serious and some inconsequential. Sometimes, a small amount of guilt can be helpful for the correction of an error (feeling badly for yelling at the kids can provide motivation for taking a parenting course or otherwise improving the situation). However, large amounts of guilt can be debilitating rather than helpful, paralyzing rather than motivating. Indeed, intense guilt can both lead to and be a symptom of clinical depression.

Besides feeling guilty for actions they've performed, parents can feel guilty for feelings they've felt. For example, they can feel guilty for feeling angry, upset, frustrated, disturbed, impatient, depressed, frightened or any other negative emotion. In fact, many parents expect themselves to feel loving, tolerant, patient, emotionally balanced and compassionate 24 hours a day—and then feel guilty when they don't!

In addition to the daily disappointing feelings that parents feel, there are sometimes "horrific" feelings that occur in parenting. Although these are normal and even common, they are not generally discussed because of the great shame they carry. Parents feel terribly guilty for this set of thoughts and emotions.

> *I know this is an awful thing to say, but I wish Melissa would just disappear, leave home, get out of my life. I can't take it anymore; I can't deal with her abuse, her acting out and her violence. I just want her to go away. Our home would be so much happier without her.*

You've probably never heard anyone admit something like this—I feel terribly guilty for thinking it—but I think we'd all be better off without Jason. He's made so many suicide attempts; each one is unbearable for him and for us. I've died a thousand deaths on the inside. Now I get panic attacks whenever I hear his voice; I have nightmares when I sleep, but a lot of the time I can't sleep. I'm always worrying about him. If he's gone out for too long, I picture him dead somewhere. I can't take any more of this. I feel constantly tormented. I don't even want to help him anymore; I'm exhausted. He'd be at peace and so would we if he would just do it already.

Feelings like these are the natural byproduct of extreme parental burnout and overwhelming pain. Nonetheless, parents often feel alarmed, ashamed and guilty when their utter exhaustion and despair expresses itself this way. Sometimes, like children, they are afraid that their "bad thoughts" will "make bad things happen." Obviously, feeling at the end of one's rope and fantasizing about freedom is not the same as plotting murder. The reality is that even when completely emotionally and physically drained, parents usually continue to struggle along with their kids.

Although all parents hold great hopes and dreams for their babies, many will suffer unbearable agony and despair in parenting before their child has completed his second decade. A child's serious and unrelenting illness, dysfunction, emotional problem or behavioral issue can tax parents beyond their ability to cope. To make matters worse, instead of supporting themselves through these intense emotions, parents often hold themselves to the impossible standard of the continuously patient, constantly happy, unconditionally loving, always energetic, endlessly giving and forgiving, forever strong, forever optimistic parent. The result is an additional burden of suppressed emotions, nervous strain and heavy guilt. Adults endure their hard parenting experiences more successfully when they learn how to face and process their own emotional pain.

Despair

The last of the "heavy" emotions we will examine is despair, and its cousins: hopelessness, depression and misery. Considering that one expects parenting to be a joyous experience, it is almost shocking to find this gruesome cluster of feelings in a list of common parenting emotions. In fact, some people who are enjoying the toddlerhood of their first and second children might consider these kinds of feelings to be freak exceptions, belonging only to a rare population of disturbed parents. Would that it were so!

Perfectly normal parents, trying their best to raise a healthy family, can encounter such emotions when their parenting efforts fail—particularly if the failure triggers old, unresolved feelings from the past. Sometimes the efforts involved are directed to the routine aspects of parenting, such as getting children to sleep through the night or conquering one's personal yelling habit.

> *I feel like such a failure. I go to all the parenting classes and read every book I can get my hands on, but I just can't seem to stop raising my voice at the kids. I'm good for a few days after I take a parenting course, but then I fall back to my old ways. I'm so afraid my children will hate me the way I hate my mother. And I'll deserve it, because I'm treating them the same way she treated me. It's just so hopeless—I should never have had kids.*

When an adult brings a history of failure, loss, abuse or depression to the job of parenting, the normal frustrations and disappointments of the task can balloon into overwhelming difficulties. Indeed, any troubled emotional history can be triggered by parenting events and lead to intensely negative feelings.

> *My father used to terrorize all of us—he was a violent man with a mean temper. Even my mother was afraid of him. Now, when Bill*

starts up with me, I get sick to my stomach. I know he's only a kid, but he's bigger than I am and when things don't go his way he slams doors and says awful things. I feel like I'm living my childhood all over again and I want to run away. I get very depressed sometimes.

Parenting involves hard work: building relationships, handling discipline, teaching a skill set for life. Things often go well, but sometimes go poorly. It is only natural to feel discouraged, distressed and disappointed at times. And when trying circumstances, past history and genetic disposition intersect, the heavier emotions of despair and devastation can also make their presence known.

There are some situations in parenting, however, that can trigger intense negative emotions even in the absence of previous history and genetic disposition. Despair sets in for almost everybody when cherished hopes and dreams depart. Parents have specific goals for their children, even if they have not always articulated these goals. However, when a child deviates strongly from the parent's path, parents can feel devastating loss and pain. For example, devoutly religious parents sometimes have to come to terms with their child's abandonment of the religious life. Heterosexual parents whose belief system does not permit options sometimes have to deal with a child's homosexual orientation. Highly educated parents may have to resign themselves to their child's refusal to go to university. Depending on how important these values and expectations are to a parent, the child's rejection of them can cause anything from mild disappointment to major grief. Loss of one's most prized values, however, can be devastating.

Family is really important to me. I always assumed that my kids would all come home to visit after they married and had children of their own. I expected everyone to be gathered around my table for the holidays. But Ronnie stopped talking to his dad three years ago and hasn't stepped in our house since. I've kept up a relationship with him—we never had any problems. But Steve and Ronnie have always clashed and their relationship finally blew up when Steve

*threw Ronnie out of the house for doing drugs. I thought it would
be a temporary thing, maybe a couple of weeks. But Ronnie hasn't
been back since. All of our holidays are celebrated now without him.
I feel like part of me has died. My family is broken up. My heart is
ripped in half.*

There are many kinds of dreams that can die along the way during the parenting journey. Normal hopes and expectations can be dashed by a child's developmental difficulties, throwing parents into a traumatic reassessment of their child's place and potential in this world. Parents who learn that their child will never function normally go through the full cycle of grieving, including denial, anger, bargaining and mourning. This learning can occur moments after birth, setting parents on a vastly different course than the one they so happily planned for. But it can also occur very gradually as a child develops, arriving in spurts and stops. Sometimes it seems that the child will be fine, and then he or she has a sudden setback; the child's recovery is followed by yet another setback. Each setback deepens the fear of the parent that perhaps all is not well and will not be well. However, as time goes by, fear may be replaced by certain knowledge that the child is not okay. At that point of final awareness and acknowledgment, despair can set in.

*We took Mindy to a lot of specialists when she was young. Some said
she was normal, just not very motivated. Some said she had attention deficit disorder. But then her school performance would pick up
and we'd forget there was ever a problem. Next thing you know, she
wasn't doing her work again—she'd just lie around. We went to more
specialists. Someone said it was chronic fatigue syndrome. Someone
else suggested depression; she was only 12 years old at the time. But
she always seemed to get over these spells—I certainly never thought
there was anything seriously wrong. But now it's clear that Mindy
isn't like other teenagers. She's been on all kinds of medications—
nothing really helps. We're still not even sure about her diagnosis. But*

our hopes for her future have gotten narrower and narrower. Where we once thought she could be a brain surgeon if she wanted to, now we're hoping she'll just be able to function. It's incredibly hard for us—we never imagined our child would be like this.

Feelings of despair, hopelessness, depression and misery can significantly affect parenting. Sometimes they increase irritability, leading to snappiness or inappropriate outbursts of anger. Temper may be directed at any member of the family, not just the challenging child. On the other hand, these feelings sometimes lead to withdrawal, causing parents to detach from parenting so as to decrease the pain they feel. This strategy, while helping the parent survive overwhelming emotion, is a form of neglect as far as the children are concerned.

Because parenting is an intense, demanding vocation, adults need to come to it with all resources intact. Let's look at ways for parents to effectively meet the challenge of all of these intensely negative emotions, removing their potentially debilitating effects on family life.

Healing Intense Emotions

Intensely negative emotions occur while one is a parent—either because of conditions in one's personal life or marriage, or because of situations triggered by parenting itself. These emotions, when unattended to, wreak havoc with family life. They can lead parents to parent poorly and to provide a poor model of adult coping. It is part of parenthood, then, to learn how to process and heal these kinds of emotions. By being competent at negotiating the darker side of life, parents will be able to continue effective parenting even under stress and duress. Moreover, they will model necessary survival tools for their youngsters, thereby helping their children acquire the gift of resilience in the face of life's difficulties.

So how does one actually help oneself during times of intense stress? How does one transform negative emotions, preserve energy and ultimately move from deep negativity back to joy? Although the passage of time sometimes helps, children cannot wait a year or a decade for parents to recoup. It is unfortunate for them if they even have to wait an hour for a parent to regain emotional balance! More active interventions are necessary if a parent wishes to avoid unnecessary harm to bystander children.

Professional Help

Intensely negative emotion that lasts more than a few weeks, or that recurs with some frequency, can almost always be effectively resolved with professional counseling. Modern parents do not wait for a nervous breakdown! They seek counseling long before they are overwhelmed by stress and grief. Early intervention with a psychotherapist (psychologist, social worker, counselor, etc.) can restore equilibrium, heal psychological vulnerabilities and wounds, prevent further stress, and also prevent the need for medical or psychiatric treatment at a later date. If "early" can no longer apply, late intervention speaks to the dictum: better later than never! When seeking professional help, the normal rules of shopping apply: do research to select a small list of appropriate potential service providers and then follow up with comparison shopping. If one counselor is not for you, this does not mean that counseling is not for you. People patiently shop for the right dentist, the right sofa and the right car, pursuing the search until they're satisfied. The same steps are required to find the right mental health provider. Sometimes medical intervention is a helpful adjunct to counseling. A professional psychologist or other licensed psychotherapist can make an appropriate assessment and referral when necessary. Family physicians and psychiatrists may also assess, treat and refer to other services.

Self-Help

Temporary and fleeting feelings of despair, anguish and other intensely negative emotions may be amenable to self-treatment. There are many types of interventions to choose from, only a few of which are described in this section. In addition, a specific self-help procedure for clearing deep emotional pain is offered in Appendix A.

One way of helping oneself with deep emotional pain is called "clearing the feeling." In order to clear it, it must first be located. A feeling can be found by noticing its effect on the body. Intensely negative emotions are experienced as actual physical sensations in various parts of the body, most often somewhere in the central core affecting the throat, chest, stomach or back. Feelings press against the heart, the head, the shoulders or other parts of the body. They can be felt as aches in each of those areas (heartache, headache, etc.) or they can be felt as an all-over weakness, sick feeling or emptiness. Although various pills, foods, beverages and activities can temporarily block the physical sensations of negative emotion, they cannot permanently release it. Release comes by attending to the feeling and helping it. There are lots of ways to do this. They all begin with finding the feeling and just accepting that it is there. Just being friendly toward it initiates a healing process. However, for those who want to effect a profound healing of a disturbed emotion, you can use the following technique. It takes a little imagination and only a few minutes.

After you've located the feeling, name it. Remember that there are only five main possibilities: happy, sad, mad, scared or confused. There are lots of shades of each category, of course, so if you happen to know the shade of emotion, then name it (e.g., "crushed" is a shade of sad; "enraged" is a shade of mad). See Appendix B for a list of feelings and their shades. Next, see if you can get a picture or a sense of the feeling by imagining how this emotion could be represented through one or more of the five senses (appearance, sound, texture, etc.). For example, suppose you are dealing with a "devastated" feeling. To get a sense of the word "devastated" you can ask yourself, "how might a person, animal or object appear when it is devastated?" Whatever image pops up is the image you will use. Perhaps it looks like a small crying child or a broken old man. Maybe it would be best captured as someone flattened on the ground. Maybe it is a devastated landscape after a tsunami. Once you've created a fitting image for your feeling, greet it. ("Hello, I see/sense you there. I'm here with you.") Now, offer to help the feeling. Simply ask the image what it needs and wait to receive an answer (don't think; just wait—your subconscious mind will do the work for you). Sometimes these wounded feelings just want to tell their story. Sometimes they need to be held. A broken old man may want a bed, blanket and tender comfort. Someone flattened on the ground may need to be put on a hospital bed with intravenous and nursing support. A tsunami may need to run its course and then settle down. Imagine yourself providing whatever the feeling needs (you can "watch" the scene unfold just as if you were watching a movie screen).

The act of "watching" this inner movie makes a deep impact on your subconscious mind. You may be amazed to find your feeling and your physical sensations changing. Changes made with the power of imagination tend to be deep and lasting ones. You can work with your emotions this way throughout life to help maintain emotional, mental and physical health. For more in-depth instructions on similar inner healing techniques, see the resource section in Appendix C.

After spending some time with the inner world of feelings, enough healing may occur to move on to the next step of self-help: making real-life changes that support further healing and recovery. Feelings in the sad category—the kinds of deep despair and anguish discussed in this chapter—usually signal some sort of weariness and loss; they need significant rest, and an eventual replacement of whatever is missing. You will know when the resting period is over and when the replacement period is beginning. It is best to follow your own feelings about this instead of listening to the instructions of other people. When you are ready, you will have the necessary energy to engage in the replacement process. Often, replacement involves something that can replenish energy and joyfulness in living. The individual follows his or her feeling to find what will work: spiritual activities, interpersonal relationships, community endeavors, creative undertakings, personally comforting and rejuvenating activities—the soul needs nourishment and refreshment after enduring hard, stressful assaults.

Other Self-Help Measures

In addition to emotional clearing of painful feelings, there are other sound steps that can be taken. Seeking support from friends can be very helpful. Seeking support within the context of a parenting group can be especially healing, informative and validating. There are also 12-step groups of every kind—parents may find the ones for codependency or emotional issues particularly relevant and helpful. Often a parenting book can offer perspective, tools and validation. Spiritual sources of support can be particularly strengthening—now may be the time to renew or discover the power of nourishing the soul.

Naturopathic support can strengthen the mind, body and emotions to deal with heavy stress. In the case of enduring deep states of emotional distress, this support should be used in conjunction with professional psychological counseling. For fleeting but intensely negative emotions, naturopathic support can be used in conjunction with emotional self-help tools. Bach Flower Therapy treats all troubled emotions, including deep despair, guilt, rage, depression, anxiety, resentment, shame, overwhelm and so forth. (See Chapter 13 for more information about Bach Flower Therapy.) Bach Flower essences can be used along with any other medical or naturopathic treatment. Acupressure, homeopathy, aromatherapy, herbal medicine, massage and many other body-based treatments can help the release and reduction of emotional stress and speed up other psychologically based interventions.

Good self-care always helps in the achievement of balanced emotions and perspective. Sleep, exercise, relaxation, pleasure and regular breaks are all important. Stretching exercises are particularly effective in the release of deep stress and tension. Personal trainers, exercise books and videos are all available sources of education for your stress-recovery program. During times of deep emotional crisis, many people abandon all self-care routines. Skipping one or two days of lifestyle management is fine—longer periods of self-neglect lead to longer periods of emotional recovery. Lack of sleep especially tends to aggravate, prolong and worsen any emotional pain. All of the interventions discussed can help stressed people get a decent night's sleep and thereby quicken their recovery.

Living with Difficult Feelings

As King Solomon said, "This, too, shall pass." Helping oneself through the hard times by using self-care strategies yields a twofold benefit: it provides a coping model for children while it enhances the actual ability of the adult to cope. Coping while raising children is essential, since long-term lack of coping will inevitably cause harm. When the going gets tough, the tough get going—by using self-help and professional help as necessary.

CHAPTER 16

Parenting in Action: Questions and Answers

QUESTION: My 4-year-old likes to play at his friends' houses, but when I come to pick him up, he doesn't want to go home. He puts up a big fuss and I find it very embarrassing in front of the other mothers. Nothing I say seems to make a difference to him. What should I do?

ANSWER: It's not surprising that nothing you say to him makes a difference. In parenting, the general rule is "talk less; do more." Children's behavior rarely changes because of what we say to them. The routine lack of success of repeated requests (nagging) especially proves this point.

To help your child leave more gracefully, try the CLeaR Method first (comment, label reward). Go straight up to him, put your hand gently on his shoulder (or hand him his sweater/jacket, if he has one) and quickly say, "You're getting ready to leave now—that's great! You're a very cooperative young man today, aren't you? I think this deserves a special story right when we get home." Some kids will go for this approach and some won't. If yours does, continue doing the same thing every time he leaves a friend's house for the next month. Start "thinning" the reward to every other visit for a few times, and then even less often until there's no need for a reward at all. Keep up the praise indefinitely. If your child does not respond positively to your strategy, let your inner compassionate parent pat you on the back for trying! Your inner parent will sit down with you later on and draw up a strategy using the 2x Rule.

252

QUESTION: I have tried the CLeaR Method with my son to help him leave his friends' homes more gracefully, and had no success. What would the 2x Rule look like in this situation?

ANSWER: Step 1 would be an information statement like this: "It's not acceptable to run away from Mommy when she comes to get you from your friend's house, because this makes it hard and tiring for Mommy and uncomfortable for your friends and their mommies. When Mommy comes, you need to say good-bye and thank you, and come quickly with me." This sentence would be said, even though you've already told him "a thousand times." Always carry out Step 1 formally.

The next time he fails to cooperate upon leaving, do Step 2 when you've got a private moment together. Repeat what you said at Step 1 and add this warning: "From now on, when you run away instead of coming quickly, you will lose visiting privileges for your next play-date; you'll have to stay home with Mommy for that time." (You would choose this negative consequence as a ticket only if you think it would be "worth $100" to your child. If not, pick something else.)

Step 3 involves applying that same consequence on three occasions and noting whether the behavior seems to be improving. If it is, continue with this consequence until he's grown up (just kidding—use it as long as necessary and as long as it works). If it doesn't seem to be making a difference, announce a different ticket and try that one for three times. Continue experimenting with tickets as necessary, until you find the one that motivates him to cooperate.

QUESTION: My child doesn't respond to any rewards or punishments that I give him. There's nothing I can do to affect his behavior. What should I do?

ANSWER: Some children are indeed difficult to reward or punish. This small group of children seem to need more intense rewards and punishments than other kids. They also need more time to respond to them. If you have one of these children, you'll need lots of patience.

Rest assured, however, that your child will respond. The trick is to use the same punishment for 10 times, rather than the usual three. After 10 times with no change in behavior, choose another ticket and use that one for 10 times. Continue until you find the ticket that works. In order to assure a viable source of tickets, do not give these children too many unearned privileges. For instance, in some homes children are allowed to watch T.V. after school. If you have a hard-to-reward/punish child, don't just allow T.V. Make it an earned privilege (reward). Do this for almost every form of entertainment and relaxation—video time, computer time, telephone time and so forth. Give your unconditional positive attention in the form of words ("I love you" messages), hugs, listening, emotional coaching, quality time and other venues, but not in the form of privileges. This helps the child have a reason to cooperate with you (i.e., if he wants any fun in life!). With this group of children, it is also a good idea to avoid head-on confrontations by limiting the issues you decide to fight over. Drop as much as you can, take the pressure off, and address only priority issues. Read Dr. Ross Greene's book, *The Explosive Child*, for an array of effective interventions with inflexible, hard-to-reach children.

QUESTION: I have a hard time getting my kids into bed at night. The process takes hours; at the end of it, I'm exhausted and completely drained. Help!

ANSWER: It's always preferable to try a "good-feeling" technique first. You might try a reward chart for this one. Break up the bedtime routine into several steps. Let's say you include items like washing up (face and/or bath), brushing teeth, getting into pajamas, being ready for story-time, and being under the covers by bedtime. On Round 1 of your chart, each child who goes to wash promptly when asked only once, earns a point. (For children who are old enough to tell time, simply designate a time by which this should be accomplished.) After 5 points are accumulated, the first prize is received. Round 2 of the chart requires both washing up and brushing teeth when asked only once. Again, the child works to acquire 5 points. Round 3 adds pajamas to the task; the prize keeps increasing as well. Continue this way until the child reaches the stage where you say "bedtime" once, and he or she goes to wash up, brush teeth, change into pajamas, and gets ready for story, after which he/she gets under the covers ready for sleep without a fuss. When the child accomplishes this last part, give the "grand prize"—something really special.

After you've finished the reward chart, maintain the behavior with lots of praise and positive programming. Every night for years on end, be prepared to say, "Wow! You're ready so quickly! That's great! You're so responsible/independent/quick/self-reliant/cooperative" or whatever positive adjective you choose.

If the behavior reverts back to a struggle, use the 2x Rule:

- At Step 1, explain that we do not ignore our parents when we're told to get washed up for bed because the parents are tired and don't like to fight. We go right away when our parents ask us to.
- At Step 2, repeat this statement and add a warning of a specific consequence if the child doesn't go within three minutes of being asked.
- At Step 3, apply the consequence if necessary.

For example, you could say, "From now on, when you don't start your bedtime routine on time, I will have to come help you get started and you will lose your story as a result."

QUESTION: My child goes to bed on time, but then comes out of his room to get me every 10 minutes. He always wants something—he says he has to go to the bathroom or he needs some water or he forgot his toy and so on. What can I do? I wouldn't want him to wet his bed!

ANSWER: Make sure that your child goes to the bathroom, has his drink and gets what he needs *before* his actual bedtime. Finish all of your routines (reading, talking, hugging, cuddling, etc.). Apply a consequence for leaving the room. Here's one idea. Once bedtime has arrived, the child may call you or leave his bed, but if he does so, he will be asked to stand in the corner for five minutes. The second time he calls, he stands in the corner for seven minutes. The third time he comes or calls, he stands in the corner for nine minutes. Keep increasing corner time by two minutes until the child gets tired enough to go to sleep. Repeat this each night until Junior learns that bedtime is bedtime.

QUESTION: My child is very emotional. Every day she has a problem with her friends or her teachers that makes her cry. I do emotional coaching but it doesn't help—she remains unhappy and is inconsolable. I don't know what to do anymore.

ANSWER: You may have to experiment a bit here. A general principle in providing emotional support is: give excellent support the first time the problem is presented, pretty good support the second time (and ask the child what solutions she is applying or help her create some), give minimal support thereafter. Remember that emotional coaching is an intense form of positive attention. It can accidentally reinforce "having a problem." If Suzy complains bitterly that her friends rejected her on Monday, she certainly deserves emotional coaching for this painful problem. She needn't be "consoled" or "cheered up." That is not the point of emotional coaching. On the contrary, emotional coaching is meant to show a child that the parent can accept her painful feelings and just "sit" with them without needing to change them into "better" feelings. After coaching, the parent can help the child find solutions to her social problems. On Tuesday, when the child comes home with the same troubles, the parent can coach again, this time a little shorter. Now the parent should focus on the solutions—what has been tried, what works and what doesn't work, what else could be done. The third day that Suzy has the same problem, the parent should acknowledge it supportively in one sentence only ("That's really difficult"), then express confidence that Suzy can apply the solutions she has, but that she needs to give it more time. The parent should only provide this sort of minimal attention for the problem from this point on, while lavishing positive attention in other areas of Suzy's life (her hobbies, her schoolwork, her family relationships, her community relationships or whatever). Suzy needs to feel that, while her parents care, they are definitely more interested in her areas of strength than in her problems.

If you've tried this approach for several weeks and your daughter's problems are not letting up, it could be that there are other issues that are bothering her at a deeper level. Could it be that she is responding to stress at home? Is anybody ill? Have you moved recently or have there been other changes? How is your marriage? Does she hear parental arguments? Is she aware of financial stress? Is one parent violent, depressed, addicted? How is her school setting—are there problems with the teacher or a particular bully? Children are often unable to express anxiety directly—instead, they act out a series of small difficulties. If you suspect that stress may be affecting her happiness, you might take her to a children's art therapist. Art therapy is a great medium for children—so much fun that they don't realize that they're involved in a serious treatment program. Family therapy or couple therapy may also be indicated.

If there are no obvious stresses in her environment, genetic or temperamental factors may be at play. Children can be born with a tendency toward depression and anxiety. A consultation with a child therapist, art therapist, psychologist, naturopath, flower practitioner or medical practitioner may be helpful.

QUESTION: My teenage daughter has suddenly become uncommunicative. She and I used to get along great, but now I don't know what's going on in her life at all. She spends all her time on the phone with her friends and doesn't even want to eat dinner with us anymore. If I press her to tell me what's happening, she either mumbles incoherently or is downright rude. How can I reach her?

ANSWER: Teenagers are a breed unto themselves. They are at an important stage of individuation—which means they're working on becoming separate individuals from their parents. In the first decade of childhood, children are busy learning about the value system of their parents. In the second decade, they broaden their scope to learn about the values of their peers and the world around them. By the end of the second decade, they will have formed a unique identity—a blend of what their parents have taught them and what they have learned from other sources: school, media, peer group and community.

As has been mentioned so many times in this book, the quality of the parent-child relationship strongly affects how much of your value-system your adult child will decide to accept. Although you are disturbed by your daughter's withdrawal, you do not want to harm whatever is left of the relationship by complaining incessantly. Nor is it the time to criticize her friends or her lifestyle—criticism is poison to any relationship. Rather, when you do see her, aim to make your communications positive. Joke around if possible. Compliment her outfits. Show obvious pleasure when she spends a few minutes with you. When she gets off the phone for a moment, mention how nice it is that she has so many friends. Don't intrude on her privacy—don't ask her who she is speaking to and what the conversation is about. Even if she seems to be making poor choices, recognize that she must learn through her own painful experiences, not through your lectures. Convey trust in her growth process. If she seems troubled, offer her help once and tell her the door is open anytime. Do not pry or pressure. When she passes you in the kitchen, trying to grab some food, ask her for help in solving one of your personal dilemmas—show her that you value her judgment. Thank her effusively for her opinion and later, give her positive feedback about how her advice worked out. Treat her with love and kindness, but *do not accept anything less from her*. If she speaks rudely, let her know that your feelings are hurt and that you don't speak to her that way and don't want her to speak to you that way. If she continues, there are many consequences that you can use with a teen—withdrawal of telephone privileges, computer privileges, car privileges, visiting privileges, allowance, and so on. Be very careful to use negative consequences only for the most serious transgressions—overuse can seriously threaten your relationship. Insist on little, but choose your battles. You can insist, for example, that she join you for dinner a certain number of evenings a week, that she help you with household responsibilities, that she keep regular hours, and so forth. However, you will not get what you want from a teenager unless your unconditional positive strokes are loud and clear. Remember to buy gifts for no reason, write love notes, do small favors. Help her to care about you and want to please you. However, also remember the limits of your control. Sometimes a child withdraws for a while and then renews interest in a relationship later on. Just do your part and pray.

QUESTION: My child hates vegetables. Every night we have a struggle at the dinner table. I absolutely insist that he eat at least one vegetable—I don't see how he will be healthy otherwise. My spouse disagrees with me, saying I shouldn't force him. What do you think?

ANSWER: This is a very common parenting question. Children seem to have different tastes in food than adults. Often their food preferences are seriously limited to a few choices. These choices may not be representative of all food types, but they almost always meet the minimal requirements for nutrition. Check with a professional nutritionist to see if your child's preferences will sustain him, and for ideas as how to disguise other foods so that they may be consumed more readily by your child.

What's worse for your child's health than lack of vegetables is routine fighting at mealtime. The stress this causes interferes with digestion, even if you do manage to force a bite of zucchini into him. No one should be forced to eat something unappealing. Would you like it if someone forced you to eat chicken livers for breakfast even if you weren't in the mood for them? To your child, your fancy meatloaf may be his morning chicken livers! Never force food. Rather, give prizes for "conducting experiments"—anyone who is willing to try a teaspoon of an unfamiliar or "unpreferred" food gets a small treat of some kind. Only do this if it feels like fun for your kids and does not create huge disappointment or pressure. Let your child eat in a relaxed, happy mood. This promotes well-being in the broadest sense. Do not offer sweets and snacks in between meals, but offer real food items like fruit, cheese, whole-grain crackers with cream cheese, toast, milk, macaroni and cheese, meatballs, eggs, fish sticks and pizza slices freely. Young children, in particular, often do better with "grazing"—eating short, frequent meals—than with full sit-down dinners. Almost every child grows into an adult who enjoys a wide variety of foods.

QUESTION: My child always fights me at homework time. He dawdles and dawdles and runs away. I just can't get him to sit down and concentrate for 10 straight minutes. What should I do?

ANSWER: Don't fight. (Surprised?)

Use the CLeaR Method: "Oh, I see you're getting your books ready to do your homework. That's really organized of you—and prompt this evening too! Good for you! I think that deserves a little treat when we finish, don't you?" You can also use lots of praise, emotional coaching and encouragement. "I know how you feel. I never liked homework either. Especially math—blah! What would make it more tolerable for you?" Another strategy would be utilizing fun and humor: "Do you want me to draw some funny pictures for you while you're doing it? No? Should I stand on my head and do somersaults? No? Then, you suggest an idea." (Remember, laughter always goes a long way—much further than nagging, lecturing, criticizing and other parental favorites.) You can also try games and rewards: "Would you like to try a mini-reward chart? We can put the buzzer on for five minutes and you work without complaint until it goes off. Each time the buzzer goes off, you'll get a sticker. Each sticker will be worth five minutes of a (game, movie, story, activity) after homework time." Finally, you can use the 2x Rule if necessary, punishing lack of cooperation. This should be your last choice after other positive interventions have failed. If you are too emotionally involved to be effective with any of these techniques, consider hiring a tutor and letting someone else take over!

QUESTION: I am raising two adolescents from my husband's first marriage and two younger children that we had together. The stepchildren have never really bonded to me and now express a lot of jealousy toward the younger two. In addition, they complain to their father that I am mean whenever I ask them to wash a dish or any small thing. I often feel like I am living in a hostile environment. I feel that I can't get any cooperation from the older girls, and I'm worried that my little ones will be affected by their obvious lack of respect for me.

ANSWER: There are so many issues to contend with in blended families. Older children often have great difficulty bonding with a stepparent. Who can blame them? What teenager wants a third (or in some cases, fourth!) parent? Two are hard enough for older kids to deal with! There can be all sorts of complicating factors as well, such as pain for the biological parent who is not a part of the new blended family unit, anger at one or both biological parents, upset at the divorce and, sometimes, dislike of the stepparent. Here are some guiding principles that may help you with your dilemma. To begin with, the 90-10 Rule is essential with every teenager. However, with adolescents who aren't your own, I suggest trying to get that closer to 95-5. Use your 5% to make simple requests and establish appropriate limits. Let the natural parents handle all routine discipline. (This would not be the case if your stepchildren were under 10; you would have to be involved in more direct guidance.) You have an opportunity to have a tremendously positive impact on these young people, who may be living in your home for almost a decade. You can do this through showing them a healthy marriage and a personal model of a mature, healthy and loving woman. Your ability to manage your own stress, frustration, anxiety and other negative emotions conveys powerful lessons to these young people. Even though they don't come to you for affection at this point, you are still a parent in that your presence in their lives will have lasting influence for good or for bad—and that is up to you, not them. Even if they are psychologically disturbed, immature and troubled, they can still see and hear you. Be careful not to use anger with them;

do not raise your voice, say unpleasant or unkind words, or otherwise model disturbed behavior of your own. Your small children will be saved from living in an ugly, conflictual environment. If your own children have questions as to a double standard that seems to be operating ("How come *they* never have to eat at the table with us?") you can answer truthfully: "They do things differently because they have their own mother and father—you two listen to the rules that your mommy and daddy make." In other words, don't pretend that everything is the same when it clearly isn't. As for the insecurities of the older ones, most will be rectified by a careful application of the 95-5 Rule. Buy those girls the occasional gift, make them the meals they enjoy, do small acts of kindness and show them compassion. How long will they be able to reject all that love? If they leave their plates on the table, ask their dad to take care of the issue until you feel that your relationship with them is strong enough to handle minor bad-feeling interactions like requests and instructions. Showing them that you understand their resentment of the situation by simply being patient and kind to them will eventually pay off. And even if it never draws them to you, you can rest assured that you did all that was possible. Many of the difficulties that stepparents experience have come as a result of their efforts to discipline and guide the older child. Once they take this task off their agenda, the difficulties melt away. Most importantly, and worth repeating once more: raise these children without raising your voice!

CHAPTER 17

Reaping the Rewards

Happy Parenting

When parents take the appropriate steps to release and relieve their stress, they bring renewed energy into their bodies and souls. There is room again for light-heartedness, humor and fun—the playful part of parenting. Children thrive in an upbeat atmosphere, as do their parents. Indeed, the sunshine of good humor feeds everyone's creativity, motivation, drive and zest for life. Happiness, like a rainbow after the storm, is a beautiful part of the tapestry of life. As we have seen, self-care, professional help and self-help are important actions that adults can take to access this important emotion. When raising children, one's good mood is not an optional personal luxury; rather, it is an essential ingredient in the healthy functioning of an entire household. It must be a consistent part of the parenting journey.

However, the storm itself is also an important part of life. Pain in every form can be—and should be—befriended as part of the normal flow of human emotion. When it is accepted, both in the parent and in the child, it moves in a healthy, life-affirming path. It brings each person to higher levels of maturity, integration and wisdom. It brings intimacy between those who can welcome and explore it together. Honoring painful emotions actually prevents destructive anger from coloring family life. Anger is usually a cover-up, hiding the more vulnerable hurting feelings beneath the surface. Addressing these feelings compassionately, both in ourselves and in our children, allows us to parent honestly and lovingly, without rage and angry defense.

Raise Your Kids Without Raising Your Voice

When all is said and done, one of the most important ingredients in the building of a healthy home is parental self-control: the ability to raise one's children without raising one's voice. Success comes with understanding what it takes to raise a human being, knowing the tools that create the best possible outcomes and clearing the emotional impediments to using those tools. The payoffs are enormous: peace and joy in childrearing and lifelong loving relationships. Even those who begin the process after many years of negativity will find that love has the capacity to heal old wounds and forge new pathways. It is never too late for those who are willing to address the pain and change their habits. On the contrary, it is always the right time to love.

As our children grow, so do we. By the time they're all grown up, we've learned a lot about ourselves and about life, about our power and about our limitations. Even before then, we learn daily about patience, about mood-management, about our deepest vulnerabilities and our greatest strengths, about self-control and about love. We teach our kids as we go along.

Our parenting journey is definitely more enjoyable and productive if we invite our inner compassionate parent along for the ride. Its patience with our impatience, and tolerance with our intolerance, helps us to be more gentle teachers to our children. It is the inner compassionate parent that supports us in our intention to raise our children without raising our voice; it is the part of us that knows that the source of power is love, and that anger betrays our weakness. It's the part that recognizes the destructive vibrations of harsh communications and the healing vibrations of respect. It can sit on our shoulder throughout the parenting day, praising our accomplishments and tapping us gently now and then to remind us to stay calm and loving toward our kids. We don't have to do this alone. This wisest, kindest and most understanding part of our inner family can light the path, providing love and healing both to ourselves and our children. In this way, we can raise ourselves as we raise our kids. The only thing we don't raise . . . is our voice!

Parenting Power Points:
A Summary

Follow the 80-20 Rule

Interactions between parent and child should feel pleasant *to the child* 80% of the time. That is, 8 out of 10 parental communications (including words, body language, facial expression and behaviors) should feel good to the child receiving them. When the 80-20 Rule is followed, children misbehave less often, have better relationships with their parents and enjoy higher self-esteem and its consequences. (The recommended ratio for teenagers is 90:10.)

Good-Feeling Communications

These include words of praise, acknowledgment, appreciation, positive labels, validation, sympathy, empathy (including naming feelings), support, humor, interest, sharing, concern, caring and love; body expressions such as smiles, holding, hugs, pats, massage and caresses; actions such as giving gifts or treats, making favorite meals, playing, doing acts of kindness, assisting, helping and listening. Love is conveyed with feel-good communications. In addition, almost all teaching and guiding should be done with feel-good communications (using the CleaR Method—comment, label, reward—and other forms of positive attention).

Bad-Feeling Communications

These include words of correction, criticism, reprimand, mockery, sarcasm, discounting, invalidation, complaint, threats, accusations, negative labels and other insults, instructions, requests and demands; body language such as frowns, angry faces, physical roughness, looks of distraction, disinterest, disapproval; actions such as disciplining, ignoring, hitting, slamming doors, hanging up, shouting, neglecting and abandoning. All of these can weaken the parent-child relationship.

Discipline Is Necessary; Anger Is Not

Discipline is an essential part of parenting, but must fit into the 10 or 20% allowance for "bad-feeling" interactions. When anger is regularly used as a tool to gain a child's cooperation, there are three typical consequences: severe damage to the parent-child relationship, loss of parental power, and damage to the child's personality. Effective discipline removes the need for anger.

The 2X Rule Is the Basis of Effective Discipline

Most discipline can be done with feel-good techniques. When it's necessary to use feel-bad strategies, proceed with caution. Pick your issues (to fit into the 20% allotment!). Don't ask many times and then scream. Use the 2x Rule: ask once. Ask a second time and give choice of compliance or negative consequence. Apply negative consequence if necessary.

Respect Is a Two-Way Street

Parents teach children how to interact successfully with people. Good modeling is required but is not enough. Parents must teach respectful behavior. The parent's motto: "I will treat you respectfully and I expect you to treat me respectfully."

Feelings and Behaviors Are Different

All feelings are acceptable—all behaviors are not. Parents name, accept and "be with" feelings—both their own and their children's. This process helps heal feelings, helps parents stay calm, builds love between parent and child, and improves children's behavior, health, emotional intelligence, academic functioning and social skills.

Techniques for
Emotional Healing

Energy Psychology

For the curious and the courageous, this section presents a revolu-
tionary self-help technique for the relief of emotional stress and the
prevention of anger. Used regularly to address any upset, anxiety or
bad mood—in fact, any state of physical or emotional discomfort—
this new technology helps break up old, dysfunctional neural pathways
in the brain (the ones that lead to angry outbursts, for example), replac-
ing them with healthier, stress-free structures. The result is greater calm,
happiness and serenity. Users report experiencing better moods and
improved physical health. Although more formal research is required
in order to establish the clinical effectiveness of this healing modality,those who suffer from stress-related health conditions such as skin
disorders, ulcers, fibromyalgia, arthritis, headaches, stomach disorders,
heart disease and high blood pressure often report that their conditions improve with the regular application of this stress-reducing technique. (We will now explore its specific use in childrearing.)

Abracadabra

Although parenting can be stressful at times, there is a way to almost
instantly reduce—and often completely remove—that stress. Whether

the problem is caused by a child who won't eat dinner or by a family tragedy, the cutting-edge techniques known collectively as Energy Psychology can help to rapidly resolve pain and promote recovery. These new techniques can be used as a self-help tool by older kids and adults and by parents to directly treat their small children. Energy Psychology helps lift worry, fear, frustration, disappointment, depression, anxiety, despair, moodiness, rage, confusion, resentment, jealousy and any other negative emotion. It can rapidly heal trauma, grief and loss. Teenagers find the techniques helpful for test anxiety, oral book reports and other performances, phobias, broken hearts, overwhelm, upsets, hormonal challenges, frightening experiences and many other issues. Parents can treat their younger children for separation anxiety, night-time fears, school refusal, homework stress, nightmares, tantrums, irritability, panic attacks, boredom, jealousy, upset, thumb sucking, bedwetting and all kinds of other challenges. And, of course, parents can use the techniques on themselves to heal and clear stress, anger and parenting pain.

There are numerous internet resources for Energy Psychology, several of which address the specific needs of children.

Acupressure for Emotional Healing

Energy Psychology techniques employ the body's meridian system—the pathways used for acupuncture and acupressure therapies. A person uses their fingers to tap lightly on the body at specific locations. Tapping itself gives nothing more than a pleasant massage. However, tapping on the right spot while tuned into a distressing thought, feeling and/or image can result in something like psychosurgery–the thoughts, feelings, images and body sensations can be permanently changed for the better. Distress is replaced with calm. The mind becomes clearer, solutions become obvious, problems lift and virtually disappear. Horrible memories melt away. Peace is restored. People are often truly amazed at the results of these simple procedures.

Acupuncture and acupressure have long been used to help stimulate physical healing. In recent decades, psychologist Dr. Roger Callahan discovered that acupressure could be used to stimulate profound emotional healing as well, and he developed a groundbreaking technique called Thought Field Therapy. Dr. Callahan's students went on to develop many variations of the technique. Although each one has a different name and protocol, they are all equally effective. Currently, research studies are assessing the clinical effectiveness of Energy Psychology techniques. However, world-wide reports from clients and other users of the techniques over the past fifteen years have confirmed the power of Energy Psychology to rapidly resolve emotional and even physical distress. These techniques are now being used in areas of war and natural disaster to help heal the deepest psychological scars experienced by mankind.

I am including a brief introduction to one form of Energy Psychology for you to use on yourself and your family. It is called WHEE, which stands for two different names: Whole Health–Easily and Effectively and Wholistic Hybrid of EMDR and EFT. The time required on your part to explore this new avenue of personal healing is minimal—a few minutes to learn the technique and a few minutes to apply it to yourself, your spouse or your child. If it works, it is then available for a lifetime of stress relief. If it doesn't, it can be put aside or explored later in greater depth through resources. You can learn all about WHEE at www.wholistichealingresearch.com.

What to Expect

Energy Psychology techniques take only minutes to apply. Before applying the technique, rate the intensity of your discomfort, upset or physical pain between zero (no discomfort) and 10 (extreme discomfort). After using the technique, rate the discomfort, upset or physical pain again. If the rating is lower or higher, this means the technique is working. (The number is sometimes higher because the real pain of the issue becomes clearer as a person is processing the emotion—treatment continues based on the new information revealed in the higher level of distress.) The change is caused by rapid psychological processing. If the rating remains the same, it's because the technique hasn't worked yet. In this case, massage a spot about two inches below the collarbone on the left side of the body, using your right hand. This area is called The Tender Spot, because it feels a bit tender or sore when rubbed. Massaging it for just a minute or so usually releases enough of an energetic block that the Energy Psychology technique will work the second time. If the technique still doesn't work after rubbing this spot yourself, you can engage an Energy Psychology professional practitioner. In fact, many people like to learn the technique from such a practitioner before using it on their own.

Improvement usually happens in stages. One round of treatment may cause a drop of 2 to 4 points on a 10-point scale. Thus, anger that was first rated as a 10 may become a 7 after one round of treatment. Continue with more rounds until you are at 0. Sometimes the emotion will seem to jump from one to another at the end of each round. For instance, a woman who starts off feeling very angry at her husband for not helping her with the children may be at a 10 for anger. After one round of treatment, she finds that her main feeling is now sadness, rather than anger. She rates her sadness at a 10. Since this is a different emotion from the one she started out with, we say that the treatment is working and rapid processing is occurring, even though she is still at 10. (If she was still at 10 with anger, however, we would say that she was energetically stuck and needed to rub that spot below the collarbone.) After her second round of treatment, she is no longer sad, but is now disappointed. She rates her disappointment at an 8. After this round of treatment she feels less disappointed—a 3. She is beginning to think of all the things that her husband does for her, even though he isn't helpful with the kids. After one more round, she is at 0 and feels totally calm. Since each round of treatment takes just seconds, the whole treatment takes only a few minutes.

Sometimes a person does go from 10 right to 0 in one round of treatment. More often, a few rounds are needed before reaching 0. After treatment, there are many common experiences. Most people have one or two of the following mental, emotional, or physical reactions:

- A feeling of exhaustion (caused by very deep psychological change)
- A feeling of deep calm and relief
- An inability to think about the issue anymore
- An inability to feel anything about the issue
- A sense that the issue is very distant, no longer personal
- A foggy or slightly light-headed physical sensation for a short time (in rare cases, this feeling can last for hours)

Sometimes, during the practice of Energy Psychology, deep wells of pain are released. You may cry during treatment. While the sudden flood of emotion may feel overwhelming, it is actually a good sign, indicating a very positive movement of negative energy out of the system. The result is often a profound shift to a higher level of emotional well-being. Nonetheless, anyone who feels concerned or frightened by strong feelings should first learn Energy Psychology techniques from a professional psychologist or other qualified mental health practitioner. Similarly, anyone who feels unduly uncomfortable after using these techniques should consult a mental health professional. Many Energy Psychology therapists listed in internet resources provide telephone services in addition to in-person consultations, making this treatment modality available virtually anywhere in the world. However, for the purposes of resolving psychological upset, you can certainly consult any competent mental health professional, whether or not that person is familiar with Energy Psychology techniques.

The WHEE Technique

Psychiatrist Daniel Benor, M.D., developed the WHEE technique. He offers workbooks and information about WHEE on his site, www.wholistichealingresearch.com. Even the simplified version described below can help you and your family relieve all kinds of upset and pain. Here is the technique:

- Think of the disturbing issue/feeling/pain/situation and rate it between 1 and 10.
- Say (out loud or silently) "Even though I (name your problem in lots of detail), I love and accept myself completely and God loves and accepts me too." (If you prefer, you can just say the phrase "I love and accept myself completely.") Here are some examples of how this might sound:

> "Even though I am upset with my sister and I don't feel like talking to her and she's always been upsetting me like this ever since we were kids, I love and accept myself completely and God loves and accepts me too.

> "Even though I'm starting to get a headache and now my day will be ruined and I won't be able to cope and the medicine won't work and I feel so helpless, I love and accept myself completely and God loves and accepts me too."

> "Even though I am very anxious about giving this presentation and I hate giving presentations and can't stand the pressure of having to do it, I love and accept myself completely and God loves and accepts me too."

> "Even though I can't stop thinking about what he said to me and I hate that he said it and I hate him for saying it, I love and accept myself completely and God loves and accepts me too."

> "Even though I miss Daddy so much and I wish he was still living here with us and I hate that Mommy and Daddy got divorced, I love and accept myself completely and God loves and accepts me too."

- Now focus your attention on the problem by repeating it again, picturing it, watching it unfold like a movie, thinking about it and so on. While doing this, tap alternately (left/right, left/right, etc.) on each side of your body. Pick any ONE of the following ways to do this alternating tapping or make up one of your own: Use your fingers to lightly tap on your eyebrow where it meets the nose—right eyebrow, then left eyebrow, right eyebrow, left eyebrow, etc. Or fold your arms with your hands under them. Now tap the left side of your body with one hand and the right side of your body with the other hand. Continue left/right, left/right, etc. Or fold your arms so that your hands are on top of your arms. Now tap on top of the left arm, then the right arm, left arm/right arm, etc. (This position is called The Butterfly.) Or hold your arms at your sides. Tap your left leg and your right leg alternately with your hands. Or close your mouth lightly. Move your tongue inside your mouth so that it touches the left teeth, then the right teeth, continue left/right, left/right, etc.

- After tapping and thinking for about 20 seconds, make a positive statement relevant to the issue and continue tapping for another 10 to 20 seconds. Positive statements are any words that bring perspective to the issue. They might sound like any of the following:

  "We always make up in the end."
  "My headache will end eventually and I'll feel better."
  "I've survived my previous presentations and I'll survive this one too."
  "He has some good points, too."
  "The pain will get weaker over time."

You have now completed one round of WHEE. Rate the intensity of your upset/pain again. Continue doing rounds until you are at 0.

WHEE in Action

Here are some examples of the technique in action:

> *"My son Sol was about to take his first drive on the highway. The night before his excursion, I couldn't sleep—I kept worrying about his safety. After a couple of hours of tossing and turning—I couldn't seem to turn my brain off—I decided to use WHEE. Within a few minutes, I realized that he'd be just fine, and I fell asleep."*

> *"My daughter Amanda had lied to me about where she was going after school. When I found out, I was furious. I knew that I wouldn't be able to speak to her without blowing up, so I decided to try WHEE to help me gain a more mature state of mind. I went through several rounds, first feeling angry, then betrayed, then hurt, then sad. Finally I felt calm and was able to handle the situation like an adult parent instead of a mad kid. It really worked and it took less than five minutes!"*

> *"Our sixteen-year-old daughter Dana crashed the family car just one month after getting her licence. At the scene of the accident, we found her hysterical, shaking and sobbing uncontrollably. Fortunately, no one was hurt and she had hit a cement pillar rather than another car. While we were waiting for the tow truck to arrive, I sat with her and treated her with WHEE. I had her repeat this sentence, "Even though I crashed the car and I am so upset and traumatized, I love and accept myself completely and my parents love and accept me and God loves and accepts me too." Then I asked her to put her arms in the Butterfly position and tap while picturing the accident happening. After about half a minute, I asked her to say, "We'll fix the car and I'll become a better driver the more I drive" and*

*then tap for another few seconds. She calmed down like some-
one had given her a sleeping pill. It was amazing."*

*"My 9-year-old is a very earnest student—too earnest. She gets
upset before every test. She was studying for her math test last
week and started crying, 'I can't do it! I just can't do it! I'm going
to fail.' She was really falling apart. So I sat her down and did
WHEE with her. I had her say, 'Even though I feel like I can't
do it and like I'm going to fail, I love and accept myself completely and God loves and accepts me too.' I showed her how to
tap left/right and after about 20 seconds I had her continue tapping while saying, 'I usually do very well on my tests and I'll probably do just fine on this one too.' She felt a little calmer after that
but still somewhat upset, so I did another two rounds until she
was at zero. Then she just sat down and finished studying and I
never heard any more about it. Naturally she got an excellent
score on the test, as usual."*

*"My baby suffers from colic. Usually there's nothing I can do to
calm him down once he starts crying. But I decided to try WHEE
on him last night. I said out loud (pretending I was him) 'Even
though I feel miserable and something hurts me and I have to
cry and cry and cry and cry, I love and accept myself and God
loves and accepts me too.' Then I tapped on his eyebrows, left/right,
left/right while I kept saying, 'I'm upset and something hurts and
I can't stop crying.' After a bit I said, 'I'll stop crying and feel better eventually.' The baby seemed calmer after I did this so I did
a few more rounds and—miracle of miracles—he fell asleep quietly in my arms!" (Try WHEE on anything and everything—it
just may work!)*

"After suffering the loss of my second child, I could barely function as a parent. I knew I had two other kids who needed me, but I was deeply inside myself with my trauma. My husband had read about new treatments—alphabet therapies like EMDR, TAT, TFT, EFT and so on—and he eventually urged me to look into this kind of help. Fortunately, there was a trauma specialist who had an office close to our home. It turned out that she was trained in the WHEE approach. She treated me with that and taught me how to use it on my own, which really helped me get through the nights. I'm so grateful to her; she gave me my life back. Nothing can bring back my little boy, but I'm at peace with that now. I can move forward for the first time in three years. I can laugh and love my family again."

Fear, rage, grief and confusion—the full gamut of emotional stress—is experienced in every family. WHEE is a technique that anyone can use to resolve and heal emotions ranging from mild upset to deep trauma. Every member of the family can benefit from this easy and truly amazing technique.

APPENDIX B

Feeling Word List

Happy

Cheerful enchanted delighted glad pleased contented gratified satisfied elated thrilled exhilarated joyful buoyant exultant appreciative
thankful excited exulted ecstatic positive relaxed calm fulfilled glad
jubilant fortunate peaceful appreciated

Sad

Despondent downcast hopeless dejected despairing disappointed dis-
illusioned upset dissatisfied disenchanted crestfallen miserable unhappy
cynical disheartened discouraged displeased depressed broken heart-
sick crushed wretched afflicted sorry regretful sickened empty lost alone
lonely rejected distressed besieged down gloomy desperate blue dis-
mayed hurt wounded pained resigned abandoned deflated exhausted
neglected ashamed unappreciated

Mad

Enraged infuriated angry annoyed frustrated irritated bothered upset
peeved vexed exasperated provoked berserk fed-up agitated disturbed
perturbed irate hysterical galled riled cross explosive aggravated uptight

troubled irked incensed furious livid goaded disgusted revolted appalled resentful offended aggrieved indignant slighted seething vengeful incensed repulsed stifled cheated

Scared

Frightened alarmed panicky frantic overwhelmed terrified shocked threatened terrorized anxious concerned worried unnerved startled nervous apprehensive tense uneasy jumpy fearful petrified intimidated demoralized unsettled vulnerable helpless exposed powerless defenseless troubled unsure shy hysterical panic-stricken guarded horrified insecure stunned

Confused

Uncertain unknowing unsure panicky puzzled disoriented perplexed mystified confounded bamboozled mixed-up unsettled disconcerted unconvinced hesitant skeptical undecided unclear unresolved in doubt ambivalent dubious incredulous off center unbalanced disturbed disorganized uncomfortable foggy bothered baffled hesitant

Resources

Books

Arenson, Gloria. *Five Simple Steps to Emotional Healing: The Last Self-Help Book You Will Ever Need.* New York: Fireside, 2001.

Benson, Herbert. *The Relaxation Response (Updated and Expanded).* New York: HarperCollins, 2000.

Bourne, Edmund J. *Natural Relief for Anxiety: Complementary Strategies for Easing Fear, Panic and Worry.* Oakland, CA: New Harbinger Publications, 2004.

Cornell, Ann Weiser. *The Power of Focusing: A Practical Guide to Emotional Self-Healing.* Oakland, CA: New Harbinger Publications, 1996.

Gendlin, Eugene T. *Focusing.* New York: Bantam Books, 1982.

Gottman, John. *The Heart of Parenting: Raising an Emotionally Intelligent Child.* New York: Simon & Schuster, 1997.

Green, Ross. *The Explosive Child: A New Approach for Understanding and Parenting Easily Frustrated "Chronically Inflexible" Children.* New York: HarperCollins, 1998.

Hay, Louise L. *You Can Heal Your Life.* Carlsbad, CA: Hay House, 1999.

Lynch, Valerie and Paul. *Emotional Healing in Minutes*. London: Thorsons, 2002.

Mountrose, Philip and Jane. *Getting Thru to Your Emotions with EFT*. Sacramento, CA: Holistic Communications, 2000.

Pratt, George, and Peter Lambrou. *Instant Emotional Healing: Acupressure for the Emotions*. New York: Broadway Books, 2000.

Scheffer, Mechteld. *The Encyclopedia of Bach Flower Therapy*. Rochester, VT: Healing Arts Press, 2001.

Seligman, Martin E. *The Optimistic Child*. New York: HarperCollins, 1995.

Videos

Mountrose, Philip. *Getting Thru to Your Emotions with EFT*. The Emotional Freedom Techniques, 2000.

Websites

Emotional Freedom Techniques, *http: //www.emofree.com*
Be Set Free Fast, *http://www.besetfreefast.com*

Acknowledgments

I am so grateful to all the people who made this book possible. Dr. Abe and Mrs. Shainey Aberback commissioned the original manuscript for their "respect project" for schoolchildren. They gave me the original opportunity to collect my thoughts in one place. Ophira Sone generously edited the manuscript and my husband Avraham spent endless hours typesetting it. The enthusiasm, determination and generosity of friends—Rochelle Bronfman, Fern Reich and Francie Kussner—helped bring this work to the next level. It became a book thanks to the vision of Iris Tupholme at HarperCollins Publishers and Michael Levine and Hilary McMahon of Westwood Creative Artists. I am so appreciative for their faith in me. Shani Tauber gave helpful feedback during the writing process and Nicole Langlois provided not only her excellent editorial skills but also humor and encouragement. My students and clients of the past 30 years, my studies in psychology, my teachers of the inner world—Ms. Mary Armstrong and Dr. Leslie Greenberg—and above all, the wisdom of Torah, are the sources for all I have written here.

Index

disrespect (*continued*)
  children showing, 124, 129, 132, 172, 181
  the "no" response, 63
  slippery slope, 124
  teaching, 63
  from teenagers, 172
disrespectful speech, 80, 122–24, 132–33, 136–37. *See also* respectful speech; words
"distract and praise," 27
distress (does not subside), 52–53
divorce, 9, 94, 230, 232, 261
drug use, 68, 166–67
duplicity, 20–22
dysfunctional behavior, 78, 88, 121, 141, 176
dysfunctional neural pathways, 268

E
earned positive attention. *See* conditional love
easy-going children, 9, 11, 13. *See also* types of children
eating. *See* food
educational environment, 9
EFT (Emotional Freedom Technique), 270, 277
80–20 Rule, 77, 79, 265
  introducing to toddlers, 149–51
  introduction to, 14–18
  rules in the context of, 71–72
EMDR (Eye Movement Desensitization and Reprocessing), 270, 277
emotional abuse and inadequacy, 200–1
emotional coaching
  accepting, 39
  acknowledgment in, 38–39
  addressing moods, 44–45
  blocking, 136–37

examples, 42–44
  hopeless example, 43
  importance of, 53
  increasing cooperation, 46–48
  introduction, 38–53
  naming the feeling, 38–39
  prompting, 134
  respectful speech, 128–34
emotional instability in teenagers, 165
emotional intelligence, 38
emotional power, 2
emotional support, undermining, 45
emotional world of the parent, 4
emotions
  deep and painful, 43
  healing, 246–49, 269
  parenting experience, 190
  suppressed, 40–42
Energy Psychology, 268–77. *See also* WHEE
  effectiveness of, 268, 270
  how to apply, 270–274
  improvement through, 270
  internet resources, 269, 270
  uses of, 268, 269
environmental factors, 9
essential oils, 91. *See also* aromatherapy; Bach Flower Therapy
examples. *See* dialogue examples
excessive criticism, 13–14
explosive behavior. *See* anger
expressing disappointment, 78

F
feel-good. *See* good-feeling
feelings. *See also* bad-feeling; good-feeling
  after acknowledgment of, 45
  bad, 40–42
  and behaviors are different, 50–51